Drupal 7

Create and operate any type of website quickly
and efficiently

David Mercer

Drupal 7

First published: April 2008

Second edition: September 2010

Production Reference: 1020910

Published by Packt Publishing Ltd.
32 Lincoln Road
Olton
Birmingham, B27 6PA, UK.

ISBN 978-1-849512-86-2

www.packtpub.com

Cover Image by Faiz Fattohi (faizfattohi@gmail.com)

Credits

Author
David Mercer

Reviewer
Diliny Corlosquet

Acquisition Editor
Sarah Cullington

Development Editor
Mayuri Kokate

Technical Editors
Sakina Kaydawala
Neha Mallik

Copy Editor
Leonard D'Silva

Indexer
Tejal Daruwale

Editorial Team Leader
Aanchal Kumar

Project Team Leader
Ashwin Shetty

Project Coordinator
Poorvi Nair

Proofreader
Mario Cecere

Graphics
Geetanjali Sawant

Production Coordinator
Shantanu Zagade

Cover Work
Shantanu Zagade

About the Author

David Mercer was born in August 1976 in Harare, Zimbabwe. As he always had a strong interest in science, he came into regular contact with computers at the university where he graduated cum laude with majors in applied math and math (although he minored in computer science).

As a programmer and professional writer who has been writing both code and books for about ten years, he has worked on a number of well known titles, in various capacities, on a wide variety of topics. His books have been translated into over nine different languages to date.

David believes that everyone should be able to benefit from the vast potential of the Internet. He founded Site prebuilder (`http://www.siteprebuilder.com`) to provide education and services to reduce the barrier to entry for Internet newcomers. The aim of Site prebuilder is to empower ordinary, non-techie people with the knowledge and skill required to run any website efficiently.

When he isn't working, which isn't that often, he enjoys playing the guitar (generally on stage and unrehearsed) and getting involved in outdoor activities ranging from touch rugby and golf to water skiing and snowboarding.

It is necessary to first thank the Packt team for making this possible, along with Diliny Corlosquet who did the review. In addition, my ever supportive family was always at hand to provide a change of pace and scenery that enabled me to work with greater effort throughout. Finally, I would like to thank my readers. The success of the first few editions of this book has made it possible (and necessary) to sit down and update it on a regular basis. I hope it does its job well.

About the Reviewer

Diliny Corlosquet is a freelance web developer who was introduced to Drupal by the vibrant community in Ireland back in 2006. Having attended several DrupalCamps and DrupalCons, she keeps up-to-date with the latest and greatest in the Drupal community and maintains several Drupal websites. She now lives in Boston, Massachusetts, with her Drupalite husband of RDF/Semantic web fame, Stéphane, and their dog Maya.

I would like to thank my husband for his constant encouragement and commitment to Drupal as a whole, without whom I would never have become so involved!

Table of Contents

Preface

The Internet is a magical place where any type of media and information can be accessed any time, day or night. Online medical diagnosis websites pander to every whim of the world's hypochondriacs, while media sites stream endless clips of the latest celebrity meltdowns. It's a huge and wildly variable place, which is great... if you're only browsing.

The second you take it upon yourself to contribute to this melee of information, the magic has a tendency to be replaced by cold, hard reality. It's no longer sufficient to learn how to create a "Hello world" web page by hand. Those days are gone, and no-one is interested anymore.

Today, no matter who you are, you have to worry about things like SEO, sessions, hackers, RSS, DNS, Flash, Analytics, bots, and thousands of other things, all at once. Things have become so complex that it's simply not possible to do this as an individual anymore. More to the point, why would you want to?

What's important is that you can *achieve* whatever you want without ever having to learn the fundamentals of session state management or OOP, for example. This is where Drupal comes in. Thousands of developers work in, on, and around the Drupal project to provide a platform that is cutting edge and does its job "under the hood".

Your job is to take Drupal and turn it into what you need in order to meet your goals—regardless of what they are. Sure, you'll need to become knowledgeable about some things, and you'll have to invest a bit of your time learning the ropes, but that isn't a very high price to pay for what you get.

Learning new concepts, techniques, and technologies can be frustrating—believe me, I know. That's why this book contains everything I would want to know about Drupal, if I was starting out again. It has a focus on practical, real world information that will turn you into an adaptable and competent Drupal 7 webmaster.

What you do with your newfound knowledge and experience after that is entirely up to you. The sky is the limit!

What this book covers

Chapter 1, Introduction to Drupal introduces you to the world of Drupal and looks at where Drupal comes from, where it's going, and what it can offer you. It then deals with how to get everything you need up and running on a development machine and also briefly looks at how all the requisite technologies gel together to produce a working Drupal site.

Once everything is up and running, and after looking over some of the more common installation problems, the chapter presents a brief tour of Drupal in order to give you an idea of what to expect in the coming chapters.

Chapter 2, Basic Functionality sees us adding important functionality to the newly created site. The focus of this chapter is on modules and blocks and how to add and enable them, and how to obtain modules that are not a part of the core distribution. Given that menus are closely associated with a site's functionality, these are also covered here.

Chapter 3, Configuration and Reports looks at the most general settings that all Drupal administrators need to contend with. Everything from specifying your site's name and dealing with filesystem settings to proper utilization of logs and reports gets treated here.

Chapter 4, Users and Access Control concerns itself with the best ways to implement a sound access control policy. Drupal has a sophisticated role-based access control system, which is fundamentally important for handling users properly. This chapter will give you the information you need to implement whatever access controls your site requires.

Chapter 5, Basic Content gets to the heart of the matter by beginning the book's coverage on content. Working with content, what content types are available, administering content, and even a discourse on some of the more common content-related modules serve as a basis for moving to more advanced content-related matters that follow in the next chapter.

Chapter 6, Advanced Content gives you the edge when it comes to creating engaging, dynamic content. In particular, Drupal 7's new field paradigm is discussed along with content types, taxonomy, and formatting.

Chapter 7, Multimedia embraces the trend towards rich, visually appealing websites. Given the increasing availability of broadband Internet, it is only fitting that a full chapter be devoted to learning how Drupal's various core and contributed modules support different media.

Chapter 8, Views is dedicated to arguably the most important topic of all. By mastering Views, Drupal webmasters can manipulate and organize their content in a way that no other platform can. This chapter shows not only how to create new basic and advanced Views, but also how to theme and manipulate them.

Chapter 9, Drupal Theming gives you a run down of how attractive, functional interfaces are created in Drupal through the use of themes. As well as discussing briefly some of the considerations that must be taken into account when planning your website, it shows how to make important modifications to your chosen theme, through the use of sub-themes.

Chapter 10, Advanced Features adds the icing on the cake by looking at a host of more advanced topics. From better and more complex theming issues, to creating a real world application by integrating several different features and technologies, this chapter gives readers their first look at how Drupal makes building genuinely world-class websites possible.

Chapter 11, Deployment and Management takes a pragmatic look at the type of tasks in which you will need to be proficient in order to successfully run and maintain a Drupal site. Whether it's considering what type of hosting service to use, or how to enhance a site's SEO, everything you need to do throughout the course of operating a live website is covered.

It also discusses the all-important topic of deployment. Because all major work should be done on a development website, this chapter presents a sound process for taking the finished product and making it available for public consumption on a live server.

Appendix looks at the JavaScript features that come as standard with Drupal using the jQuery package. By demonstrating how to incorporate jQuery effects and features into content, readers will be able to add that special something to their pages.

What you need for this book

You need to have the following:

- XAMPP (PHP, Apache, and MySQL)
- Drupal 7
- Internet connection (Online quizzes and exercises for this book are available at Site prebuilder — `http://www.siteprebuilder.com`)

Who this book is for

This book is for people with little to no experience in using Drupal. People who are not familiar with PHP, MySQL, or HTML will also be able to use the book.

Conventions

In this book, you will find a number of styles of text that distinguish between different kinds of information. Here are some examples of these styles, and an explanation of their meaning.

Code words in text are shown as follows: "It may be more expedient to create a directory, say `drupal_downloads`, to save these files to."

A block of code is set as follows:

```
h1, h2, h3, h4, h5, h6 {
  margin: 0;
  padding: 0;
  font-weight: normal;
  font-family: Helvetica, Arial, sans-serif;
}
```

When we wish to draw your attention to a particular part of a code block, the relevant lines or items are set in bold:

```
h1, h2, h3, h4, h5, h6 {
  margin: 0;
  padding: 0;
  font-weight: normal;
  font-family: Helvetica, Arial, sans-serif;
}
```

New terms and **important words** are shown in bold. Words that you see on the screen, in menus or dialog boxes for example, appear in the text like this: "click on the **Run cron** link".

 Warnings or important notes appear in a box like this.

 Tips and tricks appear like this.

Reader feedback

Feedback from our readers is always welcome. Let us know what you think about this book—what you liked or may have disliked. Reader feedback is important for us to develop titles that you really get the most out of.

To send us general feedback, simply send an e-mail to feedback@packtpub.com, and mention the book title via the subject of your message.

If there is a book that you need and would like to see us publish, please send us a note in the **SUGGEST A TITLE** form on www.packtpub.com or e-mail suggest@packtpub.com.

If there is a topic that you have expertise in and you are interested in either writing or contributing to a book on, see our author guide on www.packtpub.com/authors.

Customer support

Now that you are the proud owner of a Packt book, we have a number of things to help you to get the most from your purchase.

Errata

Although we have taken every care to ensure the accuracy of our content, mistakes do happen. If you find a mistake in one of our books—maybe a mistake in the text or the code—we would be grateful if you would report this to us. By doing so, you can save other readers from frustration and help us improve subsequent versions of this book.

If you find any errata, please report them by visiting `http://www.packtpub.com/support`, selecting your book, clicking on the **errata submission form** link, and entering the details of your errata. Once your errata are verified, your submission will be accepted and the errata will be uploaded on our website, or added to any list of existing errata, under the Errata section of that title.

Any existing errata can be viewed by selecting your title from `http://www.packtpub.com/support`.

Piracy

Piracy of copyright material on the Internet is an ongoing problem across all media. At Packt, we take the protection of our copyright and licenses very seriously. If you come across any illegal copies of our works, in any form, on the Internet, please provide us with the location address or website name immediately so that we can pursue a remedy.

Please contact us at `copyright@packtpub.com` with a link to the suspected pirated material.

We appreciate your help in protecting our authors, and our ability to bring you valuable content.

Questions

You can contact us at `questions@packtpub.com` if you are having a problem with any aspect of the book, and we will do our best to address it.

1
Introduction to Drupal

Until quite recently, the most important thing a newcomer to the Web could do in order to prepare for building a website was to buy a book on how to learn programming in any one of the major web-centric languages such as PHP or Perl. The not inconsiderable task of learning the niceties of the chosen language to a respectable degree would consume a fair chunk of time and patience. Once our hapless newcomer had sufficient mastery of the fundamentals, applying that knowledge to program efficiently and reliably, with the tenacity to stick with a job until the site was developed, could arguably be described as a Herculean accomplishment.

This state of affairs is, and quite rightly should be, entirely unacceptable to someone like yourself. It's like forcing lawyers to learn the intricacies of architecture, construction, and masonry simply because they require a courtroom to work in. It should be quite apparent that separating the technical task of *developing the software* for a website, from the *function* of that website is a very sensible thing to do; the main reason being that it allows people to focus on what they are good at without them having to devote time and energy to becoming good software developers too.

It's not surprising then, that in recent years the open source community has been hard at work pulling the programming world out of the software dark ages by providing us with flexible frameworks for building web-based enterprises. These frameworks free website creators from the intellectual burden of learning software development ideas and concepts, allowing them instead to focus more on goal/business-oriented configuration and customization tasks.

Drupal is one such result of this software development evolution, and this book seeks to provide you with the fundamental information needed in order to use it effectively. Because this book focuses more on beginner-level aspects of working with Drupal, you will be pleased to know that there will be little to no coding involved—you're not required to learn how to develop Drupal modules from scratch, for example. That's not to say this book will be elementary; on the contrary, the knowledge gained here will enable you to tackle problems beyond the scope of this material with confidence.

To further consolidate your learning and expand on the practical aspect of the various topics covered throughout the book, each chapter will have an associated self-marking online quiz with additional exercises available at the author's website: http://www.siteprebuilder.com. It is highly recommended you take advantage of this additional resource to get the maximum benefit from this book.

Before we begin building anything that resembles a website, I'm sure you have plenty of questions about the how, what, where, and why of Drupal. Consequently, this chapter will not only provide a backdrop for the rest of the book, but will also serve as an introduction to the technology as a whole, incorporating brief discussions on the following topics:

- Drupal—an overview
- How Drupal came to be
- What Drupal has to offer
- Uses of Drupal
- The Drupal community
- The Drupal license
- The server environment
- Obtaining and installing XAMPP (Apache, MySQL, and PHP)
- Obtaining and installing Drupal
- A short tour of Drupal

Before we begin, there is one crucial bit of advice to be given:

Ensure that you have access to a good, preferably broadband Internet connection, as you will be downloading a fair amount of software.

If you already have a development environment set up and running, feel free to skip the web server sections and move to the *Obtaining and Installing Drupal* section.

Drupal—an overview

Drupal is an **Open Source Content Management System**. If you are new to both computing and Drupal, then this probably doesn't clear things up very much. First of all:

 The term open source describes software whose source code is made available, most often subject to certain conditions, for use or modification by users or other developers, as they deem fit.

The specific conditions under which Drupal is made available will be scrutinized more closely in the section *The Drupal license* later in this chapter.

Besides that, what open source means for someone who intends to make use of Drupal is that there is no obligatory payment required for this unquestionably valuable software. You also join a large community (also to be discussed later in this chapter) of Drupal users, developers, and administrators who subscribe to the open source philosophy—in other words, someone out there will probably be willing to spend time helping you out, should you get stuck.

That's a pretty good deal for those who are still not convinced about open source technologies as a whole—not only do we not have to develop the entire site ourselves, but we also get to take advantage of the collective wisdom of thousands of other people.

Is there anything else we can say about open source? Sure, with an active community like the one associated with Drupal, development advances rapidly and flexibly because any problems can be spotted early and dealt with effectively. This means that you can expect a high level of stability, security, and performance from Drupal websites.

OK, but what is the Content Management System (CMS) part all about?

A content management system is software that facilitates the creation, organization, manipulation, and removal of information in the form of images, documents, scripts, and plain text (or anything else for that matter).

If you have a need to organize and display fairly large amounts of information, especially when it is likely that content will be created or delivered from a variety of different sources, then a content management system is undoubtedly what you need.

That's basically all you have to know. Drupal provides a free platform, along with its attendant community, for satisfying a wide variety of content-management requirements. Precisely what one can achieve is the subject of the *What Drupal Has to Offer* section, later in this chapter. For now though, let's turn back the hands of time and take a look at how we ended up with Drupal as we know it today.

How Drupal came to be

As with so many modern success stories, this one started in a dorm room with a couple of students needing to achieve a specific goal. In this case, Dries Buytaert and Hans Snijder of the University of Antwerp wished to share an ADSL modem connection to the Internet. They managed this via the use of a wireless bridge, but soon after, Dries decided to work on a news site, which would, in addition to the simple connection the students already shared, allow them to share news and other information.

Over time, the site grew and changed as Dries expanded the application and experimented with new things. However, it was only later in 2001, when it was decided to release the code to the public in the hope that this would encourage development from other people, that Drupal became open source software. It's clear that releasing the source to the public was the right choice because today Drupal has a well organized, thriving community of people ranging from contributors, administrators, a security team, and a global presence, to plenty of users who make invaluable additions to the Drupal project on a regular basis through bug reports and suggestions.

In only a few years, Dries and others have taken a small inter-dorm-room application and turned it into a technology that is contributing to the way in which the global society communicates through the Web. This is embodied in their brief mission statement that reads:

> *By building on relevant standards and open source technologies, Drupal supports and enhances the potential of the Internet as a medium where diverse and geographically separated individuals and groups can collectively produce, discuss, and share information and ideas. With a central interest in and focus on communities and collaboration, Drupal's flexibility allows the collaborative production of online information systems and communities.*

Ultimately, where Drupal is going and how it came to be, are also driven by the philosophies that guide those responsible for developing this technology. As you will see throughout the course of this book, it is fair to say that the Drupal community has so far succeeded in meeting its lofty targets.

What Drupal has to offer

As users of technology and software, we should never be lax in what we demand from the technologies that serve us. It is fitting, therefore, at this stage, to discuss what we expect from Drupal in order to ensure that it will satisfy our needs.

There are three different aspects of Drupal we need to consider when looking at whether it is a *good* technology to use in general. Will it be:

- **Reliable and robust**: Are there a lot of bugs in the code? Will it affect my site if I have to forever add patches or obtain updates for faulty code?
- **Efficient**: Does the software use my server's resources wisely? Am I likely to run into concurrency problems or speed issues early on?
- **Flexible**: If I change my mind about what I want from my site, will I be able to implement those changes without redoing everything from scratch?

While Drupal will always be a work in progress, it can be taken for granted that the source code, used to build your website, has been meticulously crafted and well designed. In fact, the previously listed points are taken so seriously by the developers of Drupal that they are written into their set of principles that are available at http://drupal.org/node/21945.

While it won't influence us much for the moment, it is worth noting the following:

A great advantage of Drupal is that the code itself is very well designed and written, which makes modifying it easy. This means that, as you attempt more advanced tasks, the very way in which Drupal is designed will lend you an advantage over other platforms.

The next thing we need to consider is: *what Drupal is like for us, as administrators, to use.* Naturally, things should be as easy as possible, so that we don't spend time bogged down with problems or complicated settings, or worse yet, have to modify the source code on a regular basis. Ideally, we want a system that is:

- **Easy to set up and run**: Can I start creating a site with the minimum of fuss? Do I have to learn about other technologies before I am able to use Drupal?

- **Intuitive to work with**: Once I have begun finding my way around, will it be easy to learn new things? If I am not a particularly technical person, will I struggle to administer my site?

- **Flexible and easy to extend**: I know I can make a basic site, but I really want to create a unique and sophisticated, ground-breaking site—can it be done with Drupal?

- **Secure**: Has the website been successfully used in real world applications? Are known bugs fixed quickly and regularly?

Again, these are precisely the attributes that Drupal is known for. If you have other questions that are not specifically mentioned here, try looking through the Drupal forums.

Finally, and perhaps most importantly, it is necessary to consider whether or not Drupal creates a good environment for site users. Obviously, a technology that is well designed and easy to administer would still not be very helpful if, for example, its use by visitors is prohibitively complex. The best way to find out what type of environment Drupal can provide is to go ahead and check out the Drupal home page at http://drupal.org—since it is built with Drupal and is a good example of what one can do.

It's a good idea to register an account if you have a moment or two. It's not absolutely necessary, but believe me, it will be of great benefit in the long run. Perhaps treat your registration process as a quick and easy way to see a bit of the site.

It stands to reason that if the main site that is developed in Drupal is easy to use, then you, in turn, will be able to create an easy-to-use site for your users. Ultimately, how easy a site is to use depends on how you, the creator of the site, present content and information.

Uses of Drupal

Any enterprise that requires a fair amount of working with content is a likely candidate for Drupal, but, because of its extensibility and flexibility, you are really not limited in any sense. The following list shows the most common uses at present and comes from the case studies page (`http://drupal.org/cases`) on the Drupal site:

- **Community portal sites**: If you want a news website where the stories are provided by the audience, Drupal suits your needs well. Incoming stories are automatically voted upon by the audience, and the best stories bubble up to the homepage. Bad stories and comments are automatically hidden after enough negative votes.

- **News publishing**: Drupal is great for newspapers and other news organizations.

- **Aficionado sites**: Drupal flourishes when it powers a portal website where one person shares their expertise and enthusiasm for a topic.

- **Intranet/Corporate websites**: Companies maintain their internal and external websites in Drupal. Drupal works well in these cases because of its flexible permissions system and its easy web-based publishing. No longer do you have to wait for a webmaster to get the word out about your latest project.

- **Resource directories**: If you want a central directory for a given topic, Drupal suits your needs well. Users can register and suggest new resources, while editors can screen their submissions.

- **International sites**: When you begin using Drupal, you join a large international community of users and developers. Thanks to the localization features within Drupal, there are many Drupal sites implemented in a wide range of languages.

- **Education**: Drupal can be used for creating dynamic learning communities to supplement the face-to-face classroom or as a platform for distance education classes. Academic professional organizations benefit from its interactive features, and the ability to provide public content, member-only resources, and member subscription management.

- **Art, Music, and Multimedia**: When it comes to community art sites, Drupal is a great match. No other platform provides the rock solid foundation that is needed to make multimedia-rich websites that allow users to share, distribute, and discuss their work with others. As time goes by, Drupal will only develop stronger support for audio, video, images, and playlist content for use in multimedia applications.

- **Social networking sites**: Drupal has a lot of the common features used in social networking sites. You can build a collection of social networking applications for your site or use Drupal as a white label social networking service.

Drupal can be thought of as the Internet's jack-of-all-trades—it excels in many areas, but at heart, it is a generalist. So while you can use Drupal for a great number of things, you should perhaps limit its use to those things that complement its design—like those mentioned in the previous list.

The Drupal community

Drupal has coherent and in-depth support structures that are fairly easy to learn your way around. There are a host of categories ranging from information, polls, forums, and news to support, which can be found at the home page `http://drupal.org`.

It is strongly recommended that you regularly make use of `drupal.org` and constantly use different elements and sections in order to become proficient at extracting the information and software you require—especially because the Drupal site will change from time to time!

All the information contained in the site is well organized and easy to access from the main navigation bar at the top of the page, as shown in the following screenshot:

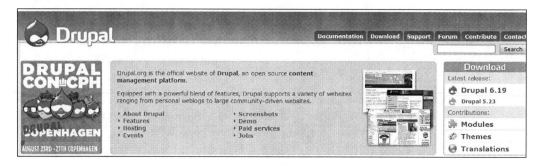

Each and every tab in the navigation bar has a host of its own links and pages; although there are some categories that contain inter-related topics. At any rate, let's go through each one quickly to see what they have to offer.

Documentation

This section is a great repository of information, catering for a wide variety of needs. The content is gathered into five main sections, some are shown in the following screenshot:

Getting started	
Understanding Drupal	Learn about Drupal concepts, technology stack, terminology, and resources.
Installation Guide	Install Drupal and its contributed modules and themes. Run multiple sites from one installation. Migrate from other content management systems and address platform issues.
Administration Guide	Manage users and content, perform backups and upgrades, secure your site, tweak performance, etc. *Audience: System and site administrators*

Creating a site	
Structure Guide	Work with content types, blocks, menus, views, panels, taxonomy, multilingual content, user profiles, and navigation. *Audience: information architects*
Site Building Guide	Add functionality and features such as ecommerce, forums, media, search, geographic data, dates, workflow, messaging, forms, social networking etc. *Audience: site builders, developers and business architects*
Theming Guide	Customize the interface using templates, CSS etc. Override the output from core or contributed modules. *Audience: designers, usability and accessibility professionals, interface experts.*

Writing your own code	
Developing for Drupal	Work with the API, JavaScript, and databases. Learn the Drupal coding standards etc. *Audience: developers.*
API Reference	Search the complete Drupal API including forms, menus, node access, theme system etc.
Examples for Developers	Examine a standard repository of sample modules that can be used to learn module development or referenced on handbook pages.

Each of these categories contains a series of links to informative pages (that, in turn, often contain links to other pages) that do a good job of explaining their respective topics. It's worth pointing out that a block appears on the left-hand side of these pages, containing links to related topics under the same category heading in order to help you navigate through the information with ease.

The following screenshot shows the **Understanding Drupal** page:

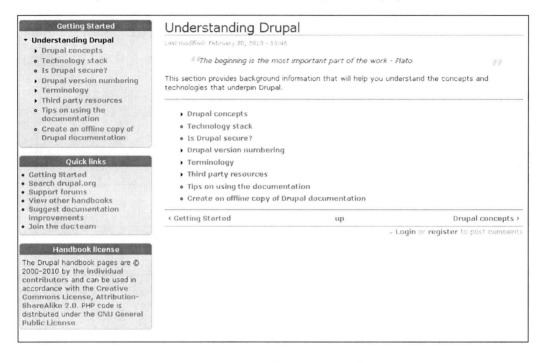

You are urged to look through at least the first section before moving on in order to learn as much about Drupal as possible. It is also a good idea to use these handbooks in tandem with this book, so that you can complement the practical advice and experience you gain here with reference-type material presented on the site.

Download

We will be visiting this section again in the following chapter when we begin to set up everything in preparation for site development. However, there are a few interesting points to note before we get there. The first is that you need to be quite careful about the Drupal version—or indeed modules and themes—you download, because each successive version makes changes and improvements on previous versions, and also sometimes messes up compatibility with other features.

If you decide to add a module (by this, I mean that at some stage you *will* want to add a module), then viewing the projects page at http://drupal.org/project/modules or clicking the **Download** tab gives the following:

You can see from the notes presented on this page, if you happen to need a module that was developed for Drupal 5.x and you are using version 6.x (the same goes for Drupal 7), then you are shortly going to experience no small amount of frustration—this is especially valid at this time, given that 7.x is brand new, and hence many modules have yet to be updated.

> Use the **Filter by compatibility** block to limit module results to only the version you require.

Problems like this can occur because modules are developed separately from the core, which means that it is up to the individual module developer to keep up to date with any changes coming from the main development team.

Naturally, not everyone will keep their modules up to date in a timely manner because, often, these developers are not getting paid and are under no obligation to do the work at all. They are simply providing us with the best code they can deliver when they can deliver it.

In terms of how to use the download pages, it is worth noting that there are four main links given in each downloadable item's box.

These are:

- Download
- Release notes
- Find out more, and
- Bugs and feature requests

The first option is pretty self-explanatory, but you should always take a look at the **Find out more** option before downloading anything to ensure that you are getting precisely what you want—often, this information will include download statistics, which can give you a good idea of how popular a module is.

For example, the **Find out more** page for the **Views** project contains information on history of **Updates** and plenty of material on **Releases**, **Resources**, **Support**, and **Development**—all of them are pretty useful if you are not sure what **Views** does to begin with.

Support

The **Support** section can be regarded as a kind of catch-all page, and actually contains a number of links to the various other community pages, many of which can also be opened by using their tabs in the main navigation bar. For example, you can navigate back to the **Drupal handbooks** (to be discussed shortly) from the **Get documentation** section to find out some basic information on Drupal.

Briefly, in this section:

- The **Get started** section offers a get started guide, training resources, and videos
- Documentation and help facilities are provided in the **Get documentation** section and include links to books and various guides
- There are also links to forums, groups, mailing lists, and commercial support in the **Get help** section.
- If you are not an English language speaker or your community predominantly speaks some other language, then it is worthwhile checking out some of the other language sites under the **Other languages** section, that includes German, French, Spanish, and Afrikaans.

If in doubt as to where to go, the **Support** page is probably the best place to start.

Forum

The forums are probably the single greatest problem-solving resource and information-based asset. Unlike the other types of information on the site (with the exception of the Freenode Drupal IRC), which are largely static, written answers or guides, the forums provide you with an interactive environment in which to learn. Of course, they also provide you with a medium for sharing whatever you have learned as well.

At the time of writing, there were in excess of 500,000 support-related posts alone. The following screenshot shows the **Forum** home page as well as the first few forum categories. It's easy to see that this is a fairly large repository of knowledge and hopefully you will take the time to add to it yourself:

Forums

Login to post new content in the forum.

Forum	Topics	Posts	Last post
Support Try **searching the forums** using the advanced search option first or a specific project's **bug reports**. Remember all support on this site is on a volunteer basis, so please visit the **forum tips** for posting hints.			
✉ Post installation Drupal is up and running but how do I ...?	103036	372784	8 min 42 sec ago by ludo1960
✉ Before you start Is Drupal a viable solution for my website? Please see the documentation **Before you start** before posting.	5003	21451	8 hours 41 min ago by bawoor
✉ Installing Drupal Installing Drupal? Please see the documentation in the handbook and the video resources for Drupal 5 and Drupal 6 for additional installation resources.	11970	51318	1 hour 30 min ago by Heine
✉ Upgrading Drupal Questions regarding upgrading an existing Drupal site. Don't forget to read the UPGRADE.txt that comes with evey Drupal download.	4197	17052	12 hours 10 min ago by yelvington
✉ Converting to Drupal Need help migrating your site to Drupal?	2064	8027	1 hour 48 min ago by pronord

Looking at the entire page, there are four main forum categories—**General**, **Support**, **Services**, and **Newsletters**—that in turn have a number of subcategories to make navigating the structure fairly easy. Notice too that there is a block on the right-hand side of the page containing a list of the most recent posts. As well as this, you can also use the search tool, shown at the top right-hand side of the page or at http://drupal.org/search/node, to search for relevant information or users.

Finally, assuming you are a registered (and logged-on) Drupal user, you can also post new topics to the forum using the link given under the page's main heading.

Before posting off hundreds of questions and salutations, please be aware that there is a certain etiquette to using these forums, and it should be followed at all times. Look at `http://drupal.org/forum-posting` before you begin writing any posts to the site:

A quick summary is as follows:

- Search the forums for your intended topic, and use those posts instead of creating redundant information.
- Make forum post titles informative and meaningful.
- Submit a good amount of system-specific information in your support queries—for example, mention the Drupal version along with the database and database version.
- Bear in mind that not everyone using the forum is a native English speaker; so some posts may be construed as rude or abrupt when that is not the intention.
- Remain polite and reasonable—even if you are frustrated over a particular problem.
- Donate some time to responding to and helping other posters.
- If you would like, enable your contact tab so that people can offer support via e-mail. Do this by editing your contact information,

Some of you may have noticed the link entitled **Recent posts** on the right-hand side of the page (assuming you are logged in). Clicking on this link brings up a list of the topics that have recently been active:

Recent posts

	All recent posts	My recent posts			
Type	Post		Author	Replies	Last updated
Forum topic	Can anyone give suggestion Please new		shaik ahmad	3 3 new	50 sec ago
Forum topic	problem with hook_menu and arguments new		titouille	3 3 new	2 min 2 sec ago
Issue	maximpodorov [maximpodorov] new		maximpodorov	12 6 new	3 min 9 sec ago
Issue	How to display sub menu tree navigation in a block consistently new		deadlyminds	12 1 new	3 min 15 sec ago
Forum topic	Anyone else think the Drupal Logo is naff and maybe needs a re-brand? new		dean.p	4 4 new	4 min 31 sec ago
Project	Multiple Email Addresses new		Josh Benner	0	5 min 19 sec ago
Issue	RonanL [ronanl] new		RonanL	6 6 new	5 min 22 sec ago
Issue	Thumbnails for Custom Video Field new		MacDennis	21 3 new	6 min 44 sec ago
Forum topic	Ubercart conditional actions and attributes!!		UNarmed	8 1 new	7 min 9 sec ago
Issue	Clock drift will cause lock system to fail new		lostchord	6 6 new	8 min 38 sec ago

If you would prefer to view the discussions that you personally have contributed to, then click the **My recent posts** tab on this page instead.

Contribute

At first glance, you might assume that there is very little to contribute to the Drupal community while you are still learning the software. This is not entirely true, so it is worthwhile seeing what is available to us:

Contribute

    View   Revisions

Thank you for your interest in contributing to the Drupal project! Contributors are Drupal's most valuable asset, and are the sole force behind improvements to the platform and the community itself. Please check out our project's mission statement and guiding principles so you can direct your efforts effectively and in line with the community's goals.

There are several areas in which you can provide assistance:

User support

Even the most gifted Drupal developers were new once, and chances are someone has helped you at some point along the way. No matter your skill level, you can give back by sharing what you know with other users needing support. It's a nice thing to do, and who knows? You might learn something, too!

Find out how to help with user support.

Documentation

Whether you're interested in providing fine-grained API documentation, writing step-by-step tutorials for the handbook, or producing multimedia screencasts to show people how Drupal works, you can help improve Drupal's documentation and provide a valuable resource to the community.

Find out how to help with documentation.

Translations

Drupal supports several languages, from Afrikaans to Turkish. If you know another language, you can offer your skills to help maintain Drupal core and contributed module translations.

Donations

Want to help but don't have the time? Want to say "thank you" to the folks who have put work into making Drupal what it is? Want to ensure that Drupal's infrastructure stays healthy and strong? Why not consider a monetary donation?.

Donate now or find out how to help with donations.

Development

Drupal thrives on developer contributions, in the form of both contributed modules and patches to core. Helping out in development helps the project move forward and stay competitive, and is the best way to ensure that Drupal can do what you need it to do on your next project!

Find out how to help with development.

Themes

Have an eye for design? Live and breathe XHTML and CSS? Contribute your knowledge to Drupal in the form of themes!

Find out how to help with themes.

For starters, the easiest way to support Drupal is by making donations—I can all but hear the sighs and groans, but bear in mind what you are getting is absolutely free. You can also help market Drupal by writing reviews, incorporating the Druplicon onto your site, and so on. There is also a constant need for people to help test, translate, support, and document Drupal.

Finally, once you have gained some experience and feel confident enough, look towards helping with Drupal development. Whatever you choose to do, any information or help you require in order to become pro-active within the community is readily available under the **Contribute** section.

Contact

The **Contact** page allows you to send an e-mail to the Drupal team, and you need to remember that no technical support queries will be addressed here — you must use the support forum for that. Select the most pertinent category from the drop-down list provided and away you go. An example is shown in the following screenshot:

That about wraps it up for our coverage of the Drupal community. You should feel fairly confident that you can use the site efficiently and find help if needs be. Before we start setting up our website, there is one more important issue we need to discuss, namely, the Drupal license.

The Drupal license

You should always be well acquainted with any legalities and responsibilities you have when it comes to using software developed by others. To this end, you will find that when you download a copy of Drupal, it will contain a license file for your perusal — it is actually required as part of the license that this copy be included.

If you're like me, then you find it challenging to remain awake when faced with the prospect of reading through licenses and other legal documents. So, instead of subjecting you to a verbatim recount of the entire license, I will instead give you the paraphrased version that is intended to provide you with the *essence* of what the license is for as it applies to Drupal.

 Please bear in mind that what I say here is in no way a legal document. You **must** read the whole license yourself if you wish to follow the letter of the law.

As odd as it may sound, one of the fundamental reasons for using the GNU GPL (General Public License) is to protect and help you—the people who use the software. The GPL is fundamentally different from the licenses of proprietary software, which, by and large, are designed to protect the rights of the corporate entities that developed and created the software.

Incidentally, the GPL is not tied specifically to Drupal; rather Drupal makes use of the GPL, which is a kind of generic license for distributing open source software. You can check out the GNU homepage http://www.gnu.org/home.html for more information on this movement.

The way things work is that the software is copyrighted and then licensed for everyone to use freely. This might strike you as a little odd at first because what is the point of copyrighting something if you are simply going to let everyone else make use of it? The reason for this is that copyrighting and licensing the software gives the developer the power to obligate people who use that software to afford everyone they hand it out to (with or without modifications) the same rights that are vested in the original software.

What this means is that, effectively, anyone who makes use of this software cannot create proprietary software from it. So, if you decide to build upon and improve Drupal in order to sell it as your own product, then you will be bound by the same terms and will have to release the source code to anyone who asks for it.

Remember though, the aim of the GPL is not to take credit for your own work by forcing you to release it under the GPL. If you have developed identifiable programs or code that are wholly your own and are independent from the original source code provided, then the GPL does not apply to your work.

A summary of some of the main points in the license is as follows:

- You are free to copy the software covered by the GPL as well as distribute these copies however you see fit. The most important thing is not to remove the licensing

- You can hack around with the source code and create whatever type of derived product you want. Again, you must pass on the same license (as you received it) with the original code, only this time you must make it very clear what changes you introduced

- You mustn't break the terms of the GPL at any stage or you will find your current license to use the software terminated

- You aren't forced to accept the conditions of the license. (You can tell this from the fact that you don't have to sign anything.) However, if you don't accept the terms of the license, you can't make use of the software

- If you do decide to redistribute the software yourself, then you can't add restrictions or modify the license in any way. You also aren't required to ensure that the parties you distribute the software to comply with it

- If you are compelled by a court ruling (or any other legal proceeding) to enforce conditions that do not meet the requirements of the GPL, then you must not distribute the software at all

- Keep an eye on the version of the license that is distributed with the software. If there is one present, then you must use that version (in some instances of the GPL, a later one is also suitable, but never an earlier one)

- There is no warranty on this software, and no one who modifies or distributes the software in terms of the GPL is responsible for anything—especially damages or failure to operate and so on

At the end of the day, the only time you do need to worry about the niceties of the GPL is when you decide to set up a business installing, configuring, and customizing Drupal websites for money, or modifying, and redistributing the original source code.

The Server environment

I know most of you will be eager to get going at the moment and might well prefer to dive straight into making modifications to your Drupal site. Before we do so, we can take a few moments to read over this section to gain an appreciation of how everything is put together behind the scenes.

Having a basic knowledge of how the various technologies co-operate in order to produce a working Drupal site will help immeasurably in the long run. While everything we need to run a server will be provided in a single package, let's take a look at each of the individual underlying technologies we will be using:

- **PHP**: PHP, or PHP Hypertext Preprocessor, is the language in which Drupal is written. PHP is widely used on the Internet for a multitude of different projects and is renowned for its ease of use.

- **Apache**: This is the web server we will use to serve web pages during the development phase. Apache is the most popular web server on the Internet, with millions of live sites using it every day. In fact, as the Apache website says: *It is more widely used than all the other web servers combined.*

- **MySQL**: This is the database software that we will use to store all the information required to keep the website running. Everything from customer details to product information and a host of other things will be stored in the MySQL database. Keeping with the trend of popularity, MySQL is also the world's most popular bit of database software with over six million active installations worldwide.

The package that we will use to get a complete web server (that includes all the above mentioned technologies) for the purposes of this book is called **XAMPP**.

 The XAMPP distribution is available at
http://www.apachefriends.org/en/xampp.html.

Now that we know *what* we are using, it is important to take a quick look at *how* it is used. The following diagram shows a simplified view of how everything works, with the shaded section denoting the package containing the Apache web server, PHP interpreter, and MySQL database, with Drupal installed on the system:

So whenever a user does anything with your Drupal site (hopefully like contributing meaningfully), here's what happens:

- The relevant information is sent to the server in the form of an HTTP (HyperText Transfer Protocol) request.

- The server receives the HTTP request and says, Ah! This is a PHP page that has been requested. I need to send it off for processing by the PHP engine. The PHP page then gets processed and executed appropriately, and any actions that are required as a result of the user's request are performed.

- Once that is done, an appropriate response is returned by the server to the user's browser, and the cycle continues.

There are quite a few methods of providing dynamic web content that don't rely on PHP server requests. Instead, processing can be done on the browser itself (features like this are often loosely termed *Web 2.0*), but what you have been shown here is fundamentally how everything works, even if there are exceptions to the rule.

Obtaining and installing XAMPP (PHP, Apache, and MySQL)

As mentioned in the previous section, we are going to make use of a package installation in order to simplify the task of creating a workable development environment. You will notice that most software installation is really about learning a single process and repeating it for whatever software you need. More often than not, you will:

- Go to the software producer's site
- Find the download page and download the appropriate package
- Unpack the software or run the executable file, depending on the method of installation
- Install and configure the software—most often you will be guided through the process in one way or another
- Test your setup

Easy enough! Head on over to `http://www.apachefriends.org/en/xampp.html` and select the appropriate download link (that is, for Windows, Linux, Solaris, and so on). Select the desired package—generally the latest stable release. At the time of writing, version 1.7.3 was the most appropriate release, but you should feel free to use a later version, if there is one, as this will not affect the installation procedure.

> Note that you should ensure that any package you use comes with versions of PHP and MySQL that are compatible with the system requirements of your Drupal installation. Drupal system requirements are available at: `http://drupal.org/requirements`

The download section should look like the following screenshot:

Version	Size	Content
XAMPP Windows 1.7.3 [Basic package]		Apache 2.2.14 (IPv6 enabled), MySQL 5.1.41 + PBXT engine, PHP 5.3.1, OpenSSL 0.9.8l, phpMyAdmin 3.2.4, XAMPP Control Panel 2.5.8, XAMPP CLI Bundle 1.6, Webalizer 2.21-02, Mercury Mail Transport System v4.72, msmtp 1.4.19, FileZilla FTP Server 0.9.33, SQLite 2.8.17, SQLite 3.6.20, ADOdb 5.10, eAccelerator 0.9.6-rc1, Xdebug 2.0.6-dev, Ming 0.4.3 For Windows 2000, XP, Vista, 7. See ☑ README
☑ EXE	51 MB	Self-extracting RAR archive MD5 checksum: 3635a1c0baf15e8a019009e6c1225339
☑ ZIP	100 MB	ZIP archive MD5 checksum: 0fe7f440a7d3af7c06981570f764d246
XAMPP Windows 1.7.3 [Upgrade 1.7.2 to 1.7.3]		
☑ EXE	45 MB	Self-extracting RAR archive MD5 checksum: 414cb9b594f90ac9257a193c6fc6057a
☑ ZIP	89 MB	ZIP archive MD5 checksum: 985d0e704bf543079e626f4adb54e9ad

Click the EXE file link and, depending on your PC's security settings, you may get the following message:

Click on **Save File** to continue. At this point, you may take a break for a cup of coffee or tea if you have a slow connection as it may take a while—the download is in excess of 50 Meg.

Once the file has been downloaded, double-click it to begin the setup procedure. Follow the dialogs and ensure that you set the XAMPP options, as shown here (Note in particular, the first two options in the **SERVICE SECTION** are selected), before clicking **Install**:

Once everything has been done, you should receive a success message and the option to reboot. Save and close whatever important documents are open before clicking **OK**. Once the machine has restarted, you should have a whole list of new and exciting options to explore from the **XAMPP** option under **Apache Friends** in the **Start** menu.

Just to ensure that everything is going according to plan, navigate to `http://localhost` in your browser:

This confirms that everything is up and running as expected. One thing to make note of as it pertains to the previous screenshot is that all pages that are visible via your local web server (at http://localhost) are contained in what is known as the root folder.

Traditionally in Apache servers, htdocs is the *root* folder, and all the web pages that are to be made available must be placed inside htdocs. If a webpage is not in htdocs, then it is not possible to browse it.

From this, we know that we will have to locate the actual folder called htdocs on the file system in order to know where to put Drupal once it is downloaded. Assuming that you have gone with the default setup, you will find htdocs in the following directory (on Windows machines) along with everything else that was installed and created during setup: C:\xampp\htdocs.

In addition, it is worthwhile taking a look at one other facility that has been provided as part of the XAMPP installation because we're going to need it when it's time to install Drupal.

phpMyAdmin is a complete database management tool for MySQL and should be available to you at http://localhost/phpmyadmin. It can make life a lot easier whenever it is necessary to deal with data directly.

 If you are struggling to log onto phpMyAdmin or any other part of the site, then try using **root** as the username without providing a password. Note that you will probably be warned that it is not good practice to have a root account with no password—remember to set a password for root (by editing it under the **Privileges** tab) as soon as possible.

If you have access to phpMyAdmin, then our work here is complete because we now have a platform from which to begin building the Drupal site. Of course, we still need Drupal, so feel free to skip the following section and get going if everything is working on your system.

Troubleshooting XAMPP installation

There is generally one major stumbling block that prevents XAMPP from serving web pages normally. It occurs because other applications hog the ports that XAMPP uses in order to operate. If you found that towards the end of the XAMPP installation process, a warning message like the following was displayed:

It is likely that something else is preventing the Apache server from starting up properly. Often, the culprits are instant messaging programs or VoIP like Skype. XAMPP comes with a utility program that can help identify which programs are using which ports, allowing you to turn them off and retry the installation.

Go to C:\xampp (or wherever you installed XAMPP) and search for the port check utility, entitled xampp-portcheck.exe, and double-click on this file to run it. If XAMPP is correctly installed, you will be able to see something like the following:

```
C:\WINDOWS\system32\CScript.exe                                       _ □ x
***********************************************************************

Please wait a moment...


RESULT
------

Service          Port    Status
=====================================================================
Apache (HTTP)      80    C:\xampp\apache\bin\httpd.exe
Apache (WebDAV)    81    free
Apache (HTTPS)    443    C:\xampp\apache\bin\httpd.exe

MySQL            3306    C:\xampp\mysql\bin\mysqld.exe

FileZilla (FTP)    21    free
FileZilla (Admin) 14147  free

Mercury (SMTP)     25    free
Mercury (POP3)    110    free
Mercury (IMAP)    143    free

Press <Return> to continue.
```

Note that Apache HTTP, Apache HTTPS, along with MySQL all have ports, exactly as required by the server. If, for some reason, the HTTP and/or the MySQL services are not displayed here, then your web server will not be able to operate correctly.

If you see any other program running on the required ports (80, 443, and 3306), then close these down and retry the installation—if the installation was successful, you might want to try starting the Apache and MySQL services before re-installing the whole thing. Use the XAMPP control panel to manage services. It is accessible from the **Start** menu in **All programs** under **ApacheFriends | XAMPP | XAMPP Control Panel**:

If the control panel is already active, it will be available from your process tray under the XAMPP icon.

Often, programs like Skype will use the default port (80) if it is available, but will simply use a different one if 80 is already in use. So, once XAMPP is correctly installed, simply turning the other programs back on should work just fine, and you should not suffer any ill effects.

Obtaining and installing Drupal

Earlier in the chapter, we covered the **Download** page on the Drupal site; so there isn't too much to present us with problems at this point. Head on over to `http://drupal.org/project/drupal` and click the Drupal version number you wish to download—generally, *the latest stable release* is the one you want. Click **Download** to grab the latest copy and save it to your `C:` drive or your `My Documents` folder (or wherever you want).

> Drupal bugfix versions are represented by an additional digit after the main release version (that is, 7.1, 7.2, and so on). Bugfix versions should be used over the initial release for obvious reasons!

Now, the Drupal download is different from the XAMPP installer in that we will install Drupal ourselves; it doesn't come with its own installer .exe file. Instead, we are asked if we would like to **Save** (or **Open**) a .tar.gz file. In the event that your PC doesn't recognize .gz files (this is for Windows users), then download a zip program like 7-zip (http://www.7-zip.org).

Once you are ready, open and decompress the downloaded tar.gz file, then extract it to the htdocs folder of your XAMPP installation. To make life easier, perhaps rename the extracted folder to something more memorable and shorter than its default name, for example, I have simply called mine drupal, as shown in the following screenshot:

With that done, open up a browser and navigate to `http://localhost/drupal`. Remember to exchange the bolded section for the actual name of your folder in the `htdocs` directory. You should be presented with the first page of the installation dialog, which looks like the following screenshot:

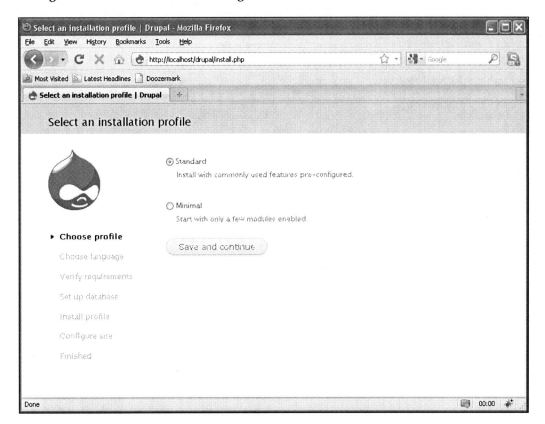

The **Standard** installation profile is fine for our purposes, so go ahead and click on **Save and continue**. For the purposes of this book, we will deal with English, but that's not to say that you can't install Drupal in a variety of different languages—simply click the **Learn how to install Drupal in other languages** link and follow the instructions. Otherwise, click on **Save and continue**.

Next, we have to ensure that Drupal's requirements are met. Drupal will present a list of what it needs, and anything highlighted in red must be dealt with before continuing:

In this case, the only serious problem is the fact that **The settings file does not exist** and further instructions are given below this message—we are to copy `default.settings.php` to `settings.php` in the `sites/default` folder.

It is not sufficient to simply rename the `default.settings.php` file, it must be a copy.

With that change implemented, we can click on **proceed with the installation**. The next batch of settings relates to the database that Drupal will use to power the site. Initially, the database does not yet exist, so let's create it quickly before continuing.

Open up a new browser, and navigate to `http://localhost/phpmyadmin`. Then enter the name of the database you would like to use for the site. Give the database either the same name as your site, or, if that is not a suitable choice for some reason, give it a sensible nickname, as shown in the following screenshot:

In this instance, you can see that I have specified a database name of `drupal`, which matches the name of the folder in which the new site is contained. Clicking **Create** brings up the following page and confirms that the new database now exists (although it still possesses 0 tables, as shown in the left-hand frame).

We can now continue with the Drupal installation. The database settings page looks something like that shown in the following screenshot:

Notice that I have referenced the database just created, specified the user as root, and provided the password I supplied upon setup of XAMPP (since this is the only user that currently exists in our pristine environment).

> Generally it is not a good practice to use the root superuser—I do so for expediency here. phpMyAdmin makes it easy to create new users from the master **Privileges** tab, and you are encouraged to add a specific user to this specific database.

Since we are using our own personal machine for testing and development, we can ignore the **Advanced options** link at the bottom of this page because the default settings are appropriate as it is. If you are using a database server that does not reside on your own machine, then these settings can be used to specify the host, port, and table prefix as required.

A table prefix is prepended to the front of each table name in the database to prevent one installation from overwriting the tables of another. This can happen if, for example, another package using the same database has table names in common with Drupal's.

The following page allows us to specify some general administrative and configuration parameters:

Ensure that you can remember whatever information is provided here because these settings specify the **Site maintenance account** details. Forgetting them could mean a real struggle to get back into the site (it's not impossible, provided you have root access to the database and can access all the information directly from phpMyAdmin). The e-mail address used here should be one that is convenient and active and does not necessarily have to be a part of your new site's domain—anything will do.

> The site maintenance account (User 1) is all powerful and has complete control over Drupal! Never use this account for everyday use of the site. Instead, create new users with specific access permissions to perform day-to-day tasks. More information on how to implement proper access control can be found in *Chapter 4, Users and Access Control*.

It's easy enough to decide on the server settings, and the final **Update notifications** section can be left activated for your convenience later on. With that, hopefully you are presented with a clean bill of health, as shown in the following screenshot:

It's also quite possible that there are some rather alarming warnings or errors written in red at this point and the most common of these are dealt with shortly in the *Troubleshooting the Drupal Installation* section.

Everything else henceforth is concerned with configuration and customization, and if you have not experienced any errors or difficulties so far, please feel free to skip the next section.

Troubleshooting the Drupal installation

In this section, we will take a look at two of the problems most likely to occur during the setup process. We will also take a look at how they manifest themselves and how to solve them quickly. It should be noted that at this early stage, there are not many things that can go wrong as the installation routine is fairly well used. This is good news because it is likely that any errors are the result of typos or something quite simple, which should be easy to rectify.

Unfortunately, we can't hope to cover absolutely everything in this section; so we will also outline a brief process that can be used to solve *any problem*, and not just the ones involved with installation. Having a sound process to follow is immeasurably more valuable than being shown solutions to each and every problem.

If, while setting up the database, you received a message like the one shown in the following screenshot:

Database configuration
The following error must be resolved before you can continue the installation process:

We were able to connect to the MySQL database server (which means your username and password are valid) but not able to select your database. MySQL reports the following message: *Unknown database 'mf4good'*.
- Are you sure you have the correct database name?
- Are you sure the database exists?
- Are you sure the username has permission to access the database?

For more help, see the Installation and upgrading handbook. If you are unsure what these terms mean you should probably contact your hosting provider.

Basic options

To set up your Drupal database, enter the following information.

Database type: *
- ⦿ mysql
- ○ pgsql

The type of database your Drupal data will be stored in.

Database name: *

`mf4good`

The name of the database your Drupal data will be stored in. It must exist on your server before Drupal can be installed.

It is likely that you have made a typo in the **Database name** field or have not correctly created a new database for Drupal to use. Check that you have not made a typo and that you have created a database with the desired name by revisiting `http://localhost/phpmyadmin`.

You might also have come across this rather ugly looking message towards the end of the installation process, as shown in the following screenshot:

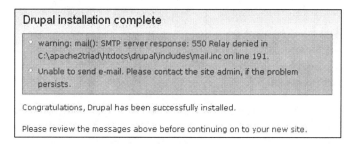

Drupal installation complete

- warning: mail(): SMTP server response: 550 Relay denied in C:\apache2triad\htdocs\drupal\includes\mail.inc on line 191.
- Unable to send e-mail. Please contact the site admin, if the problem persists.

Congratulations, Drupal has been successfully installed.

Please review the messages above before continuing on to your new site.

This error occurs when Drupal attempts to send an e-mail to confirm that the site has been set up, but finds that it is unable to do so. This problem is not critical because it doesn't prevent Drupal from completing its installation, but obviously, you would like the system to be able to send e-mails because they are useful for testing (and, of course, if you forget your password). The problem here is related to the environment itself and is not one specific to Drupal.

PHP has reported to Drupal that it is not able to send out the e-mail because it cannot find a suitable SMTP server. This is a common problem on Windows installations because unless an SMTP server is specified, there is no way PHP can decide for itself. To rectify this, open up the php.ini file located in C:\xampp\php and search for the [mail function] entries. Modify it to match an SMTP server that you have access to (for example, if you use Outlook, you can find the address of an SMTP server by viewing your account server settings):

```
[mail function]
; For Win32 only.
SMTP = mail.mysmtpserver.com
smtp_port = 25
```

Once you have made the relevant changes, save the file, and then restart the Apache server so that it can pick up the new settings.

 Restart the Apache server by opening up the **XAMPP Control Panel** from the start menu and click **Stop**; then **Start** next to **Apache**.

But what if something else has gone wrong? Another common source of errors pertains to *Permission issues*—the settings.php file in **sites/default** makes use of certain properties of PHP, and it is possible that there are conflicts here. Follow the instructions provided in the comments of this file if you suspect the problem lies here.

To see which PHP settings are possible, including whether they can be set at runtime *(such as* when `ini_set()` occurs), read the PHP documentation at `http://www.php.net/manual/en/ini.php#ini.list` and take a look at the `.htaccess` file to see which non-runtime settings are used there. Settings defined here should not be duplicated there so as to avoid conflict issues.

Further than this, the types of problems that can occur are not easily isolated, so we have outlined *how* to go about solving them. The following list of points highlight a process that can be used to troubleshoot any problems:

- Scrutinize any error messages you get and attempt to solve the problem yourself
- Visit the Drupal forums and search for similar problems
- Look through the troubleshooting FAQ at `http://drupal.org/node/199`
- View the bug list (`http://drupal.org/project/issues`) to see if your problem is a reported bug
- If you can't find bugs, similar posts, or problems, then try posting a focused and informative query on the forums and ask someone in the community to lend a hand
- To supplement this, get on Google and try using relevant keywords to locate a similar problem, hopefully a solution will be presented

For now though, you should be ready to continue with the final few tasks in the setup process, which will be performed in the following section.

Drupal's post-installation status

It's worth noting before we continue further that it is often beneficial to have several development sites in order to play around with different things without mucking up other work. The process outlined so far in this chapter can be repeated as many times as you like to set up as many development sites as you need—simply create a new database (or, alternatively, provide any new Drupal installation with a table prefix in the **Advanced options** section) and add the Drupal files to the `htdocs` directory (ensuring that they have a unique name) before browsing the new folder and repeating the installation process.

No matter what you decide, the next step is to click on the **Visit your new site** link to bring up the front page. By itself, the front page is not of much interest, since we haven't added anything to it. However, in the left-hand column, there is a link to the **Dashboard**. Click on this to bring up the following overlay and select the **BY TASK** tab:

The dashboard can be viewed either **BY TASK**, as shown here, or **BY MODULE**. At the moment, viewing the admin section **BY TASK** is probably more intuitive, but at a later stage, you might find that having direct access to specific modules is more efficient, and in this case, the **BY MODULE** view will probably be more suitable.

> The plus icon adjacent to any overlay title allows you to quickly add this page to the shortcuts menu (directly below the black toolbar menu at the top of the page). If you find that you are constantly using a specific page, it makes sense to add it to the shortcuts for quick access.

Since the **Dashboard** is where the business of building and running a Drupal site occurs, let's take a look at what that page provides and how it is organized before we quickly look at how to make use of a section by way of demonstration.

The dashboard tasks are broken up into seven default categories that cover all the aspects of running the site (note that you can click on the actual category names to bring up their default pages and not only the sub-categories), namely:

- **Content**: Search and administer all the site's content, including comments
- **Structure**: Handle content classification with taxonomies, work with layout of content and functionality via blocks, manage menus, and create and manage different content types
- **Appearance**: Work with the site's themes to produce unique interfaces
- **People**: List and administer site users
- **Modules**: Manage core and contributed modules including configuring, enabling, disabling, and uninstalling them
- **Configuration**: Access all the configuration settings for your Drupal website—including people, content, system, media, and more
- **Reports**: Keep your finger on the pulse with logs, error reports, updates, and other important report data

The price one pays for having a powerful and flexible system like Drupal is that it comes with, necessarily, a huge amount of options and parameters that need to be understood and implemented. Spending time learning and experimenting with these is one of the things that will take you from novice to pro. Ultimately, I'm sure you will agree that the organization of this array of features within Drupal makes it quite intuitive.

Right now, it's time to a have a quick look at one of the options just to get a feel of how things work. To get started, scroll down the dashboard page and check out the **Status report**—you will no doubt be presented with something that looks similar to the following screenshot (hopefully with no red involved):

This page displays information about the fundamentals of the Drupal installation. Anything showing in red needs urgent attention and action, while anything showing in yellow needs some attention. At the moment, the **Drupal core update status** is showing up in yellow, but with a close inspection of the reasons for the error, you will see that the problem is not that difficult to solve—the cron has not been run.

> Cron tasks are automated chores that Drupal needs to perform regularly in order to make sure that everything continues to run smoothly. In Drupal 7, they are handled automatically, but can also be run manually, if need be.

To deal with the cron issue, click on the **Run cron** link. This executes the cron script, and this section of the status page will now show up in green or red depending on what it finds out.

> During development, it is a good practice to periodically run the cron so that Drupal can perform its internal maintenance tasks.

While we will be going over most, if not all, the elements of the dashboard at various stages in the book, I recommend you spend a few minutes familiarizing yourself with how and where various tasks are presented. It will save you a bit of time in the future.

Creating a basic Drupal page

Let's make some modifications to the site via the admin page to confirm that everything is working normally and to highlight how easy it is to implement very powerful features at the click of a button. We'll run through a few quick steps to get some interesting features along with some new content on the site and then view it all as any visitor to the site would.

Go ahead and follow these steps:

1. Click on **Modules** in the toolbar menu. This will bring up a long list of modules that are available.
2. Select **Search**, **Poll**, and **Blog**, then scroll to the bottom of the page and click on **Save configuration**.
3. Click on **Add content** in the shortcut menu and then select the **Poll** option.
4. Fill out an arbitrary question with some options, as shown in the following screenshot, and then click **Save** (don't worry about any of the other options available for now):

5. Click on **Add content** again, but this time select the **Blog entry** option.

6. Fill out the fields available with any info that pops into your head, and click on the **Save** button (again, don't worry about any other settings or options for now).

7. Return to the **Dashboard** and select the **Blocks** option under **STRUCTURE**.

8. Scroll down the page and make changes to the table shown in the following screenshot by dragging-and-dropping a **BLOCK** to a desired **REGION**.

This page provides a drag-and-drop interface for assigning a block to a region, and for controlling the order of blocks within regions. Since not all themes implement the same regions, or display regions in the same way, blocks are positioned on a per-theme basis. Remember that your changes will not be saved until you click the *Save blocks* button at the bottom of the page. Click the *configure* link next to each block to configure its specific title and visibility settings.

Demonstrate block regions (Garland)

✚ Add block

BLOCK	REGION	OPERATIONS
Left sidebar		
✥ Search form	Left sidebar	configure
✥ Navigation	Left sidebar	configure
✥ User login	Left sidebar	configure
✥ Management	Left sidebar	configure
Right sidebar		
✥ Most recent poll	Right sidebar	configure
✥ Recent blog posts	Right sidebar	configure

9. In particular, notice that the **Most recent poll** has the **Right sidebar** region selected, as does **Recent blog posts**.

10. For convenience's sake, make sure you set **User login**. If you don't specify a **REGION** for this **BLOCK**, it will not show up when you log out and you have to manually navigate to `http://localhost/drupal/user` to get back in.

11. For now, don't worry too much about taking this all in, we will cover it in detail at a later stage—this exercise is simply going to give us our first look at a basic Drupal web page and its layout.

12. Once these changes are made, click on **Save blocks** and then **Home**.

The site should now look something like the following screenshot (minus the numbering):

There are several main areas of interest numbered in this screenshot, and we should look over them here in order to get a feel of what to expect in the chapters to come. Bear in mind that Drupal really doesn't impose many limitations on where and what you can place on any part of a web page, so the following explanation is really only a guide:

1. The toolbar menu contains links to the main administrative areas of the website.

2. The shortcuts menu can be used to add temporarily important links to help speed up navigation during administration. It can also be used by non-administrators to bookmark their favorite links.

3. The page header contains your site's logo and slogan, among other things. It also provides a link to the landing or home page.

4. (& 5) Left and right sidebars are predefined regions that contain blocks. Blocks are effectively containers of information or navigational links (or pretty much anything else you care to think of). Notice too that we now have blocks on the right-hand side (**Most recent polls** and **Recent blog posts**) because we set some of them to appear in the right sidebar earlier on. We told Drupal to display the **User login** in the left sidebar, but this is not visible because the screenshot was taken after login.

6. Content is generally displayed in this region of a site and the method of display is customizable and selective as we will see in due course. Since we did not specifically tell Drupal otherwise when we created some content, what we created is displayed automatically — we could have told it not to make the post visible here at all if we liked; we will talk about how to control content in greater detail in Chapter 6.

7. The footer often contains information that is not immediately the most important on a page but is still relevant and useful. You might get Drupal to display who is online here, but equally you could add a copyright notice, or terms of use, and so on.

This section has touched upon the power and elegance of Drupal by adding impressive features at the touch of a button and with little to no experience and certainly no programming skills required. However, it is quite possible that you don't want anything like what we have just seen. Perhaps you only want a single sidebar or none at all. Maybe you want advertising across the top of the page or content displayed in drop-shadowed boxes, whatever it may be, the coming chapters will see to it that you are equipped with the requisite information to implement your goals.

Summary

This chapter has served as an introduction to the world of Drupal as well as a backdrop for the rest of the book. The foundation from which to build a live site in the coming days and weeks has been laid. Having taken the time to set up a working development environment, you can be assured that any needless time wastage has been prevented.

With the facilities provided by XAMPP (Apache, PHP, and MySQL) installed on a test machine, we turned our attention to obtaining and installing Drupal itself — hopefully, you found that quite easy with the much improved installation features of Drupal 7.

Finally, we became acquainted with Drupal itself by adding new modules, posting some content to the site, and specifying where this content could be displayed on a typical page. In doing so, we were able to briefly discuss the anatomy of a basic Drupal page.

If you have gotten this far, then congratulations, you are ready to begin developing a new site. It's time to get your hands dirty.

2
Basic Functionality

Drupal is a modular system. Its functionality is held in modules that integrate into the main *workflow* at various points, altering the way other parts operate or even adding new features entirely. In order to build a fully functional website, we use modules that either come as part of the standard Drupal download (the *core*) or are provided by the various developers of the Drupal community.

The terms *module* and *functionality*, with respect to Drupal, are effectively synonymous from the point of view that modules provide functionality. Therefore, the discussion of Drupal functionality is really a discussion about modules.

Adding a new module is one thing, but presenting its functionality is also important and this requires us to look at menus and blocks as an integral part of our discussion on functionality. Accordingly, in this chapter, we are going to take a close look at:

- Modules
- Working with modules
- Third-party modules
- Working with blocks
- Menus, main, and secondary links

Be aware that we won't be discussing some of the content-related modules in too much depth because these will be covered in great detail in later chapters. While the focus of this chapter is on getting the basics up and running, we will also look at how to include other modules from the Drupal site in order to demonstrate its power and flexibility. This will also reveal the considerable advantage of having an entire development community at hand to help out.

Modules

To get us started, let's take a look at the definition of a module:

Modules are plugins for Drupal that extend, build, or enhance Drupal functionality. Some core modules are required by Drupal in order to function, some are optional, and others can be obtained from the Drupal community.

It is by enabling certain modules that you will be able to achieve a diverse, and more importantly, functional site. As there are plenty of modules available, I can't hope to bore you with all the ins and outs of every single one. Instead, we will enable and briefly work with some of the more interesting and useful ones to demonstrate how the module system works and how to use it.

If there is a module required by your site that is not covered here, follow the same method of enabling and testing that is discussed throughout this chapter and apply it to that specific module. You will be up and running in no time at all.

Before we begin discussing individual modules and their settings, click on the **Modules** link in the toolbar menu at the top of your page, and decide which ones to enable, based on your site's forecasted needs. Bear in mind that it is very easy to come back at a later stage and enable and disable modules — this is part of the beauty and power of Drupal.

For the purposes of this chapter, we will need the following modules enabled:

- **Forum**
- **Comment**
- **Search**

Once you have made a selection, click on **Save configuration**. At this point, it is possible that Drupal presents something like the following query, as shown in the next screenshot:

This tells us that the **Forum** module has *dependencies*. In other words, it cannot do its job without the facilities provided by the other module listed. Many modules are interdependent, and Drupal gives clues as to what relies on what on the modules page. For example, **Forum** displays the following:

In this instance, it is telling us that it requires two other modules (specifically, Taxonomy and Comment), both of which are enabled. Look at **Taxonomy**, as shown in the following screenshot:

The converse is displayed, insofar as it tells us that while **Taxonomy** itself has no dependencies, it is required by **Forum**. Note too that Drupal prevents us from disabling any module that is required by another enabled module, by disabling the checkbox next to the module's name. Disabling the **Taxonomy** module, in this case, requires us first to disable all modules that depend on it first—in this case, **Forum**.

For at least a few of these modules, we will have to put in some serious thought before they are actually implemented on the site. In particular, **Forum** needs to be discussed in some depth.

Working with modules

The inherent broadness of function associated with modules means that the configuration and use of each one can also vary greatly. Because of this, it can be quite confusing at first to find out where to go in order to administer or make use of any changes implemented by a module.

Luckily, the module listings page gives us quick access to the permissions and configuration settings for each module, as shown here:

Each module has one or more links to a **Help**, **Permissions**, and **Configuration** page. Don't confuse the configuration of a module with the administration of the functionality it provides. A module may add entire pages of administrative features that can be accessed via the **Dashboard** and these are not necessarily the same as actually configuring its settings.

For example, the **Forum** module provides a listing page where administrators can edit forum containers, topics, and so on. This is different from the settings page that allows us to specify some global options. Talking of which, let's take a look at how to configure a small sample of the modules that come with the Drupal core, starting with...

Forum

Click on **Configure,** next to **Forum** in the module list to begin working with it. This presents the following page for managing the site's forums:

Note that the forum settings can be viewed by clicking the **SETTINGS** tab at the top right of the overlay—it's fairly easy to come back here at any stage and make changes that will affect the way the forums behave. The effects will be much easier to see with some structure and content added; as we'll see in a moment.

How to organize a **forum** really depends on how broad the scope of the discussion topics is going to be, how many people will be using the forums, and the nature of the topics up for discussion. What you are aiming for is an intuitive, logical, easy-to-use structure that will facilitate and encourage discussion by allowing users to easily find information, as opposed to frustrating them with a poor structure that obscures topics—this is a general problem and not unique to Drupal.

Let's think about how to organize wildlife and conservation forum. A good idea is to draw out the structure beforehand so that you can see how everything relates and make changes before having to physically create or delete forums. For example, it may seem logical to split up forums depending on location, so that people in the US go straight to the North American forums and people in Africa go straight to the African forums.

Unfortunately, this has several drawbacks because there would be a lot of repeated topics for each continent (since wildlife issues are the same the world over). Even worse, if someone living in the US was concerned about canned lion hunting in South Africa, where would they go to discuss this, Africa or North America? It seems that partitioning forums based on location, in this instance, is probably not a good idea.

The best way to do it is by issue. People want to discuss issues or topics, so they naturally look for content based on these criteria. When looked at in this light, the meaning of the **add containers** tab becomes clear because now we can organize forum topics based on their common issues.

In Drupal, a *container* holds a grouping of forums, so adding a container based on common issues for a number of forums is a very logical way to break up forums into intuitive chunks.

Once you have a nice structure jotted down on paper or in your head, it is time to actually implement the forums on the site. Let's set about this by creating the containers first. Click on **Add container** to bring up a page to specify the name of the container, a brief description, the parent, and a weight.

Since you should have already decided on a structure, it is easy to see which container or forum has which parent. The top-level container should leave the parent as **<root>**. You can set the weight of the container or forum if you would like them to be presented in an order other than alphabetical—the smaller the weight, the closer to the top of the pile it will appear.

Keep adding containers and forums, along with helpful descriptions until the entire structure is complete. The following screenshot shows an example structure for the putative wildlife and conservation forum. (There are, no doubt, more topics that could be added or changed, but this suffices for the moment):

Now we can revisit the **SETTINGS** tab—most of the default settings here are pretty sensible, and all that is required is for you to decide on such things as how many posts to display in one go and in which order:

Once you are done, click on **Save configuration** and the forum is more or less ready to go. Not bad for a few minutes work! The best thing about this forum is that it is easily modified to adapt to how the community makes use of it—adding, renaming, or removing containers and forums is very easy. Just be careful not to continuously modify your forums because this can be frustrating for members.

In reality, you should play around with each and every module, and ensure that it is working to your satisfaction. We don't have space to do so here, so it is left to you to post some content to the forums with comments and replies to get a feel of how things work.

Comments

As the **Comment** module is needed by the **Forum** module, it's a good idea to look at it here. A comment, as the name implies, allows users to remark about content they find on the site — as simple as that. How to figure out who can make comments and on what, is the subject of *Chapter 4, Users and Access control.*

Navigate to the configuration page for **Comment** in the module list:

Drupal provides a fairly comprehensive interface for working with comments. There are a few **UPDATE OPTIONS** available in the drop-down list that delete or unpublish comments. If you never want to see a particular comment again on your site, then **Delete the selected comments** is the way to go. If you only want to prevent the comment from being displayed, without being removed entirely, then **Unpublish the selected comments** is the correct update option to use.

Assuming you have decided to unpublish a comment for some reason or the other, you will have to look for it under the **Unapproved comments** tab (towards the top of the page) instead of the main page. The approval queue allows you to search through and edit posts that have landed up here for whatever reason—it may be that they have been unpublished, or it may be that you have decided to force all comments into the **Unapproved comments** list for moderation. However the comments land up here, there are two update options available again—this time you can either delete the comment or publish it.

For completeness, it is worth discussing a number of other important settings associated with comments, namely, **Default comment settings** or **Default display mode**. These options are **attached to each specific content type** in order to provide fine-grain control over how to view and post comments for individual types. Accordingly, we must visit each different content type (in the **Content types** page under **Structure** in the main menu) in order to make the appropriate comment settings.

Select the **edit** option next to a content type you wish to work with (for example, **Basic page**), and then scroll down the page and select the **Comment settings** tab. Browse through the available options and make any changes you would like before clicking **Save content type**:

The previous screenshot shows comments set to display as a **Threaded list** in order to bunch related comments together. Deciding the best method to display comments is really up to you, and any decisions made should take into account how comments are used on the site.

Assuming you are going to allow anonymous users to post comments, decide whether they are to leave contact information with their posts. From the point of view of keeping up the standard of posts, it is probably a good idea to have postings from anonymous viewers sent to the **approval queue** so that you don't become a victim of spam attacks or cheap advertising.

Comments are also a slightly special case in that they are not really a node (like all other content), but as of Drupal 7, they have the same fields functionality and display features. When looking at any content type you will be able to work with comment fields and their display by clicking on the **COMMENT FIELDS** at the top of the page:

We're going to spend a lot of time working on fields and content display in later chapters, so just keep this new comment functionality in mind for now. Handling comment fields will be easy after the discussion on fields and content.

Incidentally, if you would like to enforce whether comments must be approved or whether they can be displayed immediately, select **Permissions** for the **Comment** module in the **Module** list. The default configuration parameters are displayed (along with those for each other module):

In this case, anonymous users are not able to post or even access comments, but changing this is simply a case of checking the relevant boxes and clicking **Save permissions**. We won't look at this in any more detail here, but as mentioned, permissions will be dealt with in detail later on in *Chapter 5, Basic Content*.

Search

This is an interesting module to configure because there are some subtle underlying issues that require consideration when adjusting settings. For a start, the indexing process that is used to search the database relies on the cron (discussed in *Chapter 3, Configuration and Reports*). Ensure that it is operating correctly on a live site if you are going to implement a search feature.

Click on **Configure**, adjacent to the **Search** module to bring up the **Search settings** page, as shown in the following screenshot:

It is possible to re-index a site manually by clicking on the **Re-index site** button at the top of the search configuration page. This will cause Drupal to go over the site's content and update its index so that any new content that you specifically wish to be included in any searches will be. From the previous screenshot, you can see that only 50 percent of the site's content has currently been indexed. Clicking on **Re-index** will index as many items as specified in the **INDEXING THROTTLE** section.

The **INDEXING THROTTLE** controls the number of items to index per cron run. This is done to prevent the indexer from taking up too many resources in one go. Instead, indexing happens in smaller batches, but this may mean that the site has to go through several cron runs before new content is indexed and available via the search.

It may be prudent to make this setting a little lower if the site experiences timeout problems. In addition, indexing shorter words (in the **INDEXING SETTINGS** section) adds load to the system because it has to index that many more words in the content. It may also clutter up the search results with unwanted matches as a result of including words like *a* or *in*.

Finally, it is possible to decide on how to rank site content based on five criteria, namely: **Number of comments, Keyword relevance, Content is sticky at top of lists, Content is promoted to the front page**, and **Recently posted**. Work out which criteria are more important and which ones can be safely downgraded in importance. For example, in the following screenshot:

Ranking indicates that a higher importance is placed on the **Keyword relevance** of the content — in other words, how closely does the content match the keywords specified in the search. This importance is almost matched by **Number of comments**, but the others are given less **Weight** and are therefore not considered quite as important as the first two criteria. Depending on your criteria, you may choose something completely different — the bottom line is to ensure that the search results are as relevant as possible to the site's users.

Third-party modules

One of the greatest things about Drupal is that the community contributions can promote and increase the diversity and features of any given project because they lower the development burden for website creators like you and me.

This means we can take a leisurely gander at a variety of modules that have been made by someone, improved on by someone else, or changed into something else, and pick and choose the best. The converse of this is, of course, that any of your own developments can also be made available for everyone else to use.

There are certain issues associated with using contributed modules such as the one we are going to incorporate into the demo. It is important to understand that people are providing useful software without enforcing payment.

 Contributions (*contribs*), like any software, are subject to bugs or errors, so make sure you back up everything, database included, before implementing any changes.

For more information on properly backing up a site, refer to *Chapter 11, Deployment and Management*. Remember, if a new module breaks your site, then you can go to the forums, bug reports, chats, and so on for help, but it is your responsibility, and not the contributor's, to keep your site operational.

Downloading and installing modules

The Drupal website houses a list of contributions that are available under the **Modules** tab of the **Download** page (`http://drupal.org/project/modules`). At the top of the **Modules** page, there is a selection of Drupal versions from which you can choose the appropriate one, and then browse the modules by category, name, or date, as shown in the following screenshot:

![Screenshot of the Drupal Modules download page showing categories, filter, search, and module listings including Views.]

The Drupal Modules page shows the following content:

Modules

You can also view an alphabetical list of projects that includes all projects but only their names.

Modules categories: - Any -   **Filter by compatibility:** - Any -   **Search Modules:**   **Sort by:** Most installed

Search

Contributed (contrib) modules are plugins for Drupal that extend, build or enhance Drupal core functionality. Use matching versions (modules released for Drupal 5.x will not work for Drupal 6.x). Contributed modules are not part of Drupal core releases and may or may not have optimized code/functionality. If a module solves your needs please consider joining forces and helping the maintainer. You can view module usage statistics for all modules to view the most popular modules used by the Drupal community.

Views

By **merlinofchaos** on the 25th of November, 2005

The Views module provides a flexible method for Drupal site designers to control how lists and tables of content (nodes in Views 1, almost anything in Views 2) are presented. Traditionally, Drupal has hard-coded most of this, particularly in how taxonomy and tracker lists are formatted.

This tool is essentially a smart query builder that, given enough information, can build the proper query, execute it, and display the results. It has four modes, plus a special mode, and provides an impressive amount of functionality from these modes.

Among other things, Views can be used to generate reports, create summaries, and display collections of images and other content.

Sidebar (Dodge): Drupalcon Copenhagen Aug 2010 · Issues · My account · My projects · Create content · Recent posts · Feed aggregator · Log out

Contributor links: Community initiatives · Queues · My issues · 485 Pending bugs (D7) · 34 Critical issues (D7) · 1549 Patch queue (D7) · 439 Patches to review (D7) · Performance issues (D7) · Usability issues (D7) · Fields in Core issues (D7)

Obtaining the correct version is important because a module developed for the 6.x family will certainly not work with the latest 7.x family. Unfortunately, the upgrading of contributions is not necessarily done at the same time as the core development; so it may be that there are some modules only built for older versions of Drupal. For development purposes, you can always download a beta version of a module to work with until a stable version is available. However, this is not recommended for a live website.

For this demonstration, we will use a contribution that you will come to rely on heavily if you intend to build a dynamic and scalable site. The **Views** module provides a smart database query builder, which is a fancy way of saying that it allows you to pick and choose lists of content (it also allows you to control their display) and is such an important topic that *Chapter 8, Views*, is dedicated to it alone.

It can be found under the **Content Display** category, but is often the first module that will show up by default due to its popularity.

 You need to be logged into the Drupal site in order to apply a version filter.

Once you have found it, you have two options (click on the **Install new module** link provided on the **Modules** page), as shown in the following screenshot:

1. Install it directly from an URL.
2. Download it from the Drupal site to your local machine and upload it to your site (also on the **Install new module** page).

The first option is fairly straightforward. Hover your mouse over the **Download** link for the version whose filename you want to see (shown in the browser's information bar at the bottom of the screen), and enter the full download link into the space provided. The URL will be in the following format:

```
http://ftp.drupal.org/files/projects/name.tar.gz
```

where `name` is replaced with the name and version of the file.

Alternatively, actually click **Download**, and save the zipped file locally. It may be more expedient to create a directory, say `drupal_downloads`, to save these files to. Once the file is downloaded on your local machine, you can upload it to your site by using the upload form at the bottom of the module install page.

Go ahead and install the *Views* module using a method of your choice. Remember that you can also simply extract the module to the `sites/all/modules` or the `sites/default/modules` folder and then enable them directly from the **Modules** list (Drupal automatically finds and adds modules stored in these folders to the list).

> To manually add modules, you will have to create a `modules` folder in the `sites/all` or `sites/default` directory first.

Before we move on, it's a good idea to take a look at the list of modules available on `drupal.org` to see what is achievable with Drupal. For example, did you know that you can use Drupal as an e-commerce website, complete with products or services and a shopping cart? Payment facilities, such as PayPal or credit cards and pretty much anything else that a fully-fledged online store would need, are readily implementable.

It's important to note that each module can have different requirements depending on how it needs to alter the system in order to function. The best way to learn about how to install modules is to simply go ahead and use them. Any module you install via the **Install new module** page will automatically be extracted to the **sites/all/modules** directory of your installation.

In the event that there is an issue preventing a module from being installed correctly, navigate to the `modules` folder on the filesystem and open up its `readme` file first. This will, more than likely, have some detailed directions on how to successfully install and utilize the module.

That's pretty much all there is to it, but we still need to ensure that we can make use of this module from the administrator's point of view. While the module is installed, it isn't yet enabled, so navigate back to the list of modules and check the enabled box next to its name before clicking on **Save configuration**.

Updating modules

Often, it is a good idea to quickly check if there are any updates available by checking manually.

In order to notify you of any important upgrades for modules and themes, Drupal requires the cron script to run (which happens automatically as of Drupal 7). Occasionally, Drupal will prompt you to view the **Available updates** page to check on the status of each of the installed modules. These warnings will be displayed at the top of the page and look something like this:

> There are updates available for one or more of your modules or themes. To ensure the proper functioning of your site, you should update as soon as possible. See the available updates page for more information and to install your missing updates.

Clicking on the **Available updates** link that leads to the **Available updates** page in the **Reports** section demonstrates that there is at least something that needs to be updated:

It's fairly easy to pick and choose the modules you want to update and click **Download these updates**. You are making regular backups before swapping out modules, right?

> Remember that the **Update** tab, in the **Modules** overlay, offers the same functionality and you can easily implement updates from there too.

Any errors that occur during the update process will be logged, and you can review them in the **Reports** section at the **Recent log entries** page. Keeping an eye on this can help you pinpoint any problems or help make decisions about which module versions to use.

Working with blocks

As we saw briefly in *Chapter 1, Introduction to Drupal*, blocks contain functionality or content that is visible in various places around the site—depending on where you choose to show them. Blocks are often generated by modules, but it is also possible to create them manually. Since many modules generate blocks automatically, it is always wise to pay the **blocks** section a visit whenever a new module has been enabled.

When we talk about working with blocks, what we are really saying is: "*How do we want to present the functionality and content of the site to the user?*" Naturally, everyone should strive to make a striking and unique site, and layout configuration is a big part of that—especially since it governs how a site is organized.

Keep in mind at all times that the overriding factors that govern setting things up, when it comes to presenting the site, relate to usability. Make sure that the site is intuitive, easy to follow, and never sacrifice clarity and ease of use for artistic reasons.

Drupal sites are already fairly sensibly laid out by default, but that doesn't mean that there is not plenty to do. You have an exceptional amount of control over where and how everything is displayed, and correspondingly, quite a lot to work on.

Adding blocks

Under **Structure** in the toolbar menu, click on **Blocks** to bring up the list of blocks that are available for the site at present. Remember that this list will change as modules are added and removed—you will probably have to revisit it more than once. The blocks page provides a list of the available blocks and several options for each one.

Drupal gives you the ability to place any of these blocks pretty much anywhere on the page. Depending on how many themes you have enabled, you can make different block settings for different themes too. Click on the theme link at the top of the blocks overlay to work on each individual theme's blocks. We will talk more about themes in *Chapter 9, Drupal Theming*.

Regardless of which theme you use, it is generally a good idea to group related information into the same places on the site, so that users can get a feel for where they might look for a specific type of content. For our current purposes, the following settings are made:

Notice that community-related information, like **Who's new** and **Who's online**, is confined to the footer area of the page. While this information might be of interest, it must be relegated to the bottom of the page to avoid detracting from the main content of the site.

All content-related blocks are grouped into the right-hand sidebar. This means that if people want to quickly take a look at what new content has been added to the site, they can find it by looking here. Additionally, information is structured such that polls appear above all other information (because we generally want to encourage people to take the time to answer a poll), but we have left the **Search form** at the top of the page because this should be one of the most useful tools, once the amount of content on the site has become substantial.

Of course, some blocks remain disabled, as the site does not need them for now. It is always easy to add or remove blocks at a later date. Provided you make sure there is a nice logical layout for the various blocks, you can chop and change what is and is not displayed as and when required. Remember not to chop and change too often once the site is live, as this impairs its usability and may lead to confusion.

Take a look at your homepage once these changes have been saved (by clicking **Save blocks**). Notice that the various blocks have now been inserted into the web pages. It's easy enough to move things around until you are totally happy with the way the page looks, but there is little point in spending hours and hours getting everything just perfect if you are going to change the theme at a later stage. Instead, make sure you understand how blocks work and come back to it after settling on a theme because different themes have different regions into which blocks can be added and removed.

You may also have noticed that there is an **Add block** tab at the top of the **Blocks** page. Clicking on this brings up a page that can be used to insert your own blocks into the site, as shown in the following screenshot:

The situation becomes more complex when we start thinking about whether certain people should be allowed to access a block or not, or whether the block should be displayed on all pages or only on selected pages. In order to find out how to deal with these issues, we must look at block configuration in some detail.

Configuring blocks

Drupal allows us to control when a block is displayed through the **configure** link at the right-hand side of each block in the list. This configuration page is split up into five main sections that deal with:

- **Block-specific settings**
- **Pages**
- **Content types**
- **Roles**
- **Users**

Combining these provides a sophisticated method of controlling when a block is shown, and to whom. Of course, some modules don't require any specific settings of their own; in which case, you are only required to make decisions about content types, roles, users, and pages.

The **Who's online** block configuration page serves as a good example. This page allows us to decide how long users can be inactive before we no longer consider them online, as well as the maximum number of people to show at any one time. That's easy enough to deal with and really depends on the needs of the site.

The other options give us something to think about though, as shown here:

This **Users** setting allows users to edit their own preference for whether they can see the **Who's online** block (alternatively, selecting **Not customizable** forces the block to be displayed for all users).

With these settings in place, users editing their account information are presented with the following checkbox that allows them to enable the block or disable it:

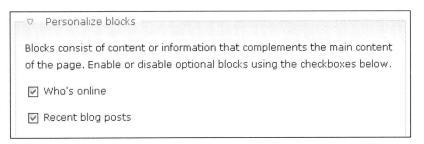

The **Roles** section also allows us to make choices based on the different groups of people using the site:

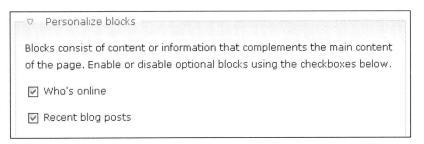

The previous screenshot shows that this block will only be displayed to authenticated users, but it serves as a more important example of how working with blocks is a fluid, dynamic task. Later, we will look at how to create different roles in *Chapter 4, Users and Access Control,* and this will require you to return to this page to re-specify the **Role-specific visibility settings**, if necessary. Any time you add new content types or roles, you will have to return and ensure that the **Visibility settings** are properly configured.

Looking at the following screenshot, notice that under **Show block on specific pages**, the **All pages except those listed** option has been selected and the text **<front>** has been entered in the text area provided:

This means that whenever someone visits the site, they are not immediately shown who is online, but as soon as they begin using the site and move away from the home page, that information becomes available. You might choose to implement completely the opposite.

As always, it is recommended that you play around and attempt to show a block on a certain page, but not the others. For example, can you prevent a block from being shown when someone is using the forums?

Completing the site's block configuration is simply a case of going through each enabled block, and making the appropriate decisions about when, where, and to whom it will be displayed. At present though, this is not quite the full picture because we have not yet discussed users, roles, and permissions; so be prepared to revisit this later.

Menus, main, and secondary links

There are five default menus that can be configured in Drupal. Clicking on **Menus** under **Structure** in the toolbar menu provides access to this menu list as well as the **Add menu** link and the menu **SETTINGS** tab, as shown in the following screenshot:

The five default menus are used for the following purposes:

- **Main menu** — add links to this menu to allow site users to quickly access the major areas of your website. For example, blog, forum, downloads, and so on.
- **Management** — this menu, shown by default on the left-hand side of the page, provides access to the Dashboard and adding content for administrative purposes.
- **Navigation** — contains links for site users to quickly access important parts of the website.
- **Secondary menu** — most themes automatically make use of the secondary menu to present links to administrative or logistical pages such as contact, terms of use or about us.
- **User menu** — provides user-specific links such as quick access to the user account or a log out link.

If, at some point, the default menus are not sufficient for your purposes, adding a new menu is quite easy. Go ahead and click the **Add menu** link on this page and provide a name and description, before adding links:

This menu will automatically be available to work with in the **Menu** section, just like the defaults. Note the additional **Custom menu** now present at the top of the list:

Remember that the new menu will not show up on the site until you tell Drupal where it should be displayed using the **Blocks** section under **Structure**. The menu block can be dragged around and worked on like any other block.

In addition to listing all the menus available on the site, the **Menus** overlay also has a **SETTINGS** tab:

The **Source for the Main links** option specifies where links that are added during content creation (for example, when creating an **About us** page) will be added. It's basically a shortcut method of adding new content to the menu because it saves you from having to post some content, find the relative path (`http://localhost/drupal/`**forum**), and then add that to the menu manually—although, we discuss this process in a moment.

These options are interesting because they control where the links displayed in a theme's main and secondary links are drawn from. For each of these you can select a range of menus, or not to show the menu at all. As a quick exercise, set the **Source for the Main links** to **User menu** and click on **Save configuration**. You should find that the **user-related** menu items are now displayed in the **Main links** menu, as shown in the following screenshot (remember to refresh the page first):

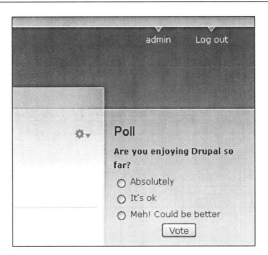

It's a bit confusing to picture what is going on before we have even looked at the Main links in any detail, so we'll clarify this in a moment. For now, ensure that you reset the **Source for the Main links** option to **Main menu** and click on **Save configuration**.

Click on the **LIST MENUS** tab, and select the **LIST LINKS** option for the **Main menu** (we're going to work on the main menu for the rest of the section but most likely there is nothing in it yet for us to explore). From here, you can add, edit, enable, disable, or in some cases, delete items as well as determine whether or not items should be expanded. In addition, items that are enabled or disabled will subsequently display a reset option that turns any configuration back to their defaults. For now , it looks a bit empty:

Click on the **Add link** option to bring up the following dialog:

In this instance, we are creating a new menu item that will take users back to the home page. The **Description** will be displayed as a tip whenever a user hovers their mouse over the link, so ensure you enter something succinct and helpful here. Since this link will not have any child links there is no point in selecting the **Show as expanded** option (for the purposes of this example) because there will be nothing to expand. The **Parent link** is, of course, set to **Main menu**, but you can alter this to another menu if you choose.

Clicking on **Save** adds this new link to the **Main menu**, and it will be available to **edit**, **disable**, or **delete** in the **LIST LINKS** section. More importantly, looking at a page now should reveal the effect this has had:

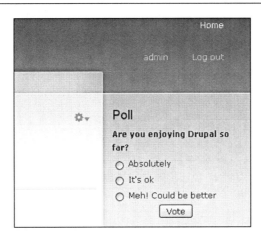

Notice there is now a **Home** link at the top right of the page. This is where the main menu is displayed in the default theme, but different themes might make any number of changes to the main menu). Clicking on **Home** should take you straight to the default front page, as specified when the link was created.

Try to add another menu item to the **Main menu** to make sure you can add any target page at will. Since we have created a forum, let's add the forum front page to the **Main menu** (can you guess the target **Path** we should specify?):

A good trick, hinted at earlier, to locate the path needed for a menu item is to navigate to it directly and then cut and paste the relative path (that is, everything in the URL after the base URL). For example, if we go to the forums on the site as it stands, the URL looks like this:

```
http://localhost/drupal/forum
```

The bold part is the relative path because `http://localhost/drupal` is the root folder (or homepage).

Now, you might decide that in addition to visiting the forum front page, you also want to add the containers to this menu so that people can go straight to their forum of choice.

After saving the forum link in the main menu, go back to the **Add item** dialog and then add the new link, as shown here:

Determining that `forum/3` corresponds to the **Conservation** container required a quick visit to the container that displayed `http://localhost/drupal/forum/3` as the URL, and from there, it is a simple matter to add this to the **Path**. Remember, that we want this link to be a child item of **Forums** within the **Main menu**, so the **Parent** link needs to be changed accordingly. Be careful here because you are able to select a parent item from any of the menus, so it is possible to choose the wrong one.

With that done, click on **Save** and then take a look at the **Main menu** at the top right of the page:

Conservation is not immediately visible because it is a child link of **Forum**. Unfortunately, clicking on **Forum** takes you to the forums and does not expose the **Conservation** link within the Main menu as you might expect—this is because the main menu does not display child links—simple as that.

However, you are not constrained to stick with the conventional setup for these particular menus either. Head on over to the **Blocks** section under **Structure** and set the **Main menu** block to display in the **Left sidebar**. With that saved, there is a new view of the **Main menu** complete with child links:

Having the ability to create unlimited menus and display them anywhere is a very powerful feature. Bear in mind that there are inevitably some limitations such as the one we have just discussed with main links not displaying child links. As always there are ways around this, and the exercises for this chapter should shed some light on a potential solution.

Summary

This chapter discussed the all-important topic of adding functionality and organizing it on the site. This is one of the most important tasks to undertake during website creation. Selecting and implementing the right functionality for the right users is a subtle art, but hopefully you found that Drupal makes it quite easy to implement.

We also got a taste of what it's like to have an entire development community to draw from, when we downloaded and installed a contributed module. Contributions are an invaluable resource for extending the functionality of a site. This facility comes with the express warning that you need to safeguard the security of your site by making backups before implementing any changes.

Drupal's power and elegance shone through when we talked about how easy it is to customize the site's menus and navigation. Having a flexible menu system is an extraordinary help when it comes to creating a well-designed and easy-to-use site.

One of the most important things you hopefully learned from this chapter is that, because Drupal is so flexible and customizable, there are a large number of ever changing settings—depending on which modules are added or removed. Keeping track of all of these might seem quite daunting at first, but it will become more familiar in time.

For now though, sit back and take a quick break, happy in the knowledge of a task well done. In the following chapter, we look at configuration—another topic crucial for your success as a Drupal website administrator.

3
Configuration and Reports

People often assume that *the basics* are easy to master and therefore, don't require much thought. Things are not quite so simple in reality because while a site's basic setup is, more often than not, easy to implement, the more subtle problem is in knowing what to implement, and how to implement it in the first place. Precisely understanding what you need from a site is particularly important for this reason; even though we cover configuration here, it is likely that you will need to revisit this chapter every now and then.

Does this mean that you should not start working directly on the site unless you know exactly what is required? Not really; like most things, it's a bit of a trade-off when it comes to starting out with the development of a Drupal website. This is because it is almost impossible to determine exactly what the site will need and how its functionality should be provided until you have been working with it for some time. Often, you will find yourself modifying the behavior of a site based on feedback from the users.

With this in mind, we are going to talk about the following Drupal site configuration topics:

- **Site information**
- **Actions and Triggers**
- **Shortcuts**
- **File system**
- **Performance**
- **Maintenance**
- **Logging and errors**
- **Clean URLs**
- **RSS Publishing**
- **Reports**

Not everything that is available in Drupal's **Configuration** section is discussed in this chapter. For example, the **People** setting will be discussed in detail separately later in the book, while others are very straightforward and really don't warrant more than perhaps a brief mention.

Before we start

It is sensible to make note of a few important things before getting our hands dirty. Make it second nature to check how the changes made to the settings affect the site. Quite often settings you modify, or features you add, will not behave precisely as expected and without ensuring that you use a prudent approach to making changes, you can sometimes end up with a bit of a mess.

 Changes to the site's structure (for example, adding new modules) can affect what is and isn't available for configuration so be aware that it may be necessary to revisit this section.

Click on **Configuration** in the toolbar menu. You should see something like the following screenshot:

| | Content | Structure | Appearance | People | Modules | Configuration | Reports | Help | | | Hello **admin** | Log out |

Add content   Find content

Configuration ⊕

Dashboard

Hide descriptions

PEOPLE

▶ Account settings
Configure default behavior of users, including registration requirements, e-mails, fields, and user pictures.

▶ IP address blocking
Manage blocked IP addresses.

CONTENT AUTHORING

▶ Text formats
Configure how content input by users is filtered, including allowed HTML tags. Also allows enabling of module-provided filters.

MEDIA

▶ File system
Tell Drupal where to store uploaded files and how they are accessed.

▶ Image styles
Configure styles that can be used for resizing or adjusting images on display

▶ Image toolkit
Choose which image toolkit to use if you have installed optional toolkits.

SYSTEM

▶ Site information
Change site name, e-mail address, slogan, default front page, number of posts per page, error pages and cron

▶ Actions
Manage the actions defined for your site

USER INTERFACE

▶ Shortcuts
Add and modify shortcut sets.

DEVELOPMENT

▶ Performance
Enable or disable page caching for anonymous users and set CSS and JS bandwidth optimization options.

▶ Logging and errors
Settings for logging and alerts modules. Various modules can route Drupal's system events to different destinations, such as syslog, database, email, etc.

▶ Maintenance mode
Take the site offline for maintenance or bring it back online.

A quick point to mention is that we aren't giving over much space to the final option—**Regional and Language**. This is because the settings here are very basic and should give you no trouble at all. There is also an online exercise available to help you with date types and formats if you are interested in customizing these.

Let's begin!

Site information

This page contains a mixed bag of settings, some of which are pretty self-explanatory, while others will require us to think quite carefully about what we need to do. To start with, we are presented with a few text boxes that control things like the name of the site and the site slogan.

Nothing too earth shattering, although I should point out that different themes implement these settings differently, while some don't implement them at all.

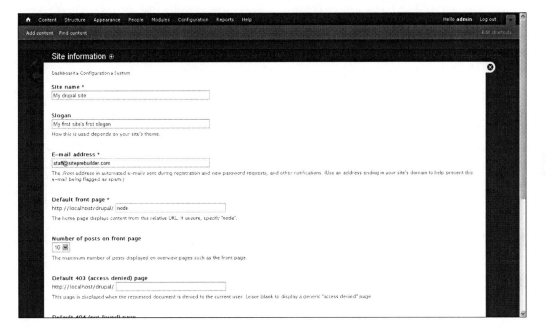

For example, adding a slogan in the default Garland theme prints it after the site name as shown in the following screenshot:

Whereas, the Stark theme places the slogan beneath the site name:

The **Default front page** setting warrants a closer look, because many people prefer to have a defined landing page from which users can then move to their desired content, as opposed to the default behavior of adding the latest published content posts to the front page.

Let's assume that there is a page of content that should be displayed by default—before anyone views any of the other content. For example, if you wanted to display some sort of promotional information or an introduction page, you could tell Drupal to display that using this setting. Remember that you have to create the content for this post first, and then determine its path before you tell Drupal to use it. For example, we could reference a specific node with its node ID, but equally, a site's blogs could be displayed if you substitute node/x (in node/ID format) for the blog.

A good way to determine exactly how to display the front page you want is to actually browse to the page (once it has been created). This could be a blog page, aggregated news feed (more about feeds later in the book), a forum, or anything.

 Once you are looking at the content intended for the front page, take note of the relative URL path and simply enter that into the text box provided.

Recall that the relative URL path is that part of the page's address that comes after the standard domain, which is shared by the whole site. For example, setting node/2 works because Drupal maps this relative path to http://localhost/drupal/node/2

The first part of this address, `http://localhost/drupal/` is the **base URL**, and everything after that is the relative URL path.

Sometimes, the front page is a slightly more complex beast and it is likely that you will want to consider Panels to create a unique front page. In this case, Panels settings can override this setting to make a specific panel page as the front page. More information on Panels in *Chapter 10, Advanced Features*.

The following settings allow you to broadly deal with the problem of two common site errors that may crop up during a site's normal course of operation—from the perspective of a site visitor. In particular, you may wish to create a couple of customized error pages that will be displayed to the users in the event of a "page not found" or "access denied" problem.

Remember that there are already pretty concise pages, which are supplied by default. However, if you wish to make any changes, then the process for creating an error page is exactly the same as creating any other normal page.

Let's make a change very quickly. Click on **Add new content** in the **Shortcuts** menu and select **Basic page**. Add whatever content you want for, say the **Page not found!** error:

Don't worry about the host of options available on this page—we will talk about all of this later on. For now, simply click on the **Save** button and make note of the URL of the page when it is displayed. Then head back to the **Site information** page, add this URL to the **Default 404 (not found) page** dialog, and then click on the **Save configuration** button:

If you navigate to a page that doesn't exist, for example, node/3333, you should receive the new error message as follows:

In this example, we asked Drupal to find a node that does not exist yet and so it displayed the **Page not found!** error message. Since Drupal can also provide content that is private or available to only certain users, it also needs the **access denied** error to explain to the would-be users that they do not have sufficient permissions to view the requested page. This is not the same as not finding a page, of course, but you can create your own access denied page in exactly the same way.

Finally, you will need to specify how often cron should run in the **Automatically run cron** drop-down at the bottom of the **Site information** page. Cronjobs are automated tasks (of any type—they could be search indexing, feed aggregation, and so on) that should run at specified intervals. Drupal uses them to keep itself up-to-date and ensure optimal operation.

> Drupal uses web page requests to initiate new cron runs once the specified interval has elapsed. If your website does not get visited regularly, cron itself cannot run regularly.

Running cron every few hours is reasonable for the vast majority of sites. Setting it to run too quickly can create a huge load on the server because each time the cron is run, all sorts of scripts are updating data, performing tasks, and consuming server resources. By the same token, run cron too infrequently and your site's content can become outdated, or worse, important module, theme, and core updates can go unnoticed, among other things.

Actions and triggers

Quite often, it happens that for specific events, it is useful to have Drupal automatically perform a specified task or action. An action, in the Drupal sense, is one of a number of tasks that the system can perform, and these usually relate to e-mailing people or acting upon user accounts or content. There are a number of simple actions that are available as well as a few more advanced ones that can be set up by anyone with sufficient permissions.

To configure actions, navigate to **Actions** in **SYSTEM** under the **Configuration** menu in the toolbar:

Default simple actions cannot be modified, so we will ignore these for the moment and focus on creating a new, advanced action. Set up a new **Send e-mail** action by selecting it from the drop-down list and click on the **Create** button, as shown in the preceding screenshot. This brings up the following page that can be set according to how this specific action will be used:

It should be clear that the intention of this e-mail is to notify the staff/administration of any new site members. The **Label** field is important in this respect because this is how you will distinguish this action from the other ones that you may create in the future. Make the description as accurate, meaningful, and concise as possible to avoid any potential confusion.

Also notice that there are several placeholder variables that can be inserted into the **Recipient**, **Subject**, and **Message fields**. In this instance, one has been used to inform the e-mail recipient of the new user name, as part of the message.

A click on the **Save** button adds this new action to the list where it can be modified or deleted, accordingly:

node	Make content unsticky		
system	Notify administrator of new user registration	configure	delete
user	Ban IP address of current user		

So far so good—we have set the action, but this in itself does absolutely nothing. An action cannot do anything unless there is a specific system event that can be triggered to set it off. These system events are, perspicaciously enough, called triggers and Drupal can look for any number of triggers, and perform the actions that are associated with it—this is how actions and triggers work together.

 Triggers are not part of the topic of Drupal configuration. However, we will discuss them here for completeness, since actions and triggers are integrally linked.

Triggers are not enabled by default, so head on over to the **Modules** section and enable the **Triggers** module. With the module enabled, there will now be a new **Triggers** link from the **Actions** page. Clicking on this brings up the following page:

Triggers are divided into five different categories, each providing a range of triggers to which actions can be attached. Assigning a trigger is basically selecting an action to apply from the drop-down list of the relevant trigger and clicking on the **Assign** button.

To continue with our example, select the **USER** tab from the top of the **Triggers** overlay and, in the **TRIGGER: AFTER CREATING A NEW USER ACCOUNT** box, select the newly defined action, as shown in the following screenshot:

Click on the **Assign** button, and the newly assigned action will show up in the relevant trigger box:

In the same way, a large number of actions can be automated depending on the system event (or trigger) that fires. To test this out, log off and register a new account—you will find that the **New User Alert** e-mail is dutifully sent out once the account has been registered (assuming your web server is able to send e-mail—see the section entitled *Troubleshooting the Drupal installation* in *Chapter 1, Introduction to Drupal* for more information).

Shortcuts

Shortcuts are a new feature of Drupal 7 and allow administrators (or anyone with sufficient permissions) to create sets of links that can be accessed by others using the shortcuts bar—directly below the toolbar menu. By default, **Add content** and **Find content** are the only two links that are provided, but you may change these regularly depending on what you are working on at any given time.

For example, it may be useful to create a set of shortcuts that involve theme-related links for quick access when it's time to theme the site. By the same token, adding links to views and displays might be more useful when working on content.

The overlay system is integrated with shortcuts, making it easy for the administrators to add links to their shortcuts. For example, let's say we wanted a set of configuration shortcuts so that all the main configuration tasks are readily accessible at a moment's notice.

To do this, we need to first add a new shortcut set. Go to **Shortcuts** in **USER INTERFACE** under **Configuration**, and click on the **Add shortcut set** link, to bring up the following page:

Now go to your account, and select the **Shortcut** tab. Select the new **Configuration** option and save the changes by clicking **Change set** to ensure that you are viewing the correct shortcut set. Now click on **Edit shortcuts** in the shortcuts bar to bring up the list of links contained in this set:

Nothing too exciting yet. In fact, this is exactly the same as the default shortcut set. We can add new shortcuts to this list manually by clicking on the **Add shortcut** link and providing a name and path manually:

Clicking on the **Save** button shows the new link added to the list and it is also now available in the shortcuts bar on the top of the page.

The other, easier way to add links is simple; click on the plus icon next to the overlay name. A small popup appears to the right of the icon while hovering over it. Take note of this because it indicates which shortcut set the link will be added to.

The new shortcut will appear along the top of the page with the rest of the links.

Anyone with sufficient permissions can create their own set of shortcuts and use them as they choose. The shortcuts system also provides a block that can be added to the site like any other block. Making effective use of shortcuts can help you cut down the wasted navigation time—just remember to select the most relevant set from your account because it is only possible to view one at a time.

File system

How you deal with the file system settings really depends on what type of content you visualize your site using. If you know that most files should be available for anyone to download, then leave the **Default download method** as **Public**. By the same token, if you want some control over who can access the files then use the **Private** method.

Public files can be accessed directly through a browser without having to go through your Drupal website. So, if someone liked a video you posted, they could reference it from their own website, allowing their visitors to see the video using your bandwidth to serve it—obviously not ideal.

> You need to keep an eye on this and find out if your host service provides some sort of hotlinking protection to combat this.

Assuming you *want* to make your download method private, you will need to specify a directory that is not directly available over the web—in other words, it is outside the document root folder.

The same technique is used for the temporary files folder that Drupal requires in order to properly handle any files you or the site users might deal with.

On your development machine, you might end up with something like the following screenshot (Public file downloads):

To make this private, create a folder outside of the web root (but still within the web server folder), add it to the **Private file system path** option, and click on the **Save configuration** button, as shown in the following screenshot:

| ⌂ Content Structure Appearance People Modules Configuration Reports Help | Hello **admin** Log out |

Add content   Find content   Edit shortcuts

Dashboard » Configuration » Media

The configuration options have been saved.

Public file system path

sites/default/files

A local file system path where public files will be stored. This directory must exist and be writable by Drupal. This directory must be relative to the Drupal installation directory and be accessible over the web.

Private file system path

C:\xampp\privatedrupalfiles

A local file system path where private files will be stored. This directory must exist and be writable by Drupal. This directory should not be accessible over the web.

Temporary directory

C:\WINDOWS\TEMP\

A local file system path where temporary files will be stored. This directory should not be accessible over the web.

Default download method

○ Public local files served by the webserver.

⦿ Private local files served by Drupal.

This setting is used as the preferred download method. The use of public files is more efficient, but does not provide any access control.

Save configuration

With the new absolute path to the private folder specified (in this case, **privatedrupalfiles**) there will now be an additional **Default download method** available for selection, entitled **Private local files served by Drupal**.

The **Default download method** is the default behavior. Individual download methods can be set on each file type field added to any content type.

Before continuing, let's confirm that we can specify a download method for any file without problems. Go to **Content types** under **Structure**, and click on the **manage fields** link next to one of the content types, say **blog entry**. Add a new field of the **File** type and save the changes. You will then be able to select **Public files** or **Private files** in the **Upload destination** section on the following configuration page, as shown in the next screenshot:

We will cover fields and content types in great depth in the coming chapters so don't worry if you aren't too sure about what we have done here. The important point is that each file uploaded to the site can be controlled on a field level basis, and more importantly on a field level per content type basis. This is a vast improvement over Drupal 6 which forced either all files to be public or all to be private.

How Drupal controls what type and the size of the files that can be uploaded is a matter for the content type specific configuration page shown in the preceding screenshot. It is not really sensible to allow any type of file to be uploaded to the site. The first thing that will happen if you do this, is that someone will upload a malicious executable file that does something nasty when it runs on the users' machines, in turn, causing them to say or do something nasty to you.

For example, you might know that for a particular content type, the only type of file that should be uploaded is a small text or .txt file. In this case, you would have something like the following settings:

In this case, we have specified that only 'txt files' of less than 50 KB can be uploaded to the blogtext sub-directory. The decisions you ultimately make should be dictated by the needs of the individual site. When in doubt, follow the tenet:

Provide only what is absolutely necessary, and no more!

The actual settings themselves are easy enough to implement, but I suggest you do not add any file extensions that you know the site will not need. Remember that it is possible to cloak nasty software within other file types, so the more variety you allow, the less secure things become.

We can test all of this out by posting a new blog and trying to upload files. Try a range of files, not just 'txt' files to see the results. For example, attempting to upload an image file gives the following result:

However, uploading a new file that does meet the criteria set, meets with success and we can check to ensure that the file is present in the proper sub-directory of the file system, as shown next:

As you can see, the site has correctly uploaded the `blogtextfile.txt` file in the `blogtext` subdirectory, as specified earlier. The field-based system for file handling in Drupal 7 represents a huge improvement over previous Drupal milestones and as soon as we have covered fields and content types in *Chapter 6, Advanced Content*, you will be able to manage files, file uploads, and access for any content type with ease.

Performance

Every once in a while, someone makes a site that becomes wildly popular. Having many people visiting all at once can put some serious strain on the server's resources and cause all sorts of problems as the congestion builds.

If you are unsure about what resources are available on your site, check with the hosting service and find out what they provide in the way of disk space, monthly transfer, and transfer speed. Many hosting services will boast unlimited bandwidth, but won't talk about connection speed. In other words, they don't meter how much water you use because they only let you switch the hosepipe on half way.

It's important to know the limitations of the hardware and network resources, but don't fall into the trap of believing this is the most important thing to know.

> Ensuring that there are facilities in place to handle a large amount of traffic will go some way in ensuring that your site scales well.

It's a time-honored tradition in the corporate world to throw extra resources at computing problems—buying the latest, fastest servers to help speed up slow applications, upgrading network hardware to allow data to travel more freely, and so on. Invariably though, poorly designed software, or software that is poorly tuned for performance always finds a way to utilize all the resources one can throw at it and still want more.

More often than not, it is better to look at why software is chewing up resources and see what can be done to either stop it or at least alleviate the problem, so that the software utilizes its resources wisely. Drupal already has several strategies in place to help you, the site administrator, decide how and when to use resource-intensive modules and how to maximize the site's efficiency.

Caching

This section provides several options to improve the performance of your site, and as nothing in this world is really free, you need to understand that, by and large, obtaining a performance boost comes at the expense of something else—namely, how up-to-date content is.

The following screenshot shows the performance page:

The first option, **CLEAR CACHE**, is useful while making modifications to a site because it helps to ensure that changes are definitely displayed and not held up while the site cache is still in operation. Having the ability to clear the cache in order to view precisely how pages are being built is useful, but comes at a price. Remember that if you have a large site with lots of content, then Drupal will have to do a lot of work to rebuild its cache, and it is possible that users may notice a slowdown during this time.

> It is important to only enable caching on a live site, and not on the development machine, because changes to a page show up only when the cache expires — causing confusion if you are expecting something else during testing.

As you know, Drupal uses PHP to build web pages that are returned to a user's browser. Most of the time, these pages are unchanged between requests, and Drupal ends up repeating the work of building the same page before sending it off to the other users who requested it. It makes sense to tell Drupal that if it has created a web page once, it should store a copy of this page and serve that copy instead of going through the trouble of recreating it.

> The process of storing copies of web pages in order to reduce the amount of effort required to repeatedly create a page is known as caching.

The trade-off when using page caching is that any changes to a page are only shown to the users once that cached version has expired and been replaced. This makes caching a suitable method for boosting performance whenever content is not updated very often or when it is not important to have new content presented immediately.

You will need to decide how long you think it is suitable to go before any updates made to a page must be shown — the longer you leave a page cached, the less work Drupal has to do, but the longer it will take for new content to show on the site. If your site is a daily blog, then by all means set the cache for up to a day at a time. If your site is a super busy, breaking news portal, then clearly you would opt for a cache time in minutes.

Drupal also has the ability to cache the content of blocks, which can be a real performance boost for authenticated users (since page caching is only available for anonymous users). Blocks are constructed independently from the page as a whole, and often require expensive database requests or other operations in order to provide the information they contain.

Enabling block caching means that blocks no longer have to query the database (or whatever else it is they are doing) each time a page refreshes. Rather, they simply serve up the cached version and save on all that work.

Again, make sure you carefully weigh up the benefits between having fresh content and having high performance.

Bandwidth optimization

BANDWIDTH OPTIMIZATION, shown at the bottom of the page in the previous screenshot, deals with how to best transfer data from your server across the Internet to the users' browsers. The way in which data is transferred plays a big role in optimizing performance. In general, the most important things to remember are:

- Keep files small
- Keep the number of files down

As shown, Drupal can aggregate and compress disparate CSS and JavaScript files in order to reduce the size and number of requests made to a server. Obviously, this has a huge number of benefits, especially if you are charged for bandwidth usage.

Again, don't aggregate files during development. Turn this feature on only once the site has gone live, otherwise you are in for some serious frustration when changes to themes or scripts don't show up or behave as expected.

Maintenance

I should make the following point very clear:

 All major development or changes to a site should be performed on the development machine and thoroughly tested before being implemented or ported to the live site.

There will be times, however, when you simply have to make some changes directly to the live site—even if it is only to implement upgrades that have already been tested out on the development server. If this is the case, then rather than allow users to browse a site under maintenance, visit the **Maintenance mode** page in the **Development** section, and select **Put site into maintenance mode**, provide a **Maintenance mode message** to display if the default one is not suitable, and get on with your work.

Be very careful when working in maintenance mode because once you have logged out you are effectively locked out too. This is because, by default, only one user (that is the administrative user) can do anything on the site while it is offline. If you log off and try logging in again, you are no longer the administrative user; you are instead anonymous and are shown only the offline message:

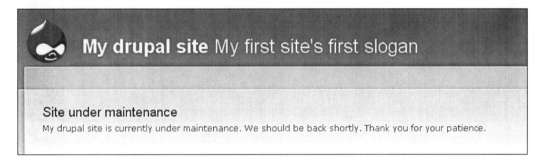

This is not very helpful if you do happen to be the site administrator; so Drupal allows the login page to be accessed as normal. Navigate to `http://localhost/drupal/user`, and you will be able to **log in** as the administrator and use the site without hindrance.

Make sure you know the administrator's password before going into maintenance mode.

Everyone else is locked out until the site is no longer under maintenance.

Logging and errors

Go to **Logging and errors** in the **DEVELOPMENT** section of the **Configuration** overlay. This page provides a few options used to control how errors are displayed and logged:

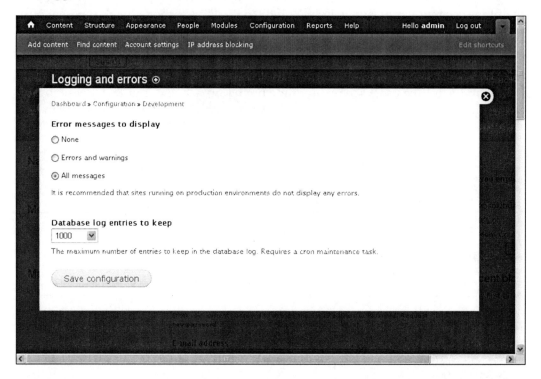

Error messages to display allows you to decide whether to write errors to the screen or not. While you are busy building the site, it's useful to view **All messages** in order to determine what has gone wrong and when. However, once it is time to go live you should change this to **None** for security reasons. Doing so prevents Drupal from displaying information to malicious users who might be able to use it in an attack on your site.

The final setting, **Database log entries to keep**, at least to begin with, is sensible. You may wish to increase or decrease the number of records stored on the system depending on how much work you have to do in order to maintain the site properly. Remember that Drupal can properly maintain the site's event logs only if the cron jobs are being run regularly.

Having only one setting to make is not that exciting, but once the site is live and messages are no longer visible through the pages, you can check the logs in the **Reports** section. Doing this on a regular basis is a good strategy to ensure that the site continues to run smoothly. Error messages, warnings, and so on are effectively windows into the operations of the site, and are indispensable tools.

Clean URLs

It is important to discuss this particular topic early on because it acts as a cog in the machinery of not only your site, but also in how your site interacts with the rest of the Internet. The simplicity of the **Clean URLs** in the **SEARCH AND METADATA** section of the **Configuration** overlay belies its importance.

Clean URLs ⊕

Dashboard » Configuration » Search and metadata

☑ Enable clean URLs

Use URLs like `example.com/user` instead of `example.com/?q=user`.

Save configuration

As you can see, the choice is simple—either enable or disable **Clean URLs**. Your system should also tell you whether or not it is possible to use clean URLs—if you see something like the following screenshot, then you have problems:

Your system configuration does not currently support this feature. The handbook page on Clean URLs has additional troubleshooting information.

> It is critical for SEO purposes that you have **Clean URLs** enabled on the live site.

The reason for this strong recommendation is because clean URLs are needed in order for your site to be properly indexed by Google and other search engines. Search engines use automated programs to traverse the web (called bots) and when they come across nice, straightforward URLs like the ones displayed by Drupal when Clean URLs are enabled, for example, `http://localhost/drupal/about-us`, they happily go about their business.

Indexing allows content to start showing up in web searches, and hence more people can find these pages (more or less). If however, they come across dynamic URLs (ones that contain query strings), then they often don't put the same effort into indexing that page, or worse, ignore it entirely. This can lead to a situation where you have a lot of lovely content just waiting to be read, but no one is able to find it because the search engines are ignoring all the pages of form: `http://localhost/drupal/?q=node/2`

The highlighted part of this URL (`?q=`) is what causes the problem. Drupal navigates around its own pages using a system of internal URLs that it finds using queries in the format shown in the previous URL. In other words, `?q=node/2` is asking Drupal to find the content or page that is held at `node/2`. The problem is that the Googlebot simply sees the dynamic query and says to itself, "This could be a nasty trick designed to make me index the same page millions of times over so I won't pay any attention to it."

> Actually, providing informative names (called aliasing) for posts is far better than relying on Drupal's default numbering system. It's worth skipping ahead and looking over the detailed section on *Path & Pathauto* in *Chapter 11, Deployment and Management* so that you get into the habit of providing user and search engine-friendly aliases for all your content.

The people at Drupal realized this is the case, so if it is possible on your web server, clean URLs are enabled by default and you don't have to worry about any of this. The problem comes during deployment because it is possible that your Internet service provider's setup does not allow for clean URLs. Now what?

If you already know who is going to host your live site, then try testing things out now by installing a copy of Drupal on the live server and ensuring that it is possible to use clean URLs (see *Chapter 11, Deployment and Management* on Deployment for more information). If you can't, consider finding another host that does. Otherwise, you will end up dealing with their system administrators and waiting until they can properly configure Apache.

Whether you can or can't use clean URLs basically comes down to a configuration setting in Apache. On your development machine, you have direct access to the `httpd.conf` file that Apache uses for its configuration—this is probably not the case on the live servers since any given host obviously doesn't want to give everyone using their servers total control to mangle everything as they see fit.

In order for Drupal to implement clean URLs, Apache needs to have `mod_rewrite` enabled. For example, open up `httpd.conf` and search for the line that reads `LoadModule rewrite_module modules/mod_rewrite.so`

This line determines whether or not Apache can implement what Drupal requires in order to implement clean URLs. If it's commented out, you will need to uncomment it and then restart Apache before any changes take effect.

If you find that at some stage you fall into the trap of having clean URLs enabled on a system that cannot implement them (causing all sorts of problems), then manually navigating to the following page should allow you to disable the clean URLs and use the site as normal: **`http://localhost/drupal`**`/?q= admin/config/search/ clean-urls`

Remember to exchange the highlighted base URL to whatever is pertinent for your setup.

RSS publishing

One of the best ways to spread the word about your website is to create and maintain a useful RSS feed. The **RSS publishing** page under **WEB SERVICES** on the **Configuration** overlay provides a few options to control the behavior of the site's feeds:

From here, it is possible to specify how many items are to be included in the feed, and what content should be shown—from the title, select the title, teaser, and full content.

There are plenty of feeds that are automatically created on your site. If you set up a blog, it will also have its own feed. In fact, each blogger has their own blog feed and visitors can subscribe by clicking the small RSS feed icon that Drupal inserts wherever a feed is available.

Clicking on the feed icon of the front page shows a mix of the latest content that has been promoted to the front page:

As you can see from the preceding screenshot, even polls can be easily aggregated into the site feed. This is a really powerful feature that can help to build up a well known and popular blog or website.

Reports

Reports are an absolutely crucial part of maintaining a healthy website. They are your eyes and ears on the ground and can often be decisive in isolating attacks or malicious users and programs that have accessed your site. They can also provide analytical information about how people are utilizing a site (through the search phrases report) or can offer some interesting benefits. For example, you might find that a certain site refers a number of people to you, and therefore, may be a good candidate for pursuing a relationship with.

Click on **Reports** in the **Toolbar** to bring up the site's list of reports and logs:

Reports ⊕

Dashboard

Status report
Get a status report about your site's operation and any detected problems.

Available updates
Get a status report about available updates for your installed modules and themes.

Recent log entries
View events that have recently been logged.

Field list
Overview of fields on all entity types.

Top 'access denied' errors
View 'access denied' errors (403s).

Top 'page not found' errors
View 'page not found' errors (404s).

Top search phrases
View most popular search phrases.

This page can change depending on which modules are installed and enabled. For example, enabling the **Syslog** and **Statistics** modules in the **Modules** section, and reviewing this page shows the newly available logs and reports:

Selecting **Recent log entries** brings up the site's log of events, and you can filter these events by clicking on FILTER LOG MESSAGES and then selecting options in the list under the heading **Type** and **Severity**, before clicking on the **Filter** button.

Each of the log records has several important features that help to determine its type and importance, who or what initiated it, and what the outcome of the event was. If you want to look at the details of any individual message, click on the link found in the **Message** column, and its details will be displayed, as shown in the following screenshot:

This logging interface gives you fairly good control over how to locate and deal with the site issues. There are several other options that you should explore on your own in the **Reports** section, the most notable being the **Available updates** and

Status report—especially at the time this book gets released, because many module developers and Drupal itself will still be undergoing upgrades, and accordingly, these two sections will be even more important than usual.

Summary

This chapter has covered a fair amount of ground in terms of setting up the site. We began by looking at some general configuration settings, like **Site information**, that are important in terms of getting the nuts and bolts in working order. Many of these settings will need to be revisited as the site develops.

While triggers aren't necessarily part of a discussion on configuration, we learned that they are inextricably linked to actions that can be configured to automate many common site tasks or chores. Again, coming back to actions and triggers every once and a while can help reduce the number of repetitive tasks that have to be completed manually.

Next, we gained the ability to control file uploads and file handling using Drupal 7's new field-based paradigm. Having fine grained control over how various files are accessed is a great improvement over past incarnations of Drupal.

While performance is not really a huge consideration at this early stage in a site's development, it serves as a good learning exercise to understand what facilities Drupal puts in place to boost performance through caching and file aggregation. Remember to return to this section once your site goes live.

Knowing that in this fiercely competitive Internet environment we need to take every SEO advantage we can find means that enabling clean URLs is important. If worst comes to worst, it may become necessary to find a new hosting service to ensure that you don't have problems with the Apache setup.

We then took a quick look at the important topics of clean URLs and explored Drupal's native RSS publishing features. As we'll find out in the section on SEO in the final chapter, having lots of valuable, fresh content is a great attribute for any website and being able to share this content quickly and effectively using RSS is an important feature for any modern site.

A look at how logs and reports serve as our eyes and ears on the ground rounded off this chapter. Remember that different modules can add different reports and logs so you aren't necessarily limited to the ones shown here.

By now, you should feel confident that you are able to skip between the various 'configuration' settings in order to get Drupal working as you need it to.

4
Users and Access Control

It's time to look at an entirely different aspect of running a Drupal website. Up until now, we have focused on adding and organizing the site's basic functionality. We have not yet given any thought to how this functionality is to be accessed or by whom. As the site grows, you will most likely feel the need to delegate certain responsibilities to various people. Alternatively, you might organize a team of people to work on specific aspects of the site. Whatever is required, at some stage, you will have to make decisions about who can do what, and Drupal makes sure that this is possible.

In the same vein as the previous chapter, having Drupal simplify the implementation of your access control policies does not mean that the task is a trivial one. There is still much thought that needs to go on behind the scenes in order to create a sophisticated, and above all, effective policy for controlling access to the site. Because of this, we will spend a bit of time exploring the ramifications of the various choices available, instead of simply listing them. Taking a holistic approach to implementing an access control policy will ensure that you don't end up with any nasty surprises later on.

Specifically, this chapter will look at the following topics:

- Planning an access policy
- Roles
- Permissions
- Users
- OpenID

Before we continue, it is worth pointing out that, at the moment, you are more than likely using the administrative user (user number 1) for all the site's development needs. That is absolutely fine; but once the major changes to the site are completed, you should begin using a normal administrative user that has only the permissions required to complete day-to-day tasks—for security purposes. The first section will highlight the general philosophy behind user access and expand on this.

Planning an access policy

When you think about how a site should work, focus on what will be required of yourself, other community members, or even anonymous users. For instance:

- Will there be a team of moderators working to ensure that the content of the site conforms to the dictates of good taste and avoids material that is tantamount to hate speech and so on?

- Will there be subject experts who are allowed to create and maintain their own content?

- To what extent will anonymous visitors be allowed to become involved, or will they be forced to merely window shop without being able to contribute?

Perhaps the site should grow organically with the community, and so you want to adopt an extremely flexible approach. But take it as given that Drupal's access policies are already flexible, so it is good practice to start out with a sensible set of access rules, even if they are going to change over time. If you need to make modifications later, so be it, but at least there will be a coherent set of rules from the start.

The first and foremost rule of security that can be applied directly to our situation is (recall that we mentioned this earlier in a slightly different context):

 Grant a user permissions sufficient for completing the intended task, and no more.

Our entire approach is going to be governed by this rule. Think about it, the last thing anyone wants is for an anonymous user to be able to modify the personal blog of a respected industry expert. Accordingly, each type of user should have carefully controlled permissions that effectively block their ability to act outside the scope of their remit.

One consequence of this is that it is better to create a larger number of specific roles—rather than creating one or two generic roles and allowing everyone to use those catch-all permissions

[A role constitutes a number of permissions that define what actions any members of that role can and can't perform.]

Drupal gives us fine-grained control over what users can accomplish, and you should make good use of this facility. It may help to think of your access control using the following figure (this does not necessarily represent the actual roles on your site—it's just an example):

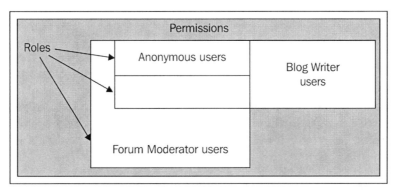

The shaded region represents the total number of permissions available for the site. Contained within this set are the various roles that exist either by default, like the **Anonymous users** role, or those you create in order to cater to the different types of users the site will require—in this case, the **Blog Writer users** and **Forum Moderator users** roles.

From the previous diagram, you can see that the **Anonymous users** role has the smallest set of permissions because they have the smallest area of the total diagram. This set of permissions is totally encapsulated by the **Forum Moderator users** and **Blog Writer users**—meaning that forum moderators and blog writers can do everything an anonymous user does and a lot more.

Remember, it is not compulsory that forum moderators encapsulate all the permissions of the anonymous users. You can assign any permission to any role — it's just that, in this context, it makes sense that a forum moderator should be able to do everything an anonymous user can.

Of course, the blog writers have a slightly different remit. While they share some privileges in common with the forum administrators, they also have a few of their own. Your permissions, as the primary or administrative user, encompass the entire set because there should be nothing that you cannot control.

It is up to you to decide which roles are best for the site, but before attempting this, it is important to ask: *What are roles and how are they used in the first place?* To answer this question, let's take a look at the practical side of things in more detail.

Roles

It may seem a bit odd that we are not beginning a chapter on users and access control with a discussion on users. After all, it is all about what *users can* and *cannot* do! The problem with immediately talking about users is that the focus of a single user is too narrow, and we can learn far more about controlling access by taking a more broad view using roles. Once we have learned everything there is to know about roles, working with users becomes far easier.

As mentioned, a user role in Drupal defines a set of rules that must be obeyed by all the users in that role. It may be helpful to think of a role as a character in a play. In a play, an actor must always be true to their character (in the same way, a user must be faithful to their role in Drupal) — in other words, there is a defined way to behave and the character never deviates.

Creating a role in Drupal is easy. Click **People** in the toolbar menu, select the **PERMISSIONS** tab, and then select the **Roles** link to bring up the following screenshot:

People ⊕

Dashboard » People

Permissions Roles ✖

Roles allow you to fine tune the security and administration of Drupal. A role defines a group of users that have certain privileges as defined on the permissions page. Examples of roles include: anonymous user, authenticated user, moderator, administrator and so on. In this area you will define the names and order of the roles on your site. It is recommended to order your roles from least permissive (anonymous user) to most permissive (administrator). To delete a role choose "edit role".

By default, Drupal comes with two user roles:

- Anonymous user: this role is used for users that don't have a user account or that are not authenticated.
- Authenticated user: this role is automatically granted to all logged in users.

NAME	OPERATIONS	
✛ anonymous user *(locked)*		edit permissions
✛ authenticated user *(locked)*		edit permissions
✛ administrator	edit role	edit permissions
[ ] Add role		

(Save order)

As you can see, we have three roles already defined by default—the **anonymous user**, **authenticated user**, and the **administrator**. It is not possible to change the first two, and so they are suffixed with **locked**. To begin with, the anonymous user (this is any user who is browsing the site without logging in) has very few permissions set, and you would more than likely want to keep it this way, despite the fact that it is possible to give them any and all permissions.

Similarly, the authenticated user, by default, has only a few more permissions than the anonymous user, and it is also sensible to keep these to a minimum because the authenticated user is any user that has created an account—not necessarily someone you completely trust with important permissions.

In order to add a new role, type in a name for the role in the space provided, click **Add role**, and you're done. But what name do you want to add? That's a key question. If you are unsure about what name to use, then it is most likely that you haven't defined the purpose of the role properly.

Let's assume we require a forum moderator who will be a normal user in every way, except for the ability to work directly on the forums (to take some of the burden of responsibility off the administrator's hands) to create new topics and to edit the content if necessary. Type in **forum moderator** and click **Add role**—actually, you might even want to more specific and use something like **conservation forum moderator** if there are going to be teams of forum moderators—you get the general idea.

Now the **roles** page should display the new role with the option to edit it, shown in the **OPERATIONS** column:

NAME		OPERATIONS
✛ anonymous user *(locked)*		edit permissions
✛ authenticated user *(locked)*		edit permissions
✛ administrator	edit role	edit permissions
✛ forum moderator	edit role	edit permissions
	Add role	

Click **edit role** in order to change the name of the role or delete it completely. Alternatively, click **edit permissions** to deal with the permissions for this specific role (we will discuss permissions in a moment).

Our work is just beginning because now we need to grant or deny the various permissions that the **forum moderator** role will need in order to successfully fulfill its purpose. New roles are not given any additional permission (above and beyond what the authenticated user already has) to begin with—this makes sense, because the last thing we want is to create a role only to find that it has the same permissions as the administrative user.

Chances are you will ultimately add several roles, depending on the needs of the site, so go ahead and add at least a **blogger** that can edit their own blog—we will need a few different types to play with later on anyway.

Let's flesh out the new forum moderator role by setting permissions.

Permissions

In order to work with permissions, click the **PERMISSIONS** tab of the **People** overlay and you should be presented with a screen much like the following screenshot (notice the new **FORUM MODERATOR** role on the right-hand side of the page):

As you can see, this page lists all of the available permissions down the left-hand column and allows you to enable or disable that permission by checking or unchecking boxes under the appropriate role. The forum moderator user already has certain permissions locked in — the exact same ones that any authenticated user has — *because a member of any role, by definition, is an authenticated user.*

It is easy enough to see that one traverses the list, selecting those additional permissions required for each role. What is not so easy is actually determining what should and shouldn't be enabled in the first place.

Notice too that the permissions given in the list on the left-hand side are grouped by module. This means that if we change the site's setup by adding or removing modules, then we will also have to change the permissions on this page.

 On most occasions when a module is added, you will need to revisit the permissions page and grant permissions, as required, for that module. By default, no permissions are granted.

What else can we learn from the permissions page shown in the previous screenshot? Well, what does each permission precisely mean? There are quite a few verbs that allow for completely different actions. The following lists the more common, generic ones, although you might find that one or two others crop up every now and then to cater to a specific module:

- **Administer**: gives the user the ability to affect the function of a module. For example, granting **Administer** rights to the `Locale` module means that the user can add or remove languages, manage strings, and even export `.po` files. This permission should only ever be given to trusted users and never to anonymous users.

- **View**: gives the user the ability to make use of a module without being able to affect it in any way. For example, granting **View** rights to the `Comment` module allows a user to view comments without being able to delete, edit, or reply to them.

- **Create**: gives the user the ability to create content of some sort. For example, granting rights to **Create** stories allows users to do so, but does not also give them the ability to edit those stories.

- **Edit any/own**: gives the user the ability to work with either anyone's content or specifically the content *they have created*—depending on whether **Edit any** or **Edit own** is selected. For example, granting **Edit own** rights to the `Blog` module means that the user can modify their own blogs at will.

- **Delete any/own**: applies to content-related modules such as `Node` and empowers users to remove either anyone's content or confines them to removing only content posted by themselves. For example, setting **Delete own blog entry** allows users to remove any blog postings that they may regret having published.

There are also other module-specific permissions available, and it is recommended that you play around and understand any new permission(s) you set.

How do we go about setting up the required permissions for the forum moderator user? If we look down the list of permissions, shown on the permission page, we see the following forum-related options (in this screenshot, the forum moderator permissions are those in the outer-most column):

Forum				
Administer forums	☐	☐	☑	☐

Enabling this option, and then testing out what new powers are made available should quickly demonstrate that this is not quite what we want. Note the message stating that we cannot post content to the forum:

Forums

○ You are not allowed to post new content in the forum.

Forum	Topics	Posts	Last post
General discussion	0	0	n/a
Conservation Topics related to conservation and how to promote it			
Ecological disasters How to effectively prevent and fight potential ecological disasters	0	0	n/a
Wildlife reserves Discuss the ins and outs of wildlife reserves and how they contribute to conservation	0	0	n/a
Hunting Topics related to hunting and how to prevent it			
Canned Discussion of canned hunting	0	0	n/a
Wildlife Advocacy			

If you are wondering how to actually test this out, you need to create a new user and then assign them to the **forum moderator** role. The following section on *Users* explains how to create new users and administer them properly. Jump ahead quickly and check that out so that you have a new user to work with, if you are unsure how it is done.

The following point might make your life a bit easier:

Use two browsers to test out your site. The demo site's development machine has IE and Firefox. Keep one browser for the administrator and the other for anonymous or other users in order to test out changes. This will save you from having to log in and log out during testing.

When testing out the new permissions, you will find that a forum moderator can access and work with all of the forums—assuming you have created any.

However, notice that there are **node module** permissions available, which is quite interesting because most content in Drupal is actually a node. How will this affect the forum moderator? Disable the **forum module** permissions for the **forum moderator** but enable all the forum content node options for the **authenticated user** before saving:

Delete any *Poll* content	☐	☐	☐	☐
Create new *Forum topic* content	☐	☑	☑	☑
Edit own *Forum topic* content	☐	☑	☑	☑
Edit any *Forum topic* content	☐	☑	☑	☑
Delete own *Forum topic* content	☐	☑	☑	☑
Delete any *Forum topic* content	☐	☑	☑	☑
Create new *Article* content	☐	☐	☑	☐

Access the forums as the **forum administrator**, and it will be clear that despite having revoked the **Administer forum** option for this user, it is possible to post to or edit anything in the forum quite easily by selecting the **Add new content** link in the main menu.

Is this what you expected, considering we have not specifically provided the forum moderator role with any of its own permissions? To elucidate, the **forum moderator** is an authenticated user, so it has acquired the permissions that come from the authenticated user.

> Any role, except the anonymous user, is automatically granted the **authenticated user** permissions.

This is why it is quite important that an authenticated user has very few permissions granted to it. If you are too liberal with what a standard authenticated user can do, it may be that a blogger can inadvertently edit a forum post because he/she has inherited the permissions from the authenticated user, for example.

While you might find that despite having a good amount of control with Drupal's native permissions, there are some things that are not easily done without help from elsewhere. Be sure to browse through the user-related modules on the Drupal website to get a feel for what other types of control you can exert over content, content types, users, roles, and their permissions.

Users

A single user account can be given as many or as few permissions as you like via the use of roles. Drupal users are not really anything unless they already have a role that defines the manner in which they can operate within the Drupal framework. Hence, we discussed roles first.

Users can be created in two ways. The most common way is by registering on the site—if you haven't already, go ahead and register a new user on your site by clicking the **Create new account** link on the homepage. Remember to supply a valid e-mail address, or else you won't be able to sign in properly. This will create an authenticated user, with any and all permissions that have been assigned to the **authenticated user** role.

The second way is to use the administrative user to create a new user. In order to do so, log on as the **administrative user** and click on **People** in the toolbar. Select the **Add user** link and follow the instructions on that page. For example, I created a new forum moderator user by ensuring that the relevant role was checked:

For each new user, you will need to supply Drupal with a username, e-mail address, password, and, if necessary, roles. Go ahead and create a few new users to play around with.

Administering users

The site's administrator is given complete access to the other users' account information. By clicking on the **edit** link, shown to the right of each user account in the **LIST** tab view of **People** (under the **OPERATIONS** column heading), it is possible to make any changes you require.

Before we do it though, it's worth noting that the administration page itself is fairly powerful in terms of being able to administer individual users or groups of users with relative ease:

The upper box, **SHOW ONLY USERS WHERE**, allows you to specify several filter conditions to cut down the result set and make it more manageable. This will become more and more important as the site accumulates more and more users. Once the various filter options have been implemented, the **UPDATE OPTIONS** allow you to apply whatever changes are needed to the list of users selected (by checking the relevant checkbox next to their name).

Having both broad, sweeping powers as well as fine-grained control over users is one of the most valuable facilities provided by Drupal, and you will no doubt become very familiar with this page in due course.

Click on the **edit** link next to the **forum moderator user** and take a look at the **Roles** section. Notice that it is possible to stipulate which roles this user belongs to. At present, there are only three roles to be assigned (yours might vary depending on which roles have been created in your setup):

Whenever a user is added to another role, they obtain the **combined permissions** of these roles. With this in mind, you should go about delegating roles in the following fashion:

1. Define the most basic user of the site by setting the **anonymous user** permissions.

2. Set permissions for a basic **authenticated user** (that is any Tom, Dick, or Harry that registers on your site).

3. Create special roles by only adding the specific additional permissions that are required by that role and no more.

4. Create new users by combining whatever roles are required for their duties or needs.

If you follow the steps above, you will be sure to always give the correct permissions to each role by avoiding redundancy and only applying permissions incrementally by role. Basically, you are building up a user's permissions from the most basic to the most complex without having to assign every single permission every time.

It should be common sense (although not a technical obligation) that a forum moderator would have all the permissions of an anonymous and authenticated user, plus a few more. Looking back to the first diagram in the *Planning an Access Policy* section, you can see that, in this case, we would:

1. Define the **anonymous user** and **authenticated user** role permissions—an authenticated user should have all the permissions of an anonymous user, plus whatever else is needed by a basic site user.

2. Create new roles with only the additional permissions needed for both the **forum moderator** and **blog user** respectively—other than those given to the authenticated user.

3. Assign blog writers to the **blog user** role (they are automatically given the permissions granted to an authenticated user), and do the same for forum moderators and their role.

Other than using that strategy for assigning roles to users, the rest, as they say, is history. Play around with any new roles you create to ensure that they behave as expected.

User settings

This section looks at how the site treats users, rather than discussing what users can and cannot do. However, you will find that some of the information in this section is important for the look and feel of the site.

Click on **Account settings** in the **People** section of the **Configuration** overlay. The following set of options is provided:

Looking at the **REGISTRATION AND CANCELLATION** section, you might want to consider which of the **Who can register accounts?** options to select quite carefully, depending on how you envisage the site functioning. For example, allowing everyone to read and post comments to the forums, or do whatever, without needing to register first, may be ideal. If this is the case, then it is likely that the only people who would need to register are going to be performing some sort of administrative duties, in which case, you would probably want to select the first option (**Administrators only**) or at least the third option (**Visitors, but administrator approval is required**).

If you do go for the third option, then check the user list regularly in order to unblock new users as soon as possible. Note that Drupal can be configured to e-mail the site administrator automatically whenever there is a new user registration application—see the *Actions & Triggers* section in *Chapter 3, Configuration and reports* for more information.

The next section deals with **PERSONALIZATION**. If you wish to enable **Picture support** for users, then select **Enable user pictures** from the list, provide a default picture (if you want one), and click **Save configuration** (the other settings are fairly self-explanatory and sensible, and you can come back at any stage to change them if they are not suitable).

Drupal will create a `pictures` folder to hold all of the pictures within your Drupal installation. Once everything is done, users will have a new section added to the **edit** tab of their `my account` page, as shown in the following screenshot:

When the picture has been successfully uploaded, it will appear on the **my account** page and with the user's blog and forum posts on the site. Remember that you can provide a default picture by supplying a valid URL address for that image in the **Default picture** setting of the **Account settings** overlay:

It is possible to control whether the user pictures are displayed in posts by selecting the **Settings** tab of the **Appearance** overlay and checking the relevant picture-related checkboxes, as shown in the following screenshot:

Allowing users to incorporate pictures into a site is a good way for people to personalize their contributions and also gives everyone something visual to associate posts with. This is a great way to foster a community, as it helps give different users an identity of sorts.

The final section on this page deals with the process of user e-mail customization for the various types of e-mails that Drupal sends out. There is an interesting facet to this in that Drupal makes certain variables available for use within the static text. Let's take a look at how to modify a line or so in order to get a feel for how it works.

By way of example, we will change the **Welcome (no approval required)** text from

Account details for [user:name] at [site:name]

to a slightly sprightlier

Congratulations [user:name], you have successfully registered with [site:name]

Nothing too complicated here! The bracketed tokens are simply placeholders for other values that are inserted into the e-mail, according to how they are set at that particular time. This gives you the ability to personalize correspondence. In this case, the subject of the welcome e-mail for a user registered as **Dave** is now displayed as shown in the following screenshot:

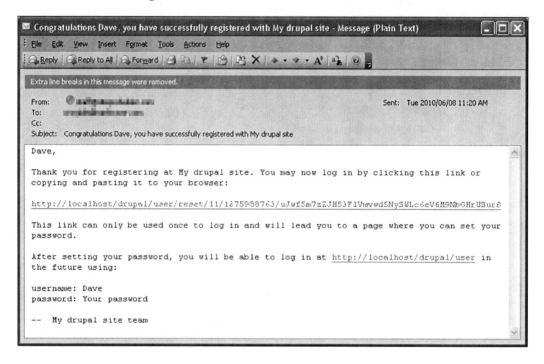

The **[user:name]** and **[site:name]** tokens have been correctly changed to reflect the contents of the variables for that particular setup. There are settings available for several standard e-mails such as **Password recovery** and **welcome (awaiting approval)**. The defaults are fairly sensible and easy to change, should you need to. Remember the placeholders that are available for each piece of text are mentioned above the section heading, so play around with them until you are comfortable with their usage.

That is pretty much the end of the line for configuring users as they stand. There are still a few more things we can do to enhance user accounts through the use of profiles.

Profiles

Given the massive growth in the social aspect of the Internet, it is likely that you are already familiar with the concept of user profiles. Almost everyone has spent a few minutes adding information about themselves on Facebook, LinkedIn, Ning, and so on.

It should come as no surprise that Drupal provides complete support for sophisticated user profiles, and, if your new site is the type that encourages a community atmosphere, then you will definitely need to spend some time in this section. A user profile allows people to share information about them. The type of information that they can share depends on what you decide is relevant for your site.

By way of example, let's assume that we want site users to be able to fill out some business information (such as web page address, title, education, skills, company, and so on) as well as some personal information (hobbies, blog address, favorite color, whatever) about themselves.

Head on over to **Modules** and enable **Profile**. Either click on the **Configure** link in the **modules** list or go to **Profiles** in the **People** section of the **Configuration** overlay. This brings up the profile field list, as shown in the following screenshot:

Adding new fields is simply a case of selecting the most suitable widget from the **Add new field** list. For example, let's allow users to enter their company home page address. Clearly, this is going to be in the form of a URL, so select **URL** from the list:

As you can see from the previous screenshot, we have:

- Supplied a **Category** — in this case, **Business**
- Given the field a **Title** — so that users filling out their profile know what information is expected from them
- Provided a **Form name** — so that Drupal can render the input correctly within the form

The **Category** is very important as Drupal will use it to group together related fields. For the sake of our example, we need two categories because all the profile information relates either to **Business** or to **Personal information**.

Next, we are required to decide on the **Visibility** of this particular field:

Visibility

○ Hidden profile field, only accessible by administrators, modules and themes.

○ Private field, content only available to privileged users.

◉ Public field, content shown on profile page but not used on member list pages.

○ Public field, content shown on profile page and on member list pages.

It is important to think carefully about this option because, depending on what type of information this field contains, you may or may not wish for other community members to view it. It may even be that this particular field is used by the site itself for one purpose or another and is not even relevant to other humans—in which case, the first option would be the most suitable.

The remaining options are fairly self-explanatory. You can decide whether or not the field is compulsory by checking **The user must enter a value** option, or you can decide to make this profile field **Visible in user registration form**. If you do make the field visible during registration, then new users can fill out this field as part of their registration:

User account

Create new account   Log in   Request new password

Account information

Username *

Spaces are allowed; punctuation is not allowed except for periods, hyphens, apostrophes, and underscores.

E-mail address *

A valid e-mail address. All e-mails from the system will be sent to this address. The e-mail address is not made public and will only be used if you wish to receive a new password or wish to receive certain news or notifications by e-mail.

Business

Company home page

Please provide a link to your company's home page.

Be careful about adding a whole lot of compulsory fields to the registration page. Even optional fields can still make user registration seem like more trouble than it's worth to the average user. It's far better to allow a quick registration with minimal effort and then allow users to fill out their profile later down the line.

With a single **Company home page** field added to the site's user profiles, we can repeat this process to add more Business information such as **Title**, **Experience**, and **Skills**. Remember to think carefully about which widget to use. For example, **Title** should only ever require a short piece of text, so a single-line **textfield** is appropriate here. However, **Skills** could be any number of different items, so the freeform **list** is probably best.

Go ahead and fill out a bunch of fields in the **Business** category. Once you're done, the **Profiles** overlay should look something like the following screenshot:

TITLE	NAME	TYPE	OPERATIONS	
Business				
✛ Company home page	profile_company_home_page	url	edit	delete
✛ Title	profile_title	textfield	edit	delete
✛ Skills	profile_skills	list	edit	delete
✛ Experience	profile_experience	textarea	edit	delete

Each field is draggable, so drag-and-drop them into the order you want. Once you're happy with the **Business** profile, do the same thing for the **Personal** profile, as shown in the following screenshot:

TITLE	NAME	TYPE	OPERATIONS	
Business				
✛ Company home page	profile_company_home_page	url	edit	delete
✛ Title	profile_title	textfield	edit	delete
✛ Skills	profile_skills	list	edit	delete
✛ Experience	profile_experience	textarea	edit	delete
Personal				
✛ Blog	profile_blog	url	edit	delete
✛ Hobbies	profile_hobbies	list	edit	delete
✛ Favorite Music	profile_favorite_music	selection	edit	delete

With all the profile fields correctly ordered in the correct categories, we can head on over to the any user account page to see what effect this has had on their account. The following screenshot shows the **Business** tab in the account edit page, providing form elements, as specified earlier:

Users can now fill out their profiles one category at a time, and depending on each individual field's setting, other users and administrators can access this information.

Before we finish with this section, it's important to note that profile functionality, as provided by the *Profile* module, is not the same as the Drupal 7 ability to add fields to users. We haven't discussed fields in any depth yet, but looking at the **MANAGE FIELDS** tab of the **Account settings** overlay in the **People** section of **Configuration**, indicates that we can add pretty much any field we like to users, regardless of whether or not the *Profiles* module is installed, as shown in the following screenshot:

The difference here is that while fields can be added to users, there is no way to categorize them. The best way to decide whether or not a field should be added directly to users, or whether to add profile fields, is to ask yourself whether the field in question applies globally to all users and does not necessarily fall into one category or another.

For example, a user's gender is not necessarily a business or personal aspect of a user, and so it might be useful to simply add it directly via the **Manage fields** overlay. If you're not entirely certain about this, come back to it once we have covered fields in the upcoming content chapters.

This completes our discussion on users. Hopefully you'll agree that there is a solid and flexible core of functionality available in Drupal to help manage your site's users efficiently.

Let's turn our attention to a module that can help attract more of said users...

OpenID

One of the biggest obstacles you will need to overcome when promoting and running a website is trying to convince people to actually make regular use of it. Adopting yet another new site is, for your run-of-the-mill Internet user, actually quite a chore, and people will do surprisingly little in terms of spending time registering or finding their way around a new domain. Ultimately, providing content that is valuable to them is the best way to keep users loyal to you, but there are a number of other things one can do to make adoption of your site easier.

At present, a new user to your site might read something that interests them and decide to post a comment about it. Assuming you are not going to allow anonymous users to post comments (I suggest finding a good anti-spam module if you do), they will need to register on the site first. This means they need to go to the registration page, enter their details (by now, most people are sick of doing this on every site they go to), wait for the confirmation e-mail, set their new password, and so on.

While it might not seem like too much work to you—after all, it only takes a minute or two—it can put a lot of people off because they only want to post their comments and don't want to create and remember a whole new set of login details. OpenID circumvents this by allowing people to sign in with their OpenID information that is stored with their OpenID operator of choice.

Please take a few moments to visit `http://openid.net/` and read about what OpenID is and how it came about. In short:

> OpenID eliminates the need for multiple usernames across different websites by providing a single digital identity in the form of a URL.

What this means is that if someone has an OpenID account, and they visit your site, they can log in straight away using their OpenID, despite having never visited you before. Of course, individual sites may still require them to enter some additional information before a new account is registered. One reason for this is that, often, a URL is not a suitable login name for websites (including Drupal), so they request one to be entered before setting up the OpenID account.

To enable OpenID support, head on over to the **Modules** section and enable the **OpenID** module before clicking **Save configuration** and logging out. Look at the login block on your web page; you should see something like this:

The OpenID module utilizes some nice Web 2.0 features to immediately convert the login form to OpenID standard, without having to refresh the page once the **Log in using OpenID** link is clicked:

Naturally, this needs to be tested, so if you don't have one already, head on over to `http://openid.net/get/` and pick a provider. For example, I opened a **myOpenID** account and created the OpenID login: `http://davidmercer.myopenid.com/`. Using this as my OpenID login on the Drupal webpage, and by clicking **Log in**, you are redirected to the following authentication page (assuming you are not already logged into your OpenID account):

After **Sign In**, the following page is presented that allows you to make a decision regarding the request for authentication from the site you are logging into:

This page is telling us it has had a request from a website (in this case, my localhost development machine) to sign in and which profile it should provide information from. This particular OpenID provider allows users to select any one of a number of profiles in order to provide that person's details for the requesting site. Using these details, one can allow requests from this URL to *always be authenticated* with the details provided, in which case, the OpenID on this particular URL never has to provide a password. Alternatively, it is possible to uncheck the sign-in option to force this page to come up each time.

Clicking **Continue** brings up the following message back on the local Drupal site:

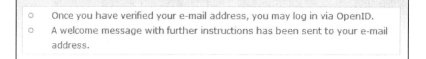

Once the e-mail address is confirmed and we have logged in using openID it's easy enough to check if the account details have been properly set up or not. Go to the account's edit page:

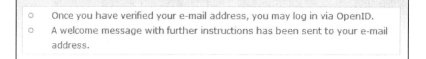

Now, any and all correspondence between this user, **Dave**, and the website will occur using the e-mail address supplied by the opened account. Note that there is little point in setting a new Password because it is easier to log in with the OpenID—especially if it is set to always authenticate for this site. If, for some reason, you really wanted to log in with the nickname (**Dave**) and a password instead of using OpenID, then go ahead and set the password as normal, and save to complete the account set-up process begun by OpenID on your behalf.

The OpenID module also provides a new tab in the **My account** section for users, so click on the **OpenID Identities** tab to bring up the following page that provides users with a list of OpenIDs used and the ability to add or remove them:

OpenID	Operations
http://davidmercer.myopenid.com/	Delete

OpenID

Add an OpenID

In conclusion, OpenID is undergoing rapid adoption all over the Web, and there are a number of really big websites that now support the standard. As time goes by, it will be more and more important for a site to implement this feature, and ultimately, in doing so, lower the "price of admission" to your community.

The fact that the OpenID module comes as part of the Drupal core is good evidence, in itself, for its growing popularity.

Summary

This chapter provided a good grounding in the basics of controlling access to your site's content. Drupal comes with a large number of facilities and options to ensure proper maintenance of the site by retaining overall control with the administrative user, as well as delegating important jobs to trusted users via the use of roles.

We looked at how to go about planning an access policy. This is not only an important requirement in terms of making sure the site runs smoothly, but also helps to solidify how the site will eventually work by forcing you to consider many eventualities. A tour of the fundamental aspects of access control in Drupal saw us discussing roles, permissions, profiles, and users.

OpenID was introduced as an additional method of accessing the site, with an emphasis on the fact that it helps reduce the barrier to entry for potential members—and this is always a good thing.

With that, we are done with access control, although you are strongly urged to spend some time on the exercises provided online for this chapter as they will expand greatly on what we have learned here.

The following chapter starts our in-depth look at content—the beating heart of Drupal!

5
Basic Content

Everything we have dealt with so far, as important as it may be in terms of creating a unique site, must take a back seat when it comes to the topic of content and content management in Drupal. After all, content *is* what this is all about!

With the explosion in the number of sites offering dynamic content, it is now an absolute necessity to provide meaningful, dynamic, and relevant information on your site in order to prosper. How this is done behind the scenes is of no concern to a site's users, but if you can make their browsing experience hassle free and relevant to their needs, they will stick with you.

Content needs to be easy to find, which in turn means it needs to be well organized. It should be well presented and easy to interact with—in other words, simple to use. Most of this is taken care of already by Drupal, and with very little additional effort, we can provide some very powerful functionality. However, before we look at adding more functionality, we must have a good understanding of how to use what is already in place.

To this end, this chapter will provide a good grounding in the basics of content management before it moves on to look at a few interesting and powerful features of Drupal. Specifically, we will look at the following:

- Content overview
- Content types
- Working with content
- Content-related modules

Once we are done with this chapter, it will be time to take what we've learned and forge ahead by putting together some neat new content types using Drupal 7's native fields, and using a range of different modules and software to create powerful new ways of presenting content.

Content overview

It's worth looking at how Drupal organizes itself in terms of presenting you, the site administrator, with a powerful content management environment. The menu system itself is dynamic in that it automatically adds and removes features and menu options that are available depending on what content-related functionality you add, enable, or remove.

While this sounds intuitive, it can make life tricky if you don't get into the habit of doing a comprehensive check whenever important changes are made (such as adding a new content type).

In fact, there are several separate areas related to content that can have profound changes on the features and functionality available:

1. **Modules**—you can add or remove the modules that implement content functionality.

2. **Content types**—add or manage different types of content such as articles, blogs, or custom types.

3. **Find content**—perform a variety of content-related administrative tasks.

4. **Add content**—add content of varying types depending on what has been enabled and/or configured.

5. **Present content**—in particular, **Views** and **Panels** are of critical importance and will be discussed in detail in the coming chapters.

6. **Taxonomy**—classify and organize content in different ways.

By way of demonstration, let's look at how enabling a module can alter another part of the site. Take a look at the **Add content** section (it should be in your **Shortcuts** menu, by default).

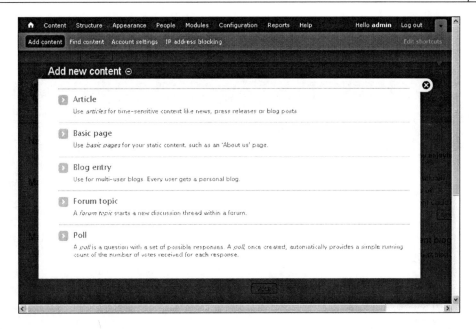

Now, go back to **Modules** and enable the **Book** module. Then look at this page once more. You should find that it now has an additional option (**Book page**), as shown in the following screenshot:

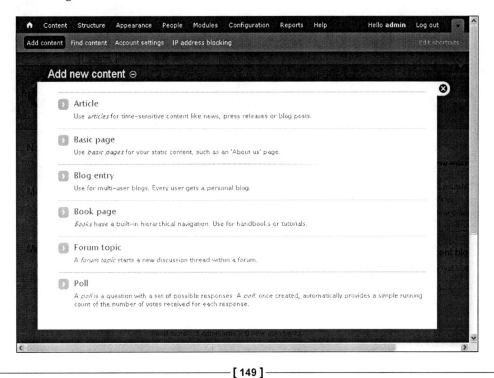

Naturally, other sections, such as the **Content types** page, also respond to whatever modules you have enabled or disabled (note the **Book page** content type is now listed):

In this instance, the **Book** module has provided an entirely new content type. However, it's important to remember that contributed content modules might have slightly different implementations. Some might deal with content display, for example, as opposed to creating new content types like the **Book** module. You should always go through the README file carefully before installing and using these.

Furthermore, the situation gets a little more complicated when you consider different types of users and the access privileges that have been granted to them. When adding a new content type, for example, you need to ensure that not only is it configured correctly, but also that you provide roles with the necessary permissions required to utilize it. We have already covered roles and access permissions, but for completeness sake, head on over to the **PERMISSIONS** page and look for the new **Book** related permissions.

Content   Structure   Appearance   People   Modules   Configuration   Reports   Help   Hello **admin**   Log out

Add content   Find content   Edit shortcuts

PERMISSION	ANONYMOUS USER	AUTHENTICATED USER	ADMINISTRATOR	FORUM MODERATOR
Block				
Administer blocks	☐	☐	☑	☐
Book				
Administer book outlines	☐	☐	☑	☐
Create new books	☐	☐	☑	☐
Add content and child pages to books	☐	☐	☑	☐
View printer-friendly books View a book page and all of its sub-pages as a single document for ease of printing. Can be performance heavy.	☐	☐	☑	☐
Comment				
Administer comments and comment settings	☐	☐	☑	☐
View comments	☐	☑	☑	☑
Post comments with approval	☐	☑	☑	☑
Post comments without approval	☐	☑	☑	☑
Edit own comments	☐	☐	☑	☐
Contextual links				
Use contextual links				

You can determine precisely who can do what from this page, depending on the needs of the site and how you want the content to be created and maintained. Remember that it is better to create a new role with its own role-specific permissions than to hand out new permissions to all authenticated users.

Understanding that content management in Drupal is a multi-faceted discipline is the key factor here. Keep an open mind because changes to one part of the system can affect other parts in different ways. Get into the habit of checking all the distinct aspects of any new content type or feature—especially permissions.

Speaking about content, let's take a look at what's available.

Content types

We need to have a good idea of the types of content that can be created in Drupal, and then look at the various ways in which these content types can be put to use. Knowing this will help you determine the best way to go about implementing the functionality you have in mind—even if it means creating your own content type.

The following table lists the content types that ship with Drupal by default (although some may not be automatically enabled):

Content type	Description
Article	This type is not meant as a standing page, like the **Basic page** type. It's something that is time-specific—like any article written for a publication. It is relevant and meaningful to its topic at that given time, but doesn't form a part of the actual structure of the website, like a "Contact us" or "Meet the team" type page.
Basic page	This page type is meant to allow you to add basic, run-of-the-mill web pages that can be found on any site. "About us" or "Terms of use" pages are good candidates for this page type. However, you can spruce these up with a bit of dynamic content and HTML.
	Just look at any website to see examples of such pages.
Blog entry	A blog, or weblog, is an author-specific content type that is used as a journal or diary, among other things by individuals. In Drupal, each blog writer can, depending on the site's settings and their permissions, add attachments, HTML, or PHP code to their blog.
	A good example of a blog can be found at http://www.siteprebuilder.com/blog, which demonstrates a Drupal blog with image handling and RSS.
Book page	A book is an organized set of book page types (actually any type can be used) that are intended to be used for collaborative authoring. Book pages may be added by different people in order to make up one single book that can then be structured into chapters and pages, or whatever structure is most appropriate.
	Because pretty much any type of data can be added to a book, there is plenty of scope for exciting content (think of narrated or visual content complementing dynamic book pages, created with PHP and Flash animations, to create a truly unique Internet-based book—the possibilities are endless).
	A good example of a book is the documentation provided for developers on the Drupal site, found at http://drupal.org/node/316. This has been built up over time by a number of different authors.
	You will notice that if you have the **Book** module enabled, an additional **outline** tag is presented above all/most of the site's posts. Clicking on this tab allows you to add that post to a book—in this way, books can be built up from content posted to the site.

Content type	Description
Forum topic	Forum topics are the building blocks of forums. Forums can only consist of forum topics and their comments, unlike books, which can consist of pretty much any content type. Information in forums is categorized in a hierarchical structure, and they are extremely useful for hosting discussions as well as community-based support and learning.
	Forums are abundant on the Internet and you can also visit the Drupal forums to get a feel for how they operate.
Poll	The poll type provides the facility to ask questions and supply a set of answers, the results of which can then be presented in graph format.
	Polls, by nature, generally have a limited life span; so you will have to search for your own examples online. Many news sites, such as Time magazine, conduct polls to determine public opinion; so these may be your best bet for seeing how polls can be put to good use.

Comments are not the same as the other node types discussed in the preceding table.

 While there may be exceptions, the terms 'node' and 'content' are synonymous with respect to Drupal.

While technically comments are content, consider the fact that one cannot create a comment without first having another node to attach the comment to. Instead, you can insert comments into other content types, and these are very popular as a means to stimulate discussion among users.

 You can see comments in action by logging into the Drupal forums, `http://drupal.org/forum`, and post or view comments on the various topics there.

It's important to check out what contribs are available to provide new content types, because as Drupal 7 matures, you can be sure that there will be some pretty neat multimedia types among many others.

Working with content

Every time some new content is created, there are several options available for you that control how that content post is managed. These options are displayed in the list that appears below the body of the post. Depending on the permissions of a given user, certain options are available and others are not. For example, if comment administration permissions are enabled for authenticated users, they will be able to decide whether to allow comments for that content or not.

As the administrator, your powers are substantial; so let's go through the default options available when creating a standard page. Be aware that different types of content may also have additional options available to them. For example, if you create a new poll, you will have to decide how long the poll is to run by setting the **Poll duration** in the poll type's unique **POLL SETTINGS** section.

To make things slightly more interesting, the choices that are made available on a content posting page not only rely on the situation, as discussed, but also change depending on which modules are enabled. This is because there are several modules that can modify how, when, and where content is displayed.

This section takes a slightly more in-depth look at how to both edit and configure content to reflect the needs of the site. We have already worked with content in previous chapters, and so are familiar with bits and pieces. However, the intention here is to provide a single, cohesive point of reference from which to learn.

We will begin by looking at how to set up the correct default options whenever you create something new. We'll also take a more in-depth look at adding and administering content.

Working with content types

It is possible to set default behavior for each enabled content type. To do this, go to **Content types** under **Structure** in the toolbar to bring up the following page:

Each content type has a set of editable configuration parameters, so to get a good idea of how they work, click on **edit** in the **Basic page** row. The edit page is broken up into six sections (which we will discuss in depth in the following section, entitled *Adding content*) dealing with the following:

- **Basic identification**—Specify the human-readable name and the name used internally by Drupal for the associated content type. It also allows you to add a description to be displayed on the content creation page.
- **Submission form settings**—Set the field name for the title field, specify previewing rules, and add submission guidelines or notes to aid users posting this content type.
- **Publishing options**—Set the default publishing behavior for this content type. Content can be **Published** automatically, **Promoted to the front page**, made to be **Sticky at the top of lists** (in other words, always appear above non-sticky content even if it is older), and it is possible to specify whether or not to **Create new revisions** each time the content is modified.
- **Display settings**—Decide whether or not to display authoring information (author's name and publish date) and how long trimmed versions of the content should be.
- **Comment settings**—Specify default comment settings such as the number of comments displayed per page, whether they are **Hidden**, **Closed**, or **Open** by default, whether or not comments are threaded (as opposed to being displayed in a flat list), and whether users are forced to preview their comments or not.
- **Menu settings**—Set the menus to which this content type can be added by the poster.

By way of demonstration, the following **Publishing options** were used for the **Basic page** content type:

Obviously, your settings may well differ depending on how you want to use your basic pages (if at all), but for example, opting to enable revisions (when there is a team of people working on a site's content) helps ensure that all changes are recorded automatically to prevent the risk of losing data or inadvertently overwriting good content with poor content.

Changes made here will be visible whenever a user attempts to post content—see the next section on *Adding content* for more information.

 Users with permission to administer a given content type can override these default settings at will.

It is also possible to add your own fields to content types and manage their display. We'll discuss fields in some depth in the next chapter, so don't worry about the array of tabs (**Manage fields**, **Manage display**, and so on) along the top of the edit page overlay for the moment.

Adding content

Drupal makes it very easy to post new content:

- Click on **Add content**
- Select the type of content you need
- Enter the content into the fields provided and set the desired properties and publishing options.

The following screenshot highlights the generic list of options available to you:

Note that as per the **Publishing options** set for the **Basic page** type in the previous section, there is a section on **Revision information** available for this content type (since you are the administrator, you have access to this regardless of what is set, but this is not necessarily the case for normal site users). Conversely, if the **Book** module were to be disabled, then the **Book outline** content option would disappear from this list.

Before we go through the list of options, I should point out that one of the usability features of Drupal 7 is that it allows easy specification of the summary content—so easy in fact that it does it automatically using a trimmed value of the full text (recall that we can set the length of the trimmed content in a content type's **Display options** section). If you want to take control of the summary, click on **Edit summary** in the **Body** field and enter what you would like to display instead.

Following directly after the **Body**, the **Text format** section is presented as follows:

By default, the **Filtered HTML** option is selected. Unless you have a good reason to use the other available options, stick with the default. Especially, be wary of allowing other users to add PHP to their content (this requires that the PHP filter module is enabled first), as this could put your site at serious risk. Remember that even the **Filtered HTML** is not entirely safe, as users can still add links to malicious web addresses within their posts, which amounts to the same thing as having it on your site.

Before continuing, I should mention that in the following chapter, we will discuss how to create custom text formats because the default options might not always be suitable for the site's requirements. It's also worth noting that not all users will be granted access to all the different text formats available, depending on the access policy and the roles in place.

The **Menu settings** section offers a **Provide a menu link** option that tells Drupal that this content is to be added to one of the site's menus. In the following screenshot, the **About us** page is being added to the main navigation panel. Equally, we could have added it to the **Main menu** or **Secondary menu** — or any other menu that was enabled in the **Menu settings** section of that content type.

Clicking on the **Save** button now adds this page to the menu, as one would expect.

Most often, content posted to the site will not form part of the menu so you can safely ignore this option. However, if you ever wish to remove or edit this menu item again, look at the same **Menu settings** section, and deselect the **Provide a menu link** option. Note too that any content can be added to a menu by using the **Menus** settings under **Structure**, as discussed in *Chapter 2, Basic Functionality*.

The **Book outline** section really forms part of the discussion on the **Book** module, so we will leave this for the section entitled *Book*, later in this chapter.

The next option, **Revision information**, allows you to specify whether Drupal should create a new version of the content if it is being updated or revised. This means that the old version of the content is retained as well as the new version. This is useful if you want to keep track of what changes are being made to documents. If a new revision has been created and tracked, then assuming you have sufficient permissions, you will notice a new **Revisions** tab on the page as follows:

Using this **Revisions** page, it is now possible to review the history of any content quite easily. For example, you can decide which revision should be the active one (displayed to the public) by clicking on **revert**, or you can **delete** the revisions altogether. Notice that the log message that was added to the content type is also displayed at the bottom of each revision. This is a very powerful feature that is quite important for maintaining good version control in content that is often modified.

Because *Path* and *Pathauto* are discussed in detail in *Chapter 11, Deployment & Management*, we won't look at the **URL Path settings** option for now (you may not currently have this option available, depending on your site's configuration). If you are curious about how to automate content aliasing for SEO purposes, skip ahead and read over that section quickly.

Next, **Comment settings** allows you to determine whether other users will be able to add comments to the content or not, as shown in the following screenshot:

Open allows all users with sufficient permissions to comment on your wonderful poetry (or whatever). The second option, **Closed**, is useful if you are posting content for which comments are not appropriate—perhaps, like me, you are averse to criticism about your poetry, or something similar. In general, for content like blog posts, comments are valuable as they contribute to your community. For a basic page, like "About us", there is little point in allowing people to post comments on it.

Authoring information has only two options. The first names the author of the content and the second gives the date on which the content was first created—these are automatically given the correct options, but there are times when it is necessary to change them. Naturally, modifying the content will not change the **Authored on** date.

The **Publishing options** can be tricky to get right, depending on how you want a particular bit of content to be handled. The following screenshot shows how they look at the moment:

In the following section on *Administering content*, it is possible to decide whether content of certain types coming from certain users needs to be moderated before it can be allowed onto the site for general consumption. If this is the case, you or a designated user will have the ability to go through a moderation queue in order to confirm that any and all the content meets the site's requirements.

In the previous screenshot, the content being added is being published directly without the need for moderation, although you could uncheck this if, for example, you wanted to leave it on the site without it being available to the general public because it may still require work.

Enabling the second option, **Promoted to front page**, will cause the content being created to appear on the front page of the website when it is first published (unless you have set a specific node to be displayed here instead).

It is unlikely that, by default, you would want, say, a new book page to appear on the front page ahead of the blogs from industry experts. Therefore, you should enable this option only for the content types that should capture the limelight.

The final option, **Sticky at top of lists**, causes the node to remain at the top of its list regardless of how many other postings are there. This is extremely useful for posting important messages to forums. For example, if there is some confusion about how to do something on a given forum, write a note explaining the procedure, and select this option to pin it to the top of that forum. In this way, you ensure that it is the first thing everyone sees, whenever they visit.

This wraps it up for default content options — there's plenty more to learn, so keep your thinking cap on as we venture into the realm of content administration.

Administering content

Assuming a user does not have **administer** permissions enabled on nodes, he or she will not have the power to modify the **Publishing options** and will simply have to click on the **Submit** button in order to send their page for moderation or publication.

To see this in action, do the following:

- Give anonymous users the ability to post pages to the site by enabling the **Create new basic page content** option under **Node** in **Permissions**. Then click on **Save permissions**.
- Edit the **Basic page** content type by disabling the **Published** option, and click on the **Save content type**.

Now, post a page as an anonymous user. You should find that the page just submitted will not appear anywhere because it has not been published. In order to see what's going on, we need to visit the **Content** overlay (click on the **Content** tab in the toolbar menu), which shows a list of all the content on the site, along with a variety of options in order to work with it, as shown in the following screenshot:

Notice that in the preceding screenshot, the final submission was posted by an **Anonymous** user. This page has not yet been published because the default settings no longer automatically publish basic pages. Before we do get around to publishing this particular post, let's explore the anatomy of the content administration page more closely.

The content filter shown towards the top of the page, **SHOW ONLY ITEMS WHERE**, is a very important tool in your administrative workshop. It allows you to display only those nodes that satisfy certain requirements. There are two filter criteria provided by default, namely, **status** and **type**. These filter all the content on the site, presenting only those items that meet the specific requirement set in the respective drop-down lists.

To locate a node that has already been published, select the **published** option from the **status** drop-down list before clicking on the **Filter** button. The content results now display only published content (Note that the anonymous post is now missing).

What if we want to show only those published posts that are of the **Blog entry** type? The way to do this is by performing a nested or refined search. This involves searching for one criteria and then refining those results using another criteria. In this case, we would do the following:

- Select the **published status**, and click on the **Filter** button
- Select the **Blog entry type**, and click on the **Refine** button

Notice that Drupal provides a readable version of the filter criteria that has been applied in order to display the current content results. It is possible to further refine the filter by selecting other filter types or even loosen the filters by one notch by clicking on the **Undo** button.

> Remember to click on the **Reset** button before starting a brand new search.

You might ask where is the moderation queue. If you look at the drop-down list provided with the **status** criterion, you will notice that there is a **not published** option. Selecting this and clicking on the **Filter** button (remember to click on the **Reset** button if you already have other filters applied) will present the following result:

As expected, there is only one posting in this category at the moment because we have only posted a single page using the anonymous user, with the default published option unselected for this content type. The results bear this out, and you can now either view the content by clicking on the title or edit it by clicking on **edit**.

Once you are happy, or even unhappy, with the posting, you can perform a number of operations by using the **UPDATE OPTIONS** from the drop-down list and clicking on the **Update** button. The options presented in this list are fairly self-explanatory, and you can do everything from add or remove stickiness ("sticky", as mentioned earlier, means the content will stick to the top of the list), force the content to be displayed, remove from your site's front page, or even delete the content entirely.

It's worth remembering that selecting **unpublish** and **delete** will have the same effect in terms of effectively removing content from the site. However, the difference is that deleting the content is irreversible—it's completely gone, while "unpublishing" is reversible and said content can be published again at a later stage.

For example, let's say we now wanted to allow the anonymous page to be published and displayed on the front page because after a bit of editing, we are happy with it. Check the box to the left of the **Title**, and then in the **UPDATE OPTIONS** section directly above the list, select the relevant option(s), as shown in the following screenshot:

Clicking on the **Update** button will ensure that the page is now published as intended. You can confirm this by viewing the page on the site normally—simply navigate to the front page to see it.

Content-related modules

It's a safe bet that there are far more content-related modules available than we have room to discuss in this chapter. However, if there is something specific you need to do, it is always worth checking out what modules are available in Drupal before attempting to build anything by yourself. There are hundreds and hundreds of modules to choose from, and even if there isn't one that does exactly what you need, you can often get fairly close with the available modules and then work from there.

This section will look over a couple of content modules that you will most likely need at some stage. They are both modules that ship with the core, but we will be downloading important content-related contributions in the coming chapters too.

Aggregator

One of the greatest opportunities available to web-based communities is the ability to readily share information. All that is required is a set of guidelines for how that information is to be presented; and once you have that, the rest is easy. So easy, in fact, it is now possible to include news and articles of interest on your site from many well known sources with just a few clicks.

What makes it so easy to include other people's news, documents, articles, or any other content is a standard called **Rich Site Summary** (**RSS**). This allows aggregators (programs that consume RSS feeds) to understand how to present content on web pages due to the way in which the RSS feed is structured. Drupal comes with one of these aggregators built in—simply enable it in the **Modules** section, and then visit the configuration overlay. You should find that a **Feed aggregator** link has been added to the **WEB SERVICES** section.

Let's assume that we want to provide Drupal-related articles on the demo site. We access `http://www.siteprebuilder.com/blog` (which publishes a Drupal-related blog feed) and look for the RSS feed icon. In this case, there is one available at the bottom-left of the blog page:

Clicking on the orange RSS icon here will bring up the following page (it may appear in a number of formats depending on your browser) — luckily Drupal takes care of all the dirty work for us, and we don't even need to understand the XML in order to utilize this feed:

This may not seem too interesting at the moment, but it serves to confirm that there is at least a feed available for use at this URL.

Head back to your site and open the **Feed aggregator** overlay in order to begin adding this feed. This will bring up the blank list of feeds along with everything else we need to manage them.

Assuming you intend to make use of a variety of feeds, it is probably prudent to categorize your content right from the start. Remember, providing access to timely and interesting news is a value-added service for your site and encourages users to return time and again. Click the **Add category** link, then enter a new category entitled **Drupal**, and then click on the **Save** button.

Click on the **List** tab to go back to the main feed overlay. You'll now be able to see the **Drupal** category in the **Category overview** section. Now click on the **Add feed** tab to bring up the following page:

As you can see, we have:

1. Specified a title for the new feed.
2. Supplied Drupal with the location of the RSS feed (check this against the URL of the RSS feed page we visited on site prebuilder a bit earlier).
3. Given an **Update interval** of one day.
4. Associated this feed with the newly created **Drupal** category.

There are a number of things to consider when aggregating feeds from different sources. First, ensure that you are not infringing any licensing issues (often these will be supplied by the creator of the source feed). If there are restrictions as to what can and cannot be done with the feed, please ensure you abide by those restrictions.

Next, there is no point in setting an update interval of one hour if you are only running the cron script once a day—cron can, at most, only update the script once a day in this case. By the same token, there is no point in using cron to update a feed every ten minutes, if the feed itself is only updated on a weekly basis—check how often the feed providers recommend it be updated.

Some feed providers will ban you from their service if you persist in querying their feeds too regularly—it is your responsibility to honor their stipulations.

Having taken these factors into account, you can now click on the **Submit** button to add the feed. Now the aggregator home page has something to tell us and should look like the following page:

As yet, there are no items in the feed because the cron hasn't been run. You can either wait for it or click the **update items** link to the right of the feed listing.

Once that is done, you should see something like the following screenshot:

Success! The feed now contains **30 items** as of the last update, which occurred **5 sec ago**. Also, you can **edit** the feed, **remove items**, or manually update it by clicking **update items**—this will update the feed to reflect any recent changes on the source site. That's all there is to it!

You can, of course, now view the content of the feed on the site by clicking the **Feed aggregator** link (most likely shown in the left sidebar by default):

All your site's users now have instant access to the content provided by site prebuilder. Nothing stops you from gathering information from any number of other feeds, and what is interesting is that provided you are not infringing any licenses, your feeds can be made available to other sites. Doing this is easy. Scroll down to the bottom of the feed page until you see the small RSS icon, and click on it:

Note that the feed contains content aggregated from site prebuilder only moments ago, but the title is now your own **My drupal site aggregator** and that the URL of this feed (in the case of the demo site) is at `http://localhost/drupal/aggregator/rss`. This is how Drupal content can be syndicated (shared with others). You aren't limited to syndicating online feeds you have obtained—any content can be syndicated.

It's worth noting that feed sources can be revealed in the navigation column by clicking on the **Sources** link under **Feed aggregator**. In this case, we are presented with the following:

This page presents us with a nice summary of feeds from each source. So far so good, but what does the **More** link do? Clicking on the **More** link for the **Site prebuilder blogs** source brings up the following page:

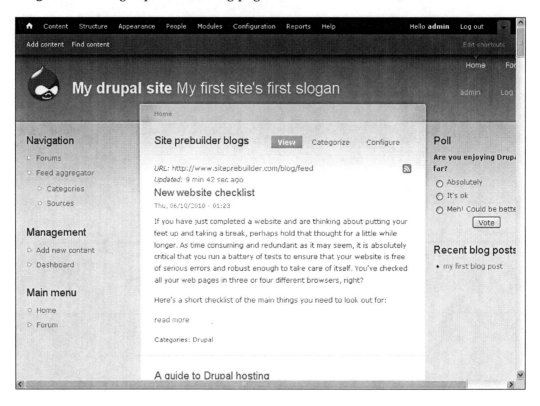

The feed items associated with this source are listed on the page below the title box for easy access. There are also two tabs at the top of this page. The **Categorize** tab opens a new dialog that allows us to put individual feed items into a variety of different categories (assuming you have created a variety of categories, in the same way we created the first one).

This following screenshot shows a feed item being assigned two categories, namely, **Drupal** and **SEO**:

In this case, the **SEO** category was created with a specific purpose in mind. Because there is news every now and then that may hold special interest for the site's readers interested specifically in SEO, all the items that are tagged in the **SEO** category should be displayed in a special block on the website (we'll see how this is done in a moment), so that every user can see the SEO news when viewing any page on the site.

Before continuing, note that the final tab on the **Sources** page, entitled **Configure**, brings up the same page that was used in order to create the feed. From here, you can make any changes you require with ease.

It is possible you would like to display some of the latest feeds in a block somewhere on the site, so **Aggregator** provides this functionality, automatically. Head on over to **Blocks** under **Structure** and enable one of the new feed blocks so that it displays its latest items.

✛	Recent comments	\<none\>	configure
✛	Recent content	\<none\>	configure
✛	SEO category latest items	\<none\>	configure
		Left sidebar	
✛	Search form	Right sidebar	configure
		Content	
		Header	
✛	Secondary menu	Footer	configure
		Highlighted content	
✛	Shortcuts	Help	configure
		Dashboard main	
✛	Site prebuilder blogs feed latest items	Dashboard sidebar	configure
		\<none\>	
✛	Syndicate	\<none\>	configure
✛	User menu	\<none\>	configure

Once this is done, you will see the new feed, along with a selection of its items on Drupal's web pages.

my first blog post

Thu, 06/03/2010 - 17:22 — admin

Read more   admin's blog   Add new comment

Are you enjoying Drupal so far?

Thu, 06/03/2010 - 17:21 — admin

○ Absolutely
○ It's ok
○ Meh! Could be better

Recent blog posts

• my first blog post

More

SEO

• Must have Drupal modules for an SEO friendly website

More

You can configure the number of news items displayed in the **Block specific settings** on its configuration page (click on **configure** to open this up)—for our purposes, the default option of five feeds is just fine.

The aggregator has one more important section to look at—configuration. If you click on the **Settings** tab of the **Feed aggregator** page under **Configuration**, the following is displayed:

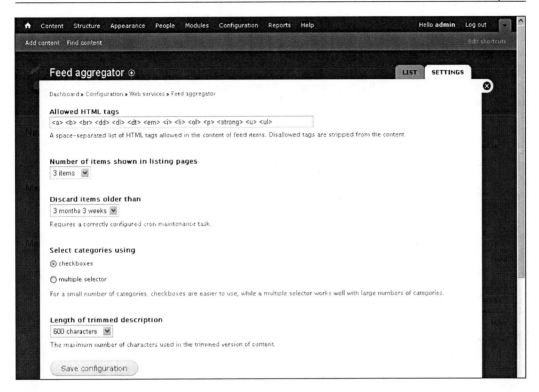

This page allows you to control the **Allowed HTML tags**, and the number of items to be shown with each feed, as well as how long to hold onto old feed items before discarding them. The **Select categories using** section stipulates whether the category selection interface should use **checkboxes** or the **multiple selector**. We have already seen **checkboxes** in use, but if **multiple selector** was enabled, the category selections would look like the following screenshot:

Before we move on, it is worth mentioning again that having interesting and informative news on your site makes it a more attractive destination for users. Further, providing your own content that others can utilize through RSS feeds builds popularity as people follow RSS feed summaries back to your site to read the full article—it's a good way of immersing your site into the Internet community as a whole.

Book

Earlier in this chapter we used the **Book** module to demonstrate how enabling a module can lead to changes in a variety of areas of the site administration. However, we neglected to give complete coverage of this useful module, so let's elaborate on this here.

A book, in the Drupal context, is a navigable structured document that can be authored collaboratively—provided that more than one person has permission to create book pages. It can consist of pretty much any type of content, including the default **Book page**, and imbues its content with a number of features that make them part of the book. For example, navigation links are added to each book page allowing readers to traverse the book structure with ease.

Creating a book is fairly easy. After ensuring that the **Book** module is enabled, click on **Add content** and select **Book page**. Adding a title for the book and a brief summary of what it is about is really no different from creating any other type of content. The difference comes in setting up where in the book's structure this page is going to be placed. Scroll down the page and open up the section entitled **Book outline**.

Selecting **<create a new book>** from the drop-down list indicates that we wish this page to be the start of a new book—Drupal dutifully informs us that this will be the top level page in the book. With that done, go ahead and save the changes—if you intend on working on the book regularly, perhaps consider adding it to the shortcut menu for easy access.

When viewing this page, it now becomes clear how the rest of the book can be built by adding pages.

Click on **Add child page** and call the new page **Chapter 1**. The important part of adding any content to a book comes in the **Book outline** section where we can specify where in the book this page must be added.

In this instance, we want this page to be part of the new book, and more importantly, its parent item must be the original book page. Click on the **Save** button, and then create a few more chapter pages so that you end up with something like the following:

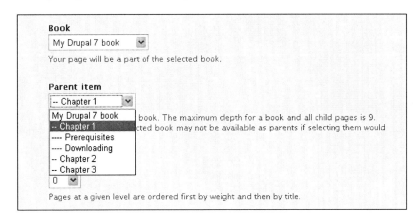

It is easy enough to then begin adding content to each chapter by adding sections or articles, and Drupal actually mentions on the content creation page that it will accept up to nine levels of depth in the content. Of course, adding content to each chapter requires us to specify the relevant chapter in the **Book outline** section.

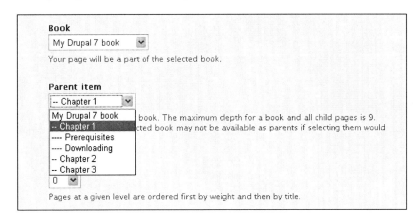

With child pages added to **Chapter 1**, the book outline indicates that there is something contained within the chapter by modifying the bullet, as shown in the following image:

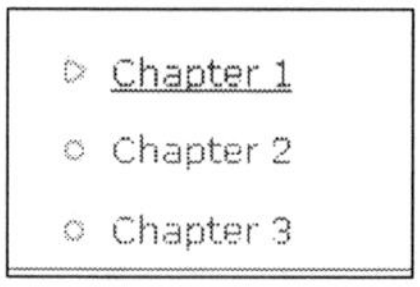

Clicking this link now brings up the child page(s) along with the book's associated navigation:

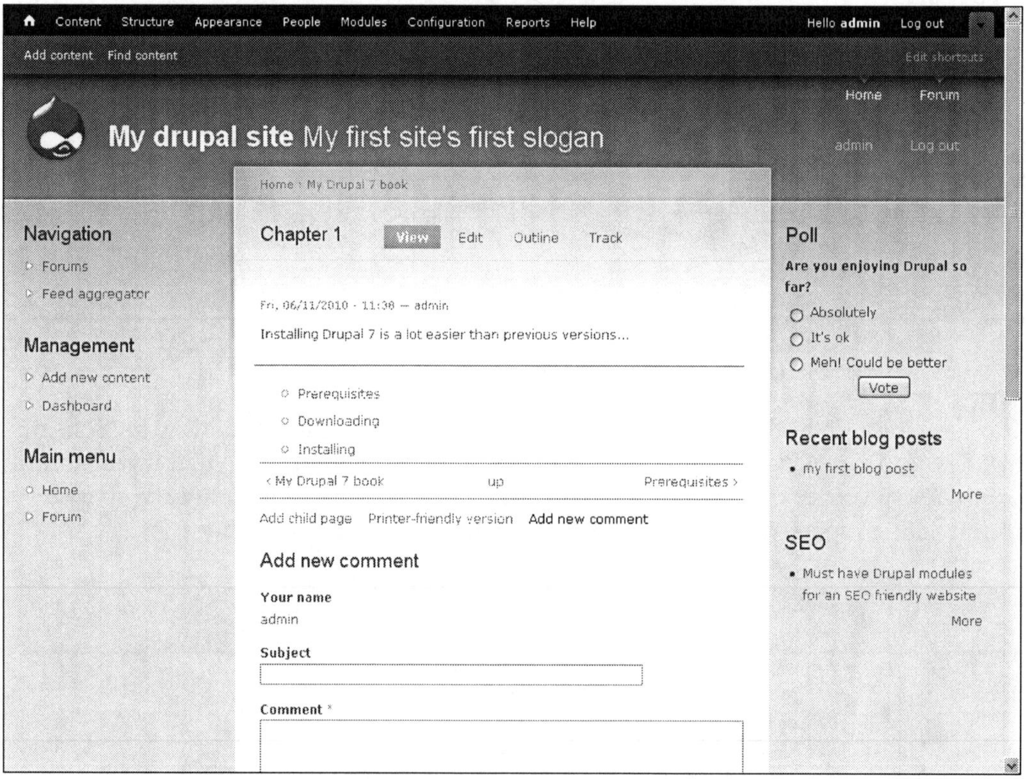

Remember that any content you like can be added to a book, so you are not limited to having to build up each piece of content in the way we have done here. Take a look at any piece of content that has been created on the site—it can be a blog post, a poll, other media, whatever—it will have an **OUTLINE** tab, which, when clicked, brings up a dialog that can be used to add the content to any part of any book on the site.

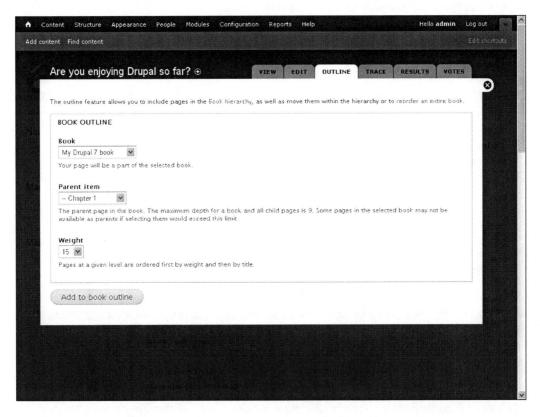

Note that this poll has been added to **Chapter 1** of **My Drupal 7 book**. It has also been assigned a large **Weight** to push it to the back of the chapter—just as one would expect in, say, an instructional document that provides questionnaires at the end of each section.

> It's easy to control the order in which content is presented in a book by modifying its **Weight** attribute. A smaller weight pushes the item up the order, and a higher weight sinks it lower in the order.

Now **Chapter 1** has the following structure:

What if, realizing that we need to add a whole bunch of questions to the end of each chapter, we now want to have a questionnaire section that contains all the polls? The answer is to add a poll's page to the chapter entitled **Questionnaires** and then edit each of the polls' **Book outline** options to insert them into the **Questionnaires** parent item.

Before we round off this section, it is important to note that the behavior of each book can be controlled by visiting the **Books** tab on the **Content** overlay. This page presents a list of all the books on the site and provides a link (**edit order and titles**) to a graphical interface utilizing drag-and-drop features for editing a book.

For example, the one we created has the following edit page:

Finally, the **Books** overlay also has a **Settings** tab that can be used to specify the default page type for books, as well as which content types are to be allowed and disallowed. As the administrator, it is possible to add any content type to a book, by default, but you may wish to consider disallowing some types, if the book is to be created collaboratively.

Summary

Knowing how to deal with content efficiently and quickly is a highly desirable trait when it comes to working with CMS systems such as Drupal. This chapter set the foundation for you to work from by giving an overview of the fundamentals. To start with, we took a brief look at the various types of content that can be implemented using Drupal and then discussed how to work with that content using the administration tools.

At the moment, content management might seem fairly straightforward, but as the site grows larger, the job becomes slightly harder. Ensuring that you spend time learning about the various content-related administrative areas will ensure that you stay on top of things as you begin attempting more complex content-oriented tasks.

The second half of this chapter demonstrated some of the powerful functionality that ships with Drupal. We saw that it is possible to create books and aggregate RSS feeds with relative ease, and in turn, syndicate content so that it is made available to other sites to consume. Having the ability to do this with only the minimum of fuss is a quantum leap for the Internet as a whole, and Drupal makes it a breeze.

Armed with a solid understanding of how to work with content, we are now ready to look at some more advanced content issues. The next chapter will talk about how to create your own dynamic and attractive content, as well as discussing how to categorize it.

6
Advanced Content

One of the most important aspects to managing content is the manner in which it is best organized for expedient retrieval — and for this, we need to discuss taxonomy. Taxonomy is what makes Drupal's classification system so powerful, and it is left for us to decide how best to implement it. We will see later on in this chapter why this faculty of Drupal is one of the features that distinguishes it from everything else out there — it's really a good thing.

Being able to categorize information is one thing, but the ability to create entirely new content types and post complex pages will also come in handy at some stage. As of Drupal 7, taxonomies are associated with content types in the same way as any other field. Accordingly, this chapter discusses the following subjects:

- Fields
- Taxonomy
- Formatting

The skills learned during the process of content classification, creation, and management will prove useful not only for this website, but also in other aspects of life — whether it is creating and managing office reports for your boss, building a new website, or even writing a book. That is because, by and large, we are now going to learn *how content should be managed and created* rather than how to enable or disable settings.

Content and fields

Up until now, we have relied on the standard content types that come as part of Drupal. Almost without a doubt, you will want to modify these or create entirely new ones to suit your particular brand of content. Creating a new content type is a cinch and ties in nicely with the topic of fields since fields can be used to modify content types (whether they are standard content types or ones made up by you).

More importantly, the use of fields plays a crucial role in more advanced management and display of content and content types when we come to utilizing arguably the most important module available in Drupal—discussed in *Chapter 8, Views*. Just to be clear:

> A field, in Drupal, is a unit of data. Fields can be added to pretty much any Drupal entity, from content types and comments to users and taxonomy terms. Fields can have any number of underlying data types, ranging from text to images and integers and have a range of associated widgets to facilitate input such as checkboxes or text fields.

It's important you understand the concept and usage of fields now so that the different ways in which they can be utilized is clear later on. Let's put them to use to get a feel for how they operate.

Creating new content types

Head over to **Content types** under **Structure**, and click the **Add content type** link to bring up the following page:

All that is really required to create the new content type is a name. However, of special interest is the **Submission form settings** below this. This is because, often, the **Title** field label should be changed to suit the content type.

In certain cases, it doesn't really make sense to have a **Title** label. For example, let's say you were building a repository of different species for a biodiversity website. It wouldn't make sense to prompt for a species' title, rather a **Common name** (as shown in the previous screenshot) makes more sense here.

Once the **Name** and **Description** fields are filled in, click **Save content type** to add this to the default list:

We are now ready to begin customizing this new type—remember that field availability and other customizations can depend on what is or is not enabled and installed on a site. It is possible to customize *any content type* that is available on Drupal, including the default ones like **Blog entry** or **Poll**, but to begin, let's work on something new and leave the default types alone.

Adding fields

To begin working on the new content type, click on **MANAGE FIELDS** in the **Species** row. We can **Add new field** or even **Add existing field**:

This dialog allows you to specify the new field's machine-readable name (**NAME**) as well as the human-readable name (**LABEL**), which is shown on a poster while they are creating new content. There is also a drop-down list providing a selection of different field types and, while this list is subject to change depending on whether you install additional field types, the default list comprises the following options:

- **Boolean, Integer, Decimal, Float**—Add numbers in various formats
- **File**—Upload a variety of different file types
- **Image**—Upload images
- **List**—Present a list of options
- **Long text, Text**—Enter text-based content
- **Term reference**—Reference taxonomy terms

Each field type comes with a set of options for how that data should be entered in the **WIDGET** column. Looking at the **Integer** type, we can see that users can be prompted for an **Integer** with a **Text field**, yet a **Boolean** type can be either a **single on/off check box** or **radio buttons**.

Be careful about how information is stored — it is important to be efficient. For example, don't store information as **Long text** when the field is used for entering a name. Certain underlying types can take up more space than others.

With the new field settings in place (the previous screenshot shows us adding a text field for the scientific name of the species), click **Save** to bring up the global **Field settings** overlay for this field. These settings affect how this field behaves in general (remember that any field can be added to any number of different content types, so global behavior is important)

In the case of a **Text** field, the only option presented here is as follows:

While this might seem a bit dull, setting the **Maximum length** is quite important. On the off chance a bot is able to post content, or a malicious attack occurs, setting a sensible size length can help limit the amount of damage that can be done. For example, if you style a list expecting only sensible data to be entered, then it can really affect your site's layout when someone adds four pages worth of content to this field (assuming you have not set the length to something small, like the default value).

Click on **Save field settings** to bring up the specific field settings as they apply to the *current* content type. From here, you can decide on how the data will be presented to the user, add help text, and decide whether or not the field itself will be compulsory, plus a number of other things:

Be aware that different field types (as well as different widget types) may present a range of different options. For example, when utilizing the **List** field type, you need to provide a list of allowed values from which users can select an option—this should make sense because there has to be a list of options from which to choose in a list widget.

For our demonstration, we need to decide whether this field is required. In other words, does the user *have* to enter a value or can they skip it. We can also decide on the **Size of textfield** presented in the form and whether or not the field should only allow plain text or whether the user may choose from the permissible text formats.

Further on, we can set a default value for this field. In the case of a species' scientific name, there is little point in having a default, but there are plenty of cases where you may be able to speed up things for content posters by providing sensible defaults.

Finally, you need to decide on the **Number of values** that can be entered. In our case, limiting this number to 1 is the correct choice since any species has only one unique scientific name. However, if this field held a species' common name, you might want to enter several or even an **Unlimited** amount since one species can be known by a huge number of names in different languages and any number of these might be entered.

Next, add a bunch of different fields to the new content type. For example, for any given species, you might want to upload an image, provide a select list of numbers in the wild, add a choice of status (endangered, thriving, extinct), and so on. Save the changes, go to the **Add content** section, and create a new **Species** post:

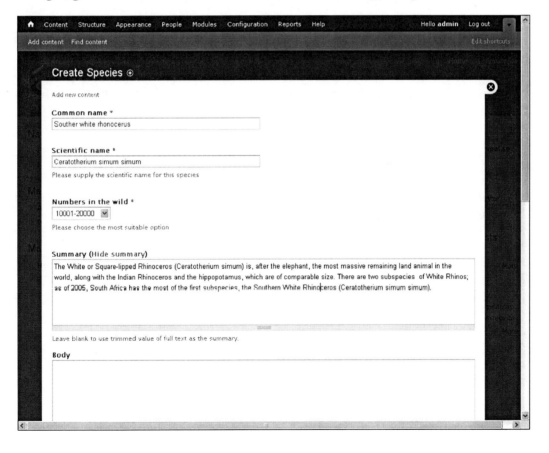

You now have, in addition to the default fields provided by Drupal, any number of fields and widgets with which to enter pertinent data. In the previous screenshot, you can see a select list allowing posters to select from a **Numbers in the Wild** range. This is a pretty powerful method of specifying this figure—as opposed to allowing people to enter this information manually into the **Body** field.

 Breaking up content into specific fields allows for greater control over how that information is presented when it comes time to utilize views and to style and format content types.

One of the great things about Drupal is that anyone can build and add custom field types that can be incorporated into your own content types. For example, by default, there is no table type field available. However, it is possible to obtain this functionality via the `TableField` module on Drupal. In time, other modules will also add to the list of possible field types.

In particular, the `CCK` module (hugely important in Drupal 6) will still, most likely, provide the node and user reference types. Being able to reference other users and nodes from within content can be a powerful tool for creating complex views. Unfortunately, we are not able to explore these at the moment (they are not available at the time of writing), but after reading *Chapter 8, Views*, you will be able to see how they may be utilized using relationships.

Displaying fields

In order to determine how input data should be displayed on screen, click on the **MANAGE DISPLAY** tab next to **MANAGE FIELDS**, when viewing a content type. This brings up a tabbed page that caters to the **Basic** display of the content type as well as how to display in **Print**, **RSS**, and **Search** results:

Basic settings control the display of the **TEASER** and **FULL CONTENT** fields and
their labels. In the same way, for example, the **Search** tab deals with the display
of this content type in the search index and search results. Each field has a **LABEL**
option to determine where the label is displayed, relative to the data it contains. The
three options are **Above**, **Inline**, or **Hidden**.

Setting the **Scientific name** to **Above**, as shown in the previous screenshot, displays
its field content like this:

Setting it to **Inline** gives:

And finally, setting it to **Hidden** displays the field content with no label whatsoever.

It's important to note that different fields have different **Format** options, depending on what underlying type they are. An example of this is the **List** type that can display the **Key** (which, obviously, would not be suitable for a plain text field, since it would never have a key).

How you choose to present content is really up to your own preferences and what is most expedient and useful for users in the context of how they utilize the site. Remember that the cron script must run before any new content will show up in search results (just in case you want to play around with the **Search** display options).

Taxonomy

If your site is never going to gather a substantial amount of content (perhaps it is only meant as a more static, placeholder webpage), then spending time working with taxonomies is probably not going to be of much advantage.

However, the aim is not generally to remain in obscurity when creating a website, so assuming that you do want to attract a community of users, you'll need to build up a reservoir of valuable content over time. The method of classifying and categorizing this content in Drupal makes it one of the most sophisticated content management systems around.

Take the time to master working with taxonomy in Drupal because not only will this help you to work out how to manage your site's content better, but it can also really set your site apart from others because of the flexible and intuitive manner in which the content is organized. These attributes allow you to manage a site of pretty much any size imaginable (just in case what you are working on is "*the next big thing*").

What and why?

Taxonomy is described as the science of classification. In terms of how it applies to Drupal, it is the *method by which content is organized* using several distinct types of relationships between terms; it's as simple as that. Before we move on, there is a bit more terminology to pick up first:

- **Term**: A term used to describe content (also known as a *descriptor* or *tag*)
- **Vocabulary**: A grouping of related terms
- **Thesaurus**: A categorization of content that describes *is similar to* relationships
- **Taxonomy**: A categorization of content into a hierarchical structure
- **Tagging**: The process of associating a term (descriptor or tag) with content
- **Synonym**: Can be thought of as *another word for* the current term.

It may help to view the following diagram in order to properly grasp how these terms inter-relate:

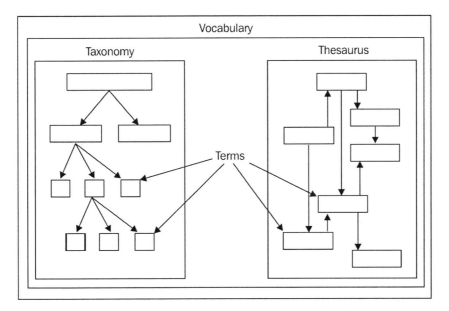

This serves to illustrate the fact that there are two main types of vocabulary. Each type consists of a set of terms, but the relationships between them are different in that a *taxonomy* deals with a hierarchy of information and a *thesaurus* deals with relationships between terms. The terms (shown as small boxes) and their relationships (shown as arrows) play a critical role in how content is organized.

We have already seen an example of a taxonomy when the **Forum** module was discussed. In this case, there was a hierarchical relationship between forum containers and the forum topics they contained. But what would we need thesauri for? For one thing, if you wanted to allow plenty of references between nodes, so that users could browse related pages (which didn't necessarily have child-parent relationships), then you would go for this type of structure — tagging on sites like Delicious are a good example of this.

What we have discussed so far is how to *control a taxonomy* from the administrator's point of view. It is also possible to pass that control onto everyone who uses the site by creating a *free taxonomy*. One of the things that makes the Drupal taxonomy system so powerful, is that it allows content to be categorized on the fly (as and when it is created). This unburdens administrators because it is no longer necessary to moderate every bit of content coming into the site in order to put it into pre-determined categories.

We'll discuss these methods in some detail in the coming sections, but it's also worth noting quickly that it is possible to tag a given node more than once. This means that content can belong to several vocabularies. This is very useful for cross-referencing purposes because it highlights relationships between terms or vocabularies through the actual nodes.

Let's begin…

Implementing taxonomies in Drupal

The best way to talk about how to implement some form of categorization is to see it in action. There are quite a few settings to work with and consider in order to get things up and running. By way of example, let's assume that the demo site has enlisted a large number of specialists who will maintain their own blogs on the website so that interested parties can keep tabs on what's new according to the people in the know.

Now, some people will be happy with visiting their blog of choice and reading over any new postings there. Others, however, might want to be able to search for specific topics in order to see if there are correlations or disagreements between bloggers on certain subjects. As there is going to be a lot of content posted once the site has been up and running for a few months, we need some way to ensure that specific topics are easy to find, regardless of who has been discussing them on their blogs.

Introduction to vocabularies

Let's quickly discuss how vocabularies are dealt with in the administration tool in order to work out how to go about making sure this requirement is satisfied. Click on the **Taxonomy** link under **Structure** to display a page listing the current vocabularies. Assuming that you have created a forum during the last few chapters, you should have something like this:

Before we look at editing terms and vocabularies, let's take a look at how to create a vocabulary for ourselves. Click on the **add vocabulary** link to bring up the following page:

By way of example, this vocabulary will deal with the topic of **Conservation**. Clicking on **Save** adds this vocabulary to the list, so that the main page now looks like this:

So far so good, but this will not be of much use to us as it stands. We need to add some terms (descriptors) in order to allow tagging to commence.

Dealing with terms

Click on the **add terms** link for the **Conservation** vocabulary to bring up the following page:

The term **Ecology** has been added here, with a brief description of the term itself. The **Parent terms** option in **RELATIONS** warrants a closer inspection, but as it relates more closely to the structure of hierarchies, we'll look at it in the *Hierarchies* section a bit later. This section will also highlight how to organize vocabularies using drag-and-drop in the **List** view.

For now, add a few more terms to this vocabulary so that the list looks something like this:

Before we can make use of these terms, we need to associate the vocabulary with one or more content types.

Adding vocabularies to content types

Go to the **Blog entry** content type under **Structure** and click **Manage fields**. In the section entitled **Add new field**, select the **Term reference** field and the **Autocomplete term widget (tagging)** option from the **Widget** column and provide a meaningful name, like so:

The autocomplete widget is handy if there are a large number of terms in the vocabulary because it allows posters to type in a few letters of their tag and obtain a list of the all the available terms from which a selection can be made. It's also used for tagging, which will be discussed in the *Tagging* section a bit later in this chapter.

The other option, **Check boxes/Radio buttons** is more suited to a vocabulary with a limited number of terms because it is easy for a poster to quickly go over the list. For example, if your website deals in, say, 10 major topics, a select list would be easier to pick from than the autocomplete widget.

Click **Save** to bring up the **Field settings** dialog that allows us to associate this term reference field with the **Conservation** vocabulary:

Click **Save field settings** and run through the content type specific field settings, as discussed earlier in the section on *Adding fields*:

As you can see, it is possible to specify whether this vocabulary is required or not. It's a good idea to enforce this option if you want to maintain a high quality of classification—otherwise, lazy posters will end up leaving everything tagged with the default descriptor (assuming you have one set) and that is not much good to anyone.

The **CONSERVATION FIELD SETTINGS** at the bottom of this page is the main area of focus because they allow you to control the number of terms a poster can use (anywhere between one and infinity) and from which vocabulary to draw the terms from:

You should have no difficulty in determining which vocabulary to draw from since it is likely that you have created one specifically for a given content type. What's not so easy to decide on is how many tags should be allowed. Only one tag per posting makes the system fairly inflexible and content might not fit perfectly under a single term. However, it makes the content simple to navigate. The more tags that are allowed, the more flexibility the system has to better classify a piece of content, but this makes navigation slightly more complex for readers.

It's a bit of a trade-off, one way or the other, and something that you should lend some thought to based on how you want or think users will utilize your content.

Posting content with taxonomy

Using any account with the requisite permissions to add blog content, attempt to post to the site. You should now be able to view the newly available taxonomy field, as shown here (this might require a bit of reordering of the field list):

Now comes the clever bit. Once this blog node has been posted, users can view the blog as normal, except that it now has its term displayed along with the post:

Where does the link take us? Click on the term, in this case **Ecology**, and you will be taken to a page listing all of the content that has been tagged with this term. This should really have you quite excited because with very little work, users can now find focused content without having to look that hard—this is what content management is all about!

Hierarchies

What we have seen so far is really only the tip of the iceberg. You can build an entire hierarchy of terms in a vocabulary. Remember that if it is a hierarchy you are building, then the broadest terms should be towards the top of the pile, with the more focused terms near the bottom. At the moment, though, we don't really have a *hierarchy*, but rather, more of a *flat* structure.

What if we wanted a set of more specific terms that would allow bloggers to tag their content (which focuses on specific types of **Ecology**, for example)? The answer lies in restructuring the vocabulary by dragging-and-dropping its terms, not only up and down the list, but from left to right as well—this is done when viewing the **list terms** link of the vocabulary (or by setting the parent terms in the **Relations** section when adding a new term).

For this example, I moved the term **Biodiversity** into **Ecology** by dragging it under and to the right of **Ecology** to indicate that it is lower in the hierarchy:

That was fairly easy to do, and now we are free to create either flat hierarchies or single depth ones (that is, one parent term with one child term — no grandchildren). If you wanted to create a deep hierarchy structure, then this is easily achieved by dragging either additional terms under **Biodiveristy** or by moving **Ecology** under something else, as shown in the following screenshot:

But what happens if your topic is slightly more complex than a straightforward hierarchy? For example, it's quite possible that the terms **Climate change** could be equally at home under both **Ecology** and **Pollution** (which in turn may also have multiple parents). In the event that one term has several parent terms, the phrase used to describe this structure is *multiple hierarchy*.

Recall that when adding terms previously, there was a **Relations** select list used to specify the parent terms for the new term. Instead of specifying a single parent, you can select several parents, but be warned that this prevents further use of the drag-and-drop interface because drag-and-drop cannot properly handle multiple parent relations. Accordingly, when specifying multiple parents, you are given the following warning:

Adding multiple parents to a term will cause the *Conservation* vocabulary to look for multiple parents on every term. Because multiple parents are not supported when using the drag and drop outline interface, drag and drop will be disabled if you enable this option. If you choose to have multiple parents, you will only be able to set parents by using the term edit form.

You may re-enable the drag and drop interface at any time by reducing multiple parents to a single parent for the terms in this vocabulary.

URL alias

Optionally specify an alternative URL by which this term can be accessed. Use a relative path and don't add a trailing slash or the URL alias won't work.

Set multiple parents   Cancel

If you want a multiple hierarchy, then the structural editing of the hierarchy must be done by hand in each term's **edit** form. For completeness' sake, go ahead and click **Set multiple parents** for a term—you might want to add a few terms and set each of these to have multiple parents to make the structure a little more complex. With that done, note that the drag-and-drop features of the list page are disabled:

✦ Add term

NAME	OPERATIONS
Advocacy	edit
Pollution	edit
Climate change	edit
Sustainability	edit
Ecology	edit
Biodiversity	edit
Climate change	edit

This hierarchical structure is useful when the topics of discussion fall fairly neatly into some sort of natural hierarchy — forums are the best example of this. However, it may well be that a given piece of content overlaps several terms and should really be tagged with more than one term. As discussed in the *Adding vocabularies to content types* section, it is easy enough to control how many or how few terms can be associated with a given content posting.

Tagging

Tagging is an interesting option because it allows posters to choose their own terms for their content. While posters effectively have free reign when it comes to tagging their posts, Drupal understands that a hundred different people might come up with a hundred different terms to describe the same post, and this can be very detrimental to the usability of the site.

In order to combat this effect, Drupal provides helpful clues to keep the tagging of posts as uniform as possible, without placing restrictions on what can and is used for tagging. Only the autocomplete widget can be used for free tagging since providing a select list or checkboxes with your own terms would defeat the purpose of tagging.

With that said, Drupal knows what terms have been used before, because any terms added by a content poster are automatically added to the vocabulary. Accordingly, there is a drop-down list of all the tags available when using the autocomplete widget (containing whatever letter(s) you type):

This means that giving people free reign to type in their own tags is not as random as it may at first seem, because they can still be guided as to what terms are already available using this drop-down list. In this way, Drupal can encourage a more coherent body of terms.

"But **Biodiversity** doesn't begin with an **E**", some of you may be remarking after inspecting the previous screenshot. That is quite correct, but **Biodiversity** contains an **e** so it is displayed here nevertheless — it's a good way to provide a range of available tags that narrows down quickly as the user types more letters.

Tagging is far more flexible than the previous methods discussed. People can tag their content exactly as they please — making the tagging system fit the content far more snugly. The problem is, however, that the vocabulary may well become unwieldy, because similar content could be tagged with entirely different terms, making it hard for users to find what they are looking for.

 Allowing free tagging is a very powerful method for categorizing content. Be wary though, it can lead to a lot of redundant tags that in turn lead to content that is hard to find.

You should make note of the fact that it is not really possible to create a hierarchy of terms using the free tagging system, because every new tag is on the same level as all the other tags. What you end up with is really a *thesaurus* instead of a taxonomy.

Note that, as things stand, users can tag their blog entry content with any *one* tag they choose. Recall that when configuring the field settings, we specified only one tag should be allowed for this content type. Most tagging systems allow several tags, so you might want to go back and change these settings to allow people to use several words or phrases to describe their content better.

Formatting

It is necessary to stipulate the type of content we will be using, in any given post. This is done through the use of the **Text formats** setting — assuming the user in question has sufficient permissions to post different format types.

In order to control what is and is not allowed, head on over to the **Text formats** link in the **Content authoring** section under **Configuration**. This will bring up a list of the currently defined formats, as shown in the following screenshot:

At the moment, you might be wondering why we need to go through all this trouble to decide whether people can add certain HTML tags to their content. The answer to this is that because both HTML and PHP are so powerful, it is not hard to subvert even fairly simple abilities for malicious purposes.

For example, you might decide to allow users the ability to link to relevant websites from their blogs. Using the ability to add a hyperlink to their text, a malicious user could create a Trojan, virus, or some other harmful content, and link to it from an innocuous and friendly looking piece of HTML like this:

```
<p>Hi Friends! My <a href="link_to_trojan.exe">homepage</a> is a great
place to meet and learn about my interests and hobbies. </p>
```

This snippet writes out a friendly sentence with a link, supposedly to the author's home page. In reality, the hyperlink **href** attribute points to a trojan, `link_to_ trojan.exe`. That's just HTML. PHP can do a lot more damage—to the extent that if you don't have proper security or disaster-recovery policies in place, then it is possible that your site can be rendered useless or destroyed entirely.

Security is the main reason why, as you may have noticed from the previous screenshot, anything other than **Filtered HTML** or **Plain text** is unavailable for use by anyone except the administrator. By default, PHP is not even present.

When thinking about what permissions to allow, it is important to re-iterate the tenet:

Never allow users more permissions than they require to complete their intended tasks.

As they stand, you might not find the text formats to your liking, and so Drupal provides some functionality to modify them. Click on the **configure** link adjacent to the **Filtered HTML** option, and this will bring up the following page:

![Filtered HTML configuration page screenshot]

Filtered HTML

A text format contains filters that change the user input, for example stripping out malicious HTML or making URLs clickable. Filters are executed from top to bottom and the order is important, since one filter may prevent another filter from doing its job. For example, when URLs are converted into links before disallowed HTML tags are removed, all links may be removed. When this happens, the order of filters may need to be re-arranged.

Name *

Filtered HTML

Roles

- ☑ anonymous user
- ☑ authenticated user
- ☑ administrator
- ☐ forum moderator

Enabled filters

- ☑ Limit allowed HTML tags
- ☐ Display any HTML as plain text
- ☑ Convert line breaks into HTML (i.e. `<br>` and `<p>`)
- ☑ Convert URLs into links
- ☑ Correct faulty and chopped off HTML

From here, you can alter the **Name** of the text format as well as specify the **Roles** which may utilize this particular format. The next two sections, **Enabled filters** and **Filter processing order**, provide a checklist of the types of **Filters** to apply to the current format and the order in which they should be applied.

Sometimes, content may not behave exactly as you expect and this can be the result of one filter acting before another. If you find that certain aspects of your content is being ignored or altered, then it's a good idea to come back and play with the filters to see if the problem can be resolved here.

Let's briefly go over the default filters:

- **Limit allowed HTML tags** — determines whether or not to strip or remove unwanted HTML

- **Display any HTML as plain text** — instead of interpreting and displaying HTML, the HTML is displayed verbatim

- **Convert line breaks into HTML** — turns standard typed line breaks (that is, whenever a poster clicks **Enter**) into standard HTML

- **Convert URLs into links** — allows recognized links and e-mail addresses to be clickable without having to write the HTML tags, manually

- **Correct faulty and chopped off HTML** — corrects any broken HTML within postings to prevent undesirable results in the rest of your page.

The line break converter is particularly useful for users, because it means that they do not have to explicitly enter `<br>` or `<p>` HTML tags in order to display new lines or paragraph breaks — this can get tedious by the time you are writing your 400th blog entry. If this is disabled, unless the user has the ability to add the relevant HTML tags, the content may end up looking squashed.

The final section, *Filter settings*, allows you to configure individual filters, as shown in the following screenshot:

The **Limit allowed HTML tags** section lets you specify which tags are not stripped. Remember that if all the tags are stripped from the content, you should enable the **Line break converter** so that users can at least arrange their content properly in paragraphs. Which tags are to be stripped is decided in the **Allowed HTML tags** text field, where a list of all the tags that are to be allowed can be entered—anything else gets the chop.

Selecting **Display HTML help** forces Drupal to provide HTML help for users posting content—try enabling and disabling this option and browsing to this relative URL in each case to see the difference: `filter/tips`. There is quite a bit of helpful information on HTML in the long filter tips; so take a moment to read over those.

> The filter tips can be reached whenever a user expands the **text format** section of the content post and clicks on the **More information about text formats** option.

The final option, **Add rel="nofollow" to all links**, is used to protect your site's reputation from being associated with websites that posters link to from their postings. The HTML attribute **rel="nofollow"** tells search engines not to build these links into how they view your website's local network; it doesn't stop normal visitors from clicking the link and going to that site. If you trust all the people posting on your website, leave this unchecked. If you are worried that someone may post links to a website that isn't in keeping with your ethics or values, then enable it.

The **Convert URL into links** option is really there to help protect the formatting and layout of your site. It is possible to have quite long URLs these days, and because URLs do not contain spaces, there is nowhere to naturally split them up. As a result, a browser might do some strange things to cater to the long string and this could make your site look odd.

Decide how many characters the longest string should be and enter that number in the space provided. Remember that some content may appear in the sidebars, so you can't let it get too long if they are supposed to be a fixed width.

This is not the end of the story, because we also need to be able to create text formats in the event we require something that the default options can't cater to. This is easy enough to accomplish by clicking on the **Add text format** link above the list of available text formats in the **Text formats** overlay. This brings up the same page as the one used to edit the default formats and all that is required is for you to make selections in exactly the same way.

Take a look at the previous screenshot that shows the **configure** page of the **Filtered HTML** text format. Notice that the `<img>` tag is not available for use. It's easy to create our own text format called **Images** and enable the **Limit allowed HTML tags** option and add the image tag to the **Allowed HTML tags** section before saving. Now any user with sufficient permissions can safely use the `<img>` tag in their posts – provided they select the **Image** format option.

We've already made use of various filters earlier in this section, but it is possible to add additional filters to content, and one in particular is important to consider — the PHP filter. Before we can look at how to use it, we must first enable the **PHP Filter** module under **Modules**. With that change saved, you will find that there is now an extra **Text format** in the list entitled **PHP code**– by default, no users have permissions to use this format.

Of importance to us is the fact that a new **PHP evaluator** option has been added to the available filters list for each text format:

Name *

PHP code

Roles

☐ anonymous user

☐ authenticated user

☐ administrator

☐ forum moderator

Enabled filters

☐ Limit allowed HTML tags

☐ Display any HTML as plain text

☐ Convert URLs into links

☐ Convert line breaks into HTML (i.e. `<br>` and `<p>`)

☑ PHP evaluator

    Executes a piece of PHP code. The usage of this filter should be restricted to administrators only!

☐ Correct faulty and chopped off HTML

Filter processing order

⊹   PHP evaluator

It's not a good idea to enable the **PHP evaluator** for either of the default options, but adding it to one of our own text formats will be ok to play with. As an example, let's assume that we need the ability to make use of PHP scripts from within content. Create a new text format as follows:

Add text format ⊕

Dashboard » Configuration » Content authoring » Text formats

Name *

Special PHP format

Roles

☐ anonymous user

☐ authenticated user

☑ administrator

☐ forum moderator

Enabled filters

☑ Limit allowed HTML tags

☑ Display any HTML as plain text

☑ Convert URLs into links

☑ Convert line breaks into HTML (i.e.
 and <p>)

☑ PHP evaluator

    Executes a piece of PHP code. The usage of this filter should be restricted to administrators only!

☑ Correct faulty and chopped off HTML

We have enabled the **PHP evaluator** option, as well as prevented the use of this format for anyone but ourselves (the administrator).

 PHP should not be enabled for anyone other than yourself or a highly trusted administrator who needs it to complete his or her work.

It's always a good idea to set the **PHP evaluator** to execute first, because, as mentioned earlier, other filters can get in the way if they are allowed to process the content first:

Filter processing order

⊹	PHP evaluator
⊹	Limit allowed HTML tags
⊹	Display any HTML as plain text
⊹	Convert URLs into links
⊹	Convert line breaks into HTML (i.e. and <p>)
⊹	Correct faulty and chopped off HTML

Now, the PHP evaluator gets *dibs* on the content and can properly process any PHP before handing it off to the other filters.

Summary

With this chapter out of the way, you should have a good understanding of how flexible and powerful Drupal really is. By creating new content types and adding and managing their associated fields, it is possible to easily create a wide range of content types to suit your every need. As we progress, you'll see that we can further manipulate our content to create powerful features and that fields play an important role in facilitating this.

While fields are important in terms of creating focused and flexible content, one of the most important aspects of content management was highlighted with the discussion on taxonomy. Drupal's taxonomy system sets it apart from other CMS technologies and provides the facilities to implement pretty much any type of structure that we can imagine for our content.

Finally, we also discussed how the actual content, entered into the website via the content types and fields discussed earlier, can be controlled through the use of text formats. By using text formats, you are able to keep a tight grasp on what can and can't be added to the site. This has important security ramifications, and we discussed the importance of limiting formats to only the essentials.

You now have the knowledge to control how content is entered, what format and structure it takes, and how it is classified. This is of critical importance for any professional website.

7
Multimedia

Earlier incarnations of Drupal didn't have very good native image and media support. This wasn't a catastrophe because, as you know, it's very easy for the community to plug any gaps by providing modules for everyone to use. The problem is that it led to a wide range of modules being produced that made it harder for new users to know which module was the right one for them.

To make matters worse, each module was created with slightly differing tasks in mind, so not only was there a lot of wasteful overlap in the functionality provided by each module, but also subtle differences that added to the learning curve. Often, several different modules were required in order to achieve a particular goal, and this meant that, inevitably, there were a lot of settings and configuration options to deal with — not ideal.

While Drupal 7 still does not have a completely unified core media handling code base, it has come a long way in terms of providing many of the most common image handling requirements. There are now very convenient and powerful image handling facilities that don't require additional downloads or configuration.

This chapter will give you a rounded view of multimedia in Drupal by looking at the following topics:

- Images
- Files
- Media
- WYSIWYG

Along the way, we'll also take into consideration resource limitations (remember, media files take up a lot more space than text or HTML content) and how to overcome or alleviate them with proper planning and general sneakiness.

Images

As broadband and high speed Internet gets faster and more prevalent, the fundamental structure of web pages must also change to capitalize on these improvements. Conventional wisdom used to state that a web page should be no more than 20 KB in total size in order for it to be downloaded at a reasonable rate. Now, it's not uncommon for a single background image (one of possibly many) to be larger than that, let alone any other content and the ever-present advertising.

However, this does not mean that we can be wasteful when dealing with images. You should still apply stringent optimization to any images that are to be displayed through your site. Often, with little discernable loss of quality, an image can have its color count reduced to 256 colors, thus reducing the overall size drastically.

If a single background image is reduced from 50 KB to 20 KB, you achieve a bandwidth saving of 30 KB per page. This might not sound like much, but if you are showing a thousand pages a day, then that is 30 Megs of bandwidth, or nearly a Gig a month. For smaller websites with limited resources, this can be significant. Naturally, your web pages will load quicker with smaller images, and this is important for any website, of any size—especially since Google now factors page upload time into its *PageRank* algorithm.

Native image support in Drupal has absorbed many features previously available in a range of contributed modules, and control over things like image resolution and type (PNG, JPG, GIF, and so on) is built directly into the image field configuration.

Let's take a look at how Drupal's native image handling works.

Fields

Images are now added to content types just like any other field. As you saw in *Chapter 6, Advanced content*, adding a field is a case of visiting the **MANAGE FIELDS** tab of a content type and entering a **LABEL**, **NAME**, **FIELD**, and **WIDGET**. In the case of an image, simply select the **Image** option from the **FIELD** drop-down list, as shown in the following screenshot:

Once saved, the added image field comes with a few global configuration settings, as shown in the next screenshot:

Since this particular image is being added to a content type, it is likely that you will want to make the file public. Unless you have a specific reason to hide the image from certain groups of people, this should always be set to **Public files** to avoid overhead. On the other hand, if this is a content type reserved for, say, paying customers, then you may want to show this image only to people with access to the content type itself—in this case, **Private files** is the way to go.

After clicking on the **Save field settings** button, we are presented with a number of configuration options that allow you to control several important features such as size, resolution, and type:

Also note that you can help to organize images by specifying a new folder in which to add images for an image field on a specific content type. This can help keep everything orderly instead of having one catch-all images folder that can get large and unwieldy.

It's not too important to be restrictive in terms of dimension at this juncture because Drupal 7 has the ability to perform a number of operations on images, including scaling and cropping, and these can be used to control the size of the image that is served. For example, you might want to allow images to be uploaded at a width of 800 px, even if the space on a page is only 500 px. This is because Drupal can handle the scaling automatically without you (or other posters) having to manually manipulate the image before uploading to the site.

The **Preview image style** drop-down menu, about half way down the image configuration page, gives us a clue as to how images are controlled - using 'styles'. Looking at this drop-down menu, you can see that there are three styles available at present, namely, **thumbnail**, **medium**, and **large**.

Save your configuration settings, and then click on the **MANAGE DISPLAY** tab at the top of the overlay. You can now see a list of the different fields in this content type, each with a **LABEL** and **FORMAT** option:

Looking specifically at the **FORMAT** drop-down list for the image field (entitled **Image** in this instance), you can see that the options provided are 'directly related to the image styles' mentioned earlier and each image style has three options—it can be the **plain** image style, **linked to content**, or **linked to file**.

These options allow us to control exactly the way in which the image behaves in the content. We can use the original image, we can apply any available style, and we can decide whether the image should be linked to the content posting or to the actual image file.

The option you choose depends on when and where the image is being displayed. For example, if we are talking about showing the image in the actual posting itself, there's no point in linking it to the content since the viewer is already at the content. In this instance, there may be a reason to link it to the file because if you have shrunk the image to fit into the page, the viewer may wish to view the full image separately.

Conversely, if we are talking about a thumbnail image in a teaser, then linking it to the content is a good idea. This is because people often click on an image thumbnail expecting to be taken to the full content post.

In order to fully utilize this system, we need to understand how to create and work with styles.

Styles

Click on **Configuration** in the toolbar menu and scroll down the page to the **Media** section. Then click on **Image styles** to bring up the default list of styles and a link to **Add style**, as shown in the following screenshot:

Thumbnail, **medium**, and **large** are provided as part of the core Image module and can't be directly edited (although they can be overridden). Let's leave the defaults as it is. Click on **Add style** and enter a meaningful name. By meaningful, I mean a name that will lend itself to the intended usage of the image to which the style applies. For example, you might want images in blog posts to have their own style, so it makes sense to name the style something like **full_blog_image**. I prefixed this with **full** because you may want to use a different *teaser* style for blog images, and these could be called, for example, **teaser_blog_image**.

Click on **Create new style** to bring up the **Edit** dialog, as shown in the following screenshot:

The images at the top of the page represent a control image (left) and the image, as it appears after the various "effects" are added to the style. There are several important points to remember here like the following:

- A style is made of one or more effects. The basic effects are:
    - **Crop**—cut an image down to size
    - **Desaturate**—reduce coloring
    - **Resize**—change the dimensions of an image to the specified settings without necessarily maintaining the aspect ratio (width to height ratio)
    - **Rotate**—change the orientation of an image's display
    - **Scale**—change the dimensions of an image while maintaining the aspect ratio
    - **Scale and crop**—combination of the scale and crop effects

- Each style creates its own copy of any given image and stores it separately from the original. This is why it is no longer as important to define stringent size restrictions on uploaded images because those originals are not necessarily the images that will be uploaded to viewers.

Let's assume that we have decided to show grayscale versions of an image, rotated 30 degrees to the right, of width 300px in our full blog posts. We can achieve this image manipulation by doing the following:

- Add the **Desaturate** effect.
- Add the **Scale** effect, and set the **Width** only to 300 px.
- Add the **Rotate** effect, and set this to 30 degrees.

Your resulting edit page should now look like the following:

Click on the **Update style** button to finish the process. Now, whenever you add an image field to a content type, it will be possible to select this option from the drop-down list when managing the image field's display. Drupal will handle everything for you behind the scenes, including creating the new image file, styling, and saving it.

Of course, you have to tell the content type to use the new style, using the **MANAGE DISPLAY** overlay, otherwise nothing will happen.

Your blog posts using this image style will now look like the following screenshot:

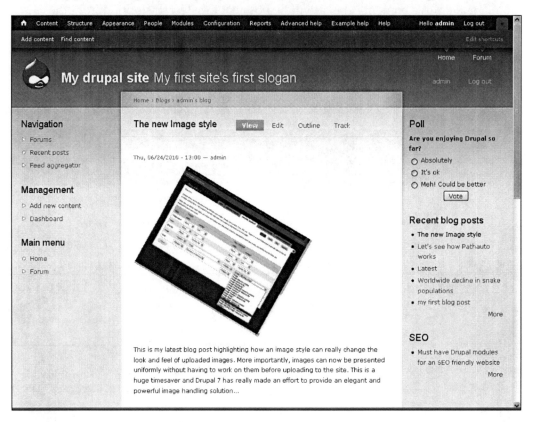

Of course, you might still want images to be presented in different parts of a page instead of it being planted in the middle of the page, as it is in the previous screenshot. Manipulating image layout and positioning falls into the realm of theming, since it requires the use of CSS in order to specify how the image container should be placed on a page.

For example, you may wish to have the image shown in line with your blog post text, floating to the right of it. In this case, you would need to specify a css class (the specific CSS class depends on on what you have named the image style, and using Firebug to inspect the field container classes is an easy way to find your way around) like the following:

```
field-name-field-blog-image{
float: right;
margin: 0 0 3px 3px;
}
```

This will display the image in the blog post, as shown in the following screenshot:

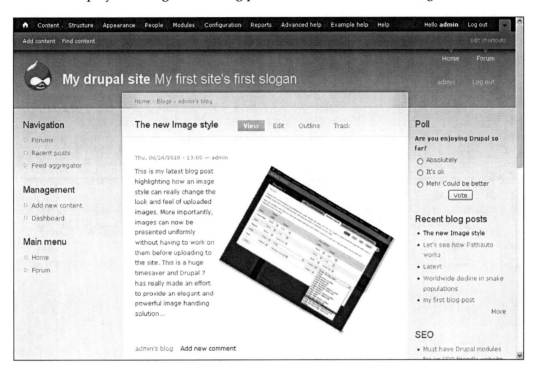

I'm sure you'll agree that this looks far more natural with the image integrated into the content. If you aren't familiar with CSS or how it can be manipulated in Drupal, then come back to this after reading the chapter on *Drupal Theming* a little later on.

There are other ways to add images to content, as we'll see in the section on *WYSIWYG* a bit later in this chapter.

Files

We have already discussed the difference between private and public download methods in *Chapter 3, Configuration*. Accordingly, we won't waste any time discussing these configuration options when it comes to adding specific file fields.

The good news is that **File** fields are added to content types in exactly the same way as any other fields (including images), so we already know precisely how to go about adding file handling facilities to content types. In the **MANAGE FIELDS** overlay for a content type, select the **File** field type from the **FIELD** column, as shown in the following screenshot:

Click on the **Save** button to bring up the global **FIELD SETTINGS** dialog:

Decide whether or not users should be allowed to control whether a file is displayed and whether to keep the file public or set it to private, and click on the **Save field settings** button. This will bring up the specific **FILE FIELD SETTINGS** for this particular content type, as shown in the following screenshot:

Most of these settings are fairly self-explanatory with the exception of the **Allowed file extensions** setting. This has direct implications for security, and you should only allow those file types you are expecting—try to limit these to non-executable files or scripts. The most harmless is **.txt** as this is a straightforward text file, which won't automatically execute something on a visitor's machine. Remember that even standard file types can harbor malicious code—in particular, Microsoft Word documents.

As an organizational matter, you can also use a specific directory for files posted to this content type in order to separate them from any and all the other files that might otherwise clutter up a single folder.

Unlike images, it is more important for you to carefully consider limiting the maximum file size. Allowing massive files can really eat up your bandwidth and slow everything down. A 4 Meg music file downloaded a few thousand times adds Gigabytes of transfer to your web server account and can become costly in the end. There are ways around this problem, as we'll see in the following section.

With the file field configured and saved to the content type, any poster who has sufficient permissions can now upload a file (or image from the previous section) in the same way:

With the content posted, you should now see the file available as a link:

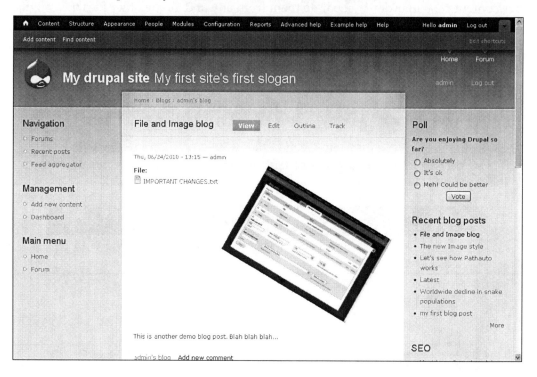

This is the default display behavior and can be changed from the **MANAGE DISPLAY** overlay for that content type. There are several options available to use including the following:

- Table of files — presented in table format with file size information
- Generic file — the default behavior
- URL to file — shows the full URL to the file but not linked
- Hidden — not visible at all

That's all there is to it. I'm sure that anyone familiar with earlier incarnations of Drupal will agree that the new methods of native image and file handling support are far more sophisticated and elegant — even if they are based on functionality from other modules.

Advanced media handling

Drupal's native media handling ends at images and files. There is still a lot we can do in terms of adding a wide range of different media to Drupal-based sites. It's important for you to first make a decision about how you envisage your website's media handling to work.

For example, are you going to show video or audio content directly from the local server? Take into consideration the fact that if you intend to host media files, you will need a hosting package that provides a lot of disk space and plenty of high speed bandwidth.

That's not your only option. There are several others that can be even more effective, depending on your particular requirements. You can upload media files to a service like YouTube and then use their native embed code to manually add the video to your own pages.

Alternatively, create an account at a file sharing website (like FileDen), which will provide a given amount of disk space and high speed transfer—the amounts vary depending on the account level you purchase. By distributing the load to other sites that are specifically designed for high speed file transfer, you reduce the load on your own server and increase the speed at which files can be transferred. The fact that you are linking to a file on another server (as opposed to your own local server) is not an issue—people and companies distribute their content like this all the time.

There are also a fairly wide variety of different Drupal contributions available to make life easier, regardless of which method you choose to make media files available through your website. Let's take a quick look at how each option might work.

Embedded media

If you have visited YouTube at all, you will be familiar with the embed code they make available, usually just below the video in question:

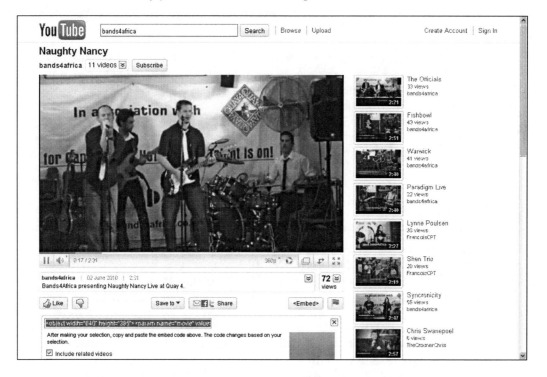

This code can be used virtually anywhere and only requires a cut and paste of the embed code into a node in order to work. Let's give it a go...

Select a video on YouTube and click the **Embed** link to bring up the embed configuration dialog. Don't worry about any settings for now, simply copy and paste the actual code into a new piece of content, like the following screenshot:

Note that YouTube makes use of the `<object>` HTML tag in order to embed videos into other web pages. It's important to remember to set the **Text format** to **Full HTML**, otherwise the `<object>` tag will be disallowed by Drupal. Click on the **Save** button to finish editing the page, and you should be presented with something like the following screenshot:

Et voila! You now have a video file viewable directly from your web pages. The beauty of this system is that you incur no performance or resource penalties because the video being shown has nothing to do with your web server. YouTube bears the burden of serving the video content.

The default dimensions and color schemes may not be suitable for your website and some media sharing sites provide a graphic interface for editing the video before it is embedded. Look at a basic YouTube embed code:

```
<object width="480" height="385"><param name="movie"
value="http://www.youtube.com/v/cGqfJdeSBdM&hl=en_GB&fs=1&"></
param><param name="allowFullScreen" value="true"></param><param
name="allowscriptaccess" value="always"></param><embed src="http://
www.youtube.com/v/cGqfJdeSBdM&hl=en_GB&fs=1&" type="application/x-
shockwave-flash" allowscriptaccess="always" allowfullscreen="true"
width="480" height="385"></embed></object>
```

The second set of `width` and `height` settings control the actual embedded file dimensions. Edit these to something like `width="240" height="190"`, and save the changes to see the difference:

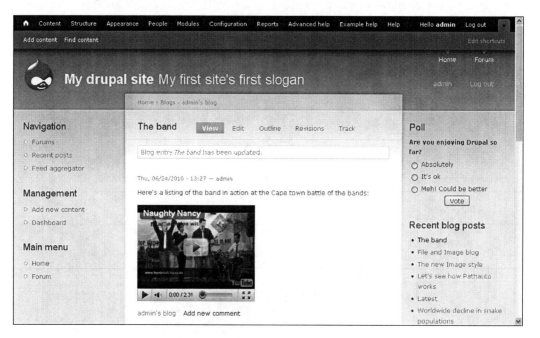

It can be a bit of a pain to manually edit this code to suit the exact dimensions required — especially if you have to do it for plenty of videos. For this reason, it is worth considering downloading and installing the `Video Filter` module from Drupal, as this provides a quick syntax to use in order to embed video files and can help speed up the process if you are going to be working with embedded media often enough.

Once installed, `Video Filter` allows media from a range of sites to be embedded using this standard syntax:

```
[video:url width:X height:Y align:left/right autoplay:1/0]
```

Assuming you required a standard video dimension, it would be easy to copy and paste this statement (with X and Y dimensions already specified) into any page, and simply change the URL (the web address of the media file) to whichever file you want to display. Note that it is possible to `align` the media to the left or right of the page and set it to `autoplay`. All attributes, except `video`, are optional and can be left out of the statement with no harmful effects.

WYSIWYG

Currently, in order to format the actual content of a posting, you'll have to use HTML. For example, let's say that we wanted to create a section that contained a list of items that looked like the following:

You'd have to know how to write out the HTML to create a header and an unordered list:

```
Body (Edit summary)
This is a content post that utilizes a bit of HTML to give the content a bit of structure.

<h3>My favorite things</h3>

<ul>
<li>Music</li>
<li>Snowboarding</li>
<li>Touch Rugby</li>
<li>France going out of the world cup after Henry cheated to get past Ireland</li>
</ul>

It's not too hard, and with practice it can be just as quick as using WYSIWYG...


Text format   Full HTML
    • Web page addresses and e-mail addresses turn into links automatically.
    • Lines and paragraphs break automatically.
```

In this instance, the h3, ul, and li tags were manually typed out in order to provide the content with its structure. Many people, however, find it easier to use a client-side editor that mimics editing software such as Microsoft Word or Open Office's Writer. Editors that provide a visual interface, which shows you what the page will look like while you are creating it, are called WYSIWYG (What you see is what you get) editors.

It's important to remember that using a WYSIWYG editor means that you don't have to manually type in HTML. It doesn't mean the content itself doesn't use HTML. The WYSIWYG editor is basically a wrapper that takes instruction through its graphical user interface and converts that into HTML in the underlying content (more about this in a while).

There are a host of open source WYSIWYG editors available and Drupal comes with the WYSIWYG module that integrates with these scripts to allow users posting content to your site to make use of them. The real advantage of these editors is that they completely obviate the need for any type of HTML experience, which is handy if you, or anyone else who is going to be creating content on your site, is not familiar with HTML.

Download and enable the WYSIWYG module from the Drupal site, and then visit the **CONTENT AUTHORING** section of the **Configuration** overlay:

Click on the newly added **Wysiwyg profiles** link that provides a list of all the available and installed editor libraries:

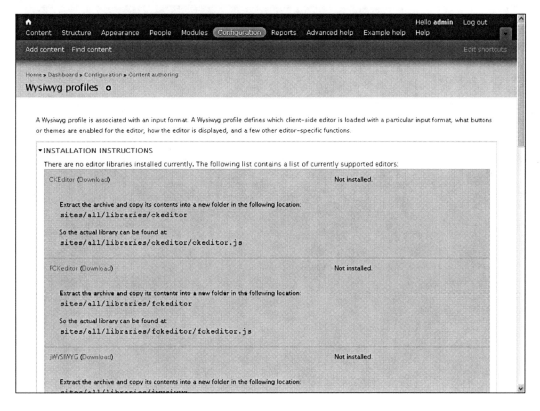

At least one library must be downloaded and installed so that the WYSIWYG functionality can be implemented. Also, there are instructions as to where the editor library files should be extracted to and a download link for each library is also available—you'll have to create a new `libraries` directory in `sites/all`.

For our purposes, the **CKEditor** was chosen and extracted to the `libraries` directory. Remember that the most important thing is to ensure that the actual editor script file is available where Drupal expects it. For the **CKEditor**, we are told that the file should exist at: `sites/all/libraries/ckeditor/ckeditor.js`

If your extracted editor folder contains version information (that is, `ckeditor-2.x`) you will have to rename it `ckeditor` so that Drupal can locate it. Once the editor is correctly installed, refreshing the **Wysiwyg Profiles** overlay should confirm that the **CKEditor** is now available:

Added above the list of editor libraries (which, incidentally, show the installed **CKEditor** in green) is now a list of the text formats for which you can assign an editor. By default, none of the text formats have the new editor assigned to them.

Plain text probably never needs an editor since it can only have plain text and no HTML anyway. You may or may not want to assign an editor to **Filtered HTML**, since this is quite limited in terms of what HTML is allowed. For the sake of this demonstration, let's assign the new editor to the **Full HTML** text format:

Once the changes are saved, the **CKEditor** will have **EDIT** and **REMOVE** (delete) operations available for the **Full HTML** format. Click on the **EDIT** link to bring up the setup and configuration options for this editor:

Of particular importance is the **BUTTONS AND PLUGINS** section that allows you to select which features are available in the editor's interface. Run through the list, and select all the options that you think will come in handy at some stage. You can also work on the **BASIC SETUP, EDITOR APPEARANCE, CLEANUP AND OUTPUT,** and **CSS** settings. However, most of the default settings are fine to begin with.

With the changes saved, we are ready to test out the new editor. Remember that we have set this editor to operate only on **Full HTML**, so users who do not have permission to use this text format won't see the editor.

Click on **Add content** and select a **Blog entry**. More than likely, the default text filter is set to **Filtered HTML**, so you may not notice anything different about the **Body** section:

Changing the **Text format** to **Full HTML** opens our eyes to a whole new world of content creation:

Now, depending on which features you enabled earlier, you can format text, add links, images, flash animations, tables, and all sorts of other goodies—all without having to touch HTML. To demonstrate how the editor works, add a whole bunch of weird and wonderful styles and elements to your page, and then click the **Disable rich-text** link at the bottom of the editor. You should see something like the following screenshot:

This is the HTML code that the editor has created behind the scenes, and you can work on this directly in the event you cannot get something working just as you want it. As mentioned, *only the HTML that is allowed by the text format will display correctly in the page*—even if the editor shows it working normally during creation time.

Summary

With the advent of Drupal 7, media handling has become far more unified and elegant. In particular, the field-based paradigm, combining with native image handling support has made it super easy to organize and handle how images are styled and presented on a site.

Above and beyond images and files, we also saw how easy it is to leverage third party services, like YouTube, to embed different media types directly into web pages. This is not the only way to serve media files and while Drupal does not have video playing facilities built into the core, there are modules that can help you to serve files from your local or file sharing server. In particular, `Media` and `Video` are two that are available for Drupal 7.

Finally, we looked at how to completely remove the need for any type of HTML experience for users posting rich content to the site. By using a WYSIWYG client-side editor script (in our case, **CKEditor**), we made an important leap from manually entering HTML code into our content, to using a graphical user interface akin to commonplace content editing software.

8
Views

At some stage, the focus on creating and managing content must shift to how best to display it. Having an intuitive and well organized site is absolutely critical to online success, and as a result, being able to show the *right content* in the *right place* becomes equally important.

While Drupal already comes with a powerful set of tools for creating and managing content, it's not nearly flexible enough on its own to cater to everyone's content display requirements. It needs *Views*!

Views is arguably Drupal's most important contributed module, and while the topic is big enough to be the subject of several large books, this chapter is going to give you a firm understanding of what Views is, how it works and how to use it properly. Accordingly, we discuss the following topics:

- Introduction to Views
- Views user interface
- Creating a basic View
- Creating an advanced View
- Theming Views
- Importing and exporting Views

With a good understanding of Views, your ability to create powerful content-based websites will increase exponentially. From creating generic lists of content to focused, themed blocks, searchable indexes, and much more, you'll not only be able to master your content, but integrate your Views into virtually every other part of the website—including *Panels* (discussed in *Chapter 10, Advanced Features*).

Introduction to Views

Views is defined on the Drupal website as:

> *...essentially a smart query builder that, given enough information, can build the proper query, execute it, and display the results.*

What this means is that by using instructions from you, as supplied through the comprehensive Views user interface, Views builds up MySQL queries that it runs against the Drupal database to return whatever information you require. This could be a list of the latest articles sorted by date, it could be all the content on the site that contains a specific term, or it could be the titles of all the newest pages in a given book linked to their node. Pretty much anything you want.

Because Views offers such a wide range of possible query options, the user interface in itself takes a bit of time to get used to. This can make using Views seem a bit overly complicated at first. Always keep in mind that at its heart, Views:

- Takes instructions from you
- Converts them into MySQL queries to run against the Drupal database
- Allows you to manipulate the results to suit your display requirements

 I strongly recommend getting to know Views as well as possible because it is quite likely that you will be able to use this tool to meet virtually any content display requirements you have in the future.

Views proficiency can really free you from having to comb through lists of other contributions that provide similar functionality. For example, there are plenty of modules that provide related content—often displayed in blocks adjacent to a given post. With a bit of effort, you will have no trouble implementing this, using Views by yourself.

Views user interface

If you haven't done so already, go to the Drupal website, download and install the `Views` module. The Views download actually provides three separate modules, as shown in the following screenshot:

All of them should be enabled before you continue.

With Views installed, you can now click on **Structure** in the toolbar menu, and then select the newly added **Views** option from the list. This brings up the **LIST** of available views in the **Views** overlay:

Any new views you create will be added to this master list, and it's easy to **Enable** or **Disable** them from here, as well as choose any one to **Edit**, **Clone**, or **Export**—more about these options a bit later. You'll also notice that Drupal provides a message at the top of the screen mentioning the `advanced help` module. This can be really useful because the vast amount of documentation that comes with Views is not available to you otherwise—so take a moment to install that at some stage.

Before we start working on our own views, let's enable one of the default views to get a sense of what we're letting ourselves in for. Scroll down the page and click on **Enable** for the **tracker** view. As soon as it is enabled, the view will jump to the top of the list and will be displayed along with its additional options, as shown in the following screenshot:

Notice from the previous screenshot that the **tracker** view has a linked **Path** attribute (below the name) entitled **tracker**. Clicking on the **tracker** link will display the output of the view—in this case, it is a table of all the most recent posts on the website:

Going back to the list of views, click on the **Edit** option in the **tracker** view to bring up the edit interface:

From the sentence at the top of the page, you can see that we are looking at the **tracker** view, displaying node items—this is important because it is possible to make views of comments, users, and other things. Below this, in the main body of the page, appear a host of settings, filters, relationships, arguments, and a variety of other criteria used in the retrieval and display of the Views content.

The left of the page contains a list of the available displays, with an **Add display** button and an **Analyze** button. To the right is a categorized page of display settings. We'll discuss how to add displays shortly, but it's worth noting that the **Analyze** button gets Views to analyze a given display and report back any problem it finds.

Note in particular that a display is divided into three columns, with the outer-right column responsible for data retrieval and manipulation, the middle responsible for output, and the left-most column responsible for more generic settings.

Before digging into all the settings, let's take a look at a few important aspects of this page in some depth.

Displays

Displays allow for a layered approach to creating views, starting with a default view that can be used to create a blueprint for more focused views. For example, it is fairly commonplace to have a node view that shows off results in a page, and perhaps a block view that shows a more limited range of results in a sidebar. In this case, the default display can be used to obtain generic results, and successive displays can focus and format these results according to their individual requirements.

In effect, each successive display can inherit any one or more of the specifications made in the default display. Looking at our **tracker** example, you can see that we have a **Defaults** and **Page** display:

Click on **Page**, below **Defaults**, and notice how the settings in the main view area change. In particular, much of the text in the **Page** display is italicized. This is an indication that those settings are *inherited* from the **Defaults** display settings. Click on any of the italicized box headings, for example, **Sort criteria**, and we are presented with an option to override the default settings at the bottom of the display:

Advanced settings	Empty text + ↑↓	Sort criteria + ↑↓
Use AJAX: No	*None defined*	*Node: Last comment time asc*
Distinct: No		
Use grouping: No	Fields + ↑↓	Filters + ↑↓
Caching: None	*Node: Type Type*	*Node: Published Yes*
	Node: Title Title	
Style settings	*User: Name Author*	
Style: Table ⚙	*Node: Comment count Replies*	
CSS class: None	*Node: Last comment time Last Post*	
Theme: Information	*Node: Has new content*	
	Node: New comments	
Exposed form		
Exposed form in block: No		
Exposed form style: Basic ⚙		
Page settings		
Path: tracker		
Menu: Normal: Recent p...		

Page: Configure sort criteria

Status: using default values   (Override)

(Update default display)   (Cancel)

Clicking on the **Override** button tells views that we are going to handle this setting ourselves, and the **Sort criteria** are no longer presented in italics and inherited from **Defaults**. That change is now enforced while working on this view, but it isn't permanent until the **Save** button is clicked. While we don't have to worry about making this particular change permanent, it's worth remembering:

> Always click on the **Save** button in order for any changes to be saved permanently.

However, note that we can just as easily operate in reverse and apply settings we make in one display to the **Defaults** display. We'll learn more about this in the following section on *Configuring categories*.

When adding a new display, Views gives us four options that help control
the output:

- **Attachment**—as the name implies, these displays can be attached to other
  displays within the View in order to be able to present multiple displays in
  one go. Useful if, for example, you wish for certain results to be formatted
  differently from others.

- **Block**—results are automatically rendered within a block that can be
  accessed and used, just like any other block. Great for providing previews,
  latest, or most popular content.

- **Feed**—powerful option for creating customized RSS feeds. Perfect for
  wielding fine-grained control over the RSS output of your site.

- **Page**—standard display type that shows results on a normal site page. This
  is the best way to show lists and tables of content that would otherwise be
  tricky to display using standard Drupal functionality.

By adding any number of displays to a generic default view, it is possible to create an
array of specialized results in a variety of formats.

One of the most powerful features that arises from Views and its displays is the
integration into other modules and areas of the site. In fact, this is where its real
power lies. We'll work on this later in (in *Chapter 10, Advanced Features*) when we
embed Views into Panels to create dynamic pages.

Configuring categories

We've looked briefly at how to click on a display item and override it. Clicking
on any category's name allows us to specify whether it inherits from the **Defaults**
view or whether we want to override the settings. A similar process is used to add,
remove, and manage the specific details of each category.

Through an example, let's take a look at the **Filters** category. Note that there is a plus
icon and a two-way arrow icon adjacent to the name:

Filters	+ ↑↓
Node: Published Yes	

Clicking on the plus icon allows us to add details by selecting them from a range of options. Each item has its own set of options, and these can vary greatly, depending on what is and isn't installed on your website, among other things. The following screenshot shows the list of options available in the **Filters** section:

For now, don't worry about what **Filters** are and how they are used; we will discuss all of that shortly when we come to creating our first view.

The **Groups** drop-down list provides a categorized list of all the possible filters we can add such as **Comment, Fields, Node**, and **User**. Select one to show the available options in that group, like **Node**, as shown in the following screenshot:

Adding the new filter is simply a case of checking the appropriate box and clicking on the **Add** button. This immediately brings up a configuration dialog for that option such as the one shown here for **Node: Comment count**:

Page: Configure filter *Node: Comment count*

Status: using default values.   Override

This item is currently not exposed. If you **expose** it, users will be able to change the filter as they view it   Expose

Operator   **Value**

○ Is less than   10
○ Is less than or equal to
○ Is equal to
○ Is not equal to
○ Is greater than or equal to
◉ Is greater than
○ Is between
○ Is not between

Update default display   Cancel   Remove

Notice that there are five options scattered around this dialog (these can change depending on whether you are working on **Defaults** or another display). Three along the bottom—**Update default display**, **Cancel**, **Remove**—and two at the top-right—**Override** and **Expose**. Unless you want to alter the **Defaults** display settings you created initially, you will have to click **Override**; otherwise you might end up affecting all the other displays that inherit their settings from **Defaults**.

> If you are going to be doing a lot of modifications to a specific category, then it is best to click on the name and override the whole thing in one go. This will change the **Update default display** option to a simple **Update**, making it far less likely you will inadvertently change the **Defaults** display settings.

The **Expose** button forces Views to give control of the configuration input to the end user of the view (in other words, the site visitor, who is looking over the list, has that particular option *exposed* to them for direct manipulation). This is a powerful technique to use when you know a view will return a lot of data, and you can *expose* a detail to empower the visitor to effectively *search* for the information they need. We'll see this in action later in the section entitled *Sort Criteria*.

Clicking on the two-way arrow icon exposes the list of options already added to a category and allows them to be re-ordered using drag-and-drop or removed completely. This is very useful in the **Fields** section, as it allows easy control over the order in which specific fields appear in the results.

Live preview

At the bottom of each view page is a **Live preview** section that allows you to select a display from the drop-down list on the left (the available options depend on the displays you have added to that particular view). Add any arguments you want and view the results along with some important information about the MySQL query generated by views.

The following screenshot shows the live preview of the **Page** display for the **tracker** view:

First in the results list is the actual result of the query (pictured in the preceding screenshot), which, in this case, is a table of the latest content. Below this appears the MySQL statement responsible for interrogating the database along with some additional information about the display and the query itself:

Basic page	Anonymous page new	Anonymous (not verified)		Fri, 06/11/2010 - 10:31
Basic page	Page not found! new	admin		Mon, 06/07/2010 - 16:10
Poll	Are you enjoying Drupal so far? new	admin	5	Fri, 06/04/2010 - 16:14
Blog entry	my first blog post new	admin		Thu, 06/03/2010 - 17:22

| Query | ```
SELECT node.type AS node_type, node.title AS node_title, node.nid AS nid, users.name AS users_name,
users.uid AS users_uid, node_comment_statistics.comment_count AS node_comment_statistics_comment_count,
node_comment_statistics.last_comment_timestamp AS node_comment_statistics_last_comment_timestamp,
history.timestamp AS history_timestamp, node.created AS node_created, node.changed AS node_changed
FROM
{node} node
INNER JOIN {users} users ON node.uid = users.uid
INNER JOIN {node_comment_statistics} node_comment_statistics ON node.nid = node_comment_statistics.nid
LEFT OUTER JOIN {history} history ON node.nid = history.nid AND history.uid = :views_join_condition_0
``` |
Title	Recent posts
Path	tracker
Query build time	13.67 ms
Query execute time	3.01 ms
View render time	96.11 ms

By regular and careful analysis of results and other stats provided by the **Live preview**, you can finely tune your displays to obtain exactly the right results and output before saving and committing the changes. This creates an easy and quick method of prototyping new views.
```

Creating a basic view

It's now time to turn our focus onto creating a brand new view. To do this, click on the **Add new view** tab at the top of the views page. This brings up a basic dialog that can be used to create the general settings for this view, as shown in the following screenshot:

Choose a meaningful name (only alphanumeric characters and underscores) and take the time to add a brief description on this page. Often, a website will end up with a fair number of different views, and it can be tricky to remember which view is for what if you haven't named and described them accurately from the start.

Towards the bottom of this page, the **View type** option provides a list of the different types of data the new view will deal with. Already, this should be an indication of the power that views have. This is because we aren't limited to returning content like pages or blogs, so we can show views of users, files, comments, and just about anything else that is stored in a Drupal website. For now, let's focus on **Node** types of data.

With your selections made, click on the **Next** button to bring up the familiar views editing interface:

Note that, at present, we have a blank **Defaults** display and nothing else. We're going to work on the **Defaults** display in this section and use it as a basis for a more advanced display later on.

First things first—we need to tell views what type of **Filters** we want.

Filters

Think of a filter as a condition against which Drupal content is tested in order for it to make it into the result set. Clicking on the plus icon in the **Filters** category brings up the list of possible filters that can be used—it's a big list, so it is broken up into different groups that can be selected using the drop-down list, as seen earlier in the section on *Configuring categories*.

It pays to plan carefully ahead in this section. There are often several ways to obtain the data you are looking for, and some will be more efficient than others. It may help to think about which conditions would cut down the possible result set as quickly as possible.

At the very least, you should be able to specify a number of things about the information you want to retrieve. For this example, we are going to show the "latest blog posts" that have been published to the site. By looking at the **Node** group in the **Filters** dialog, we can set most of these conditions quite easily:

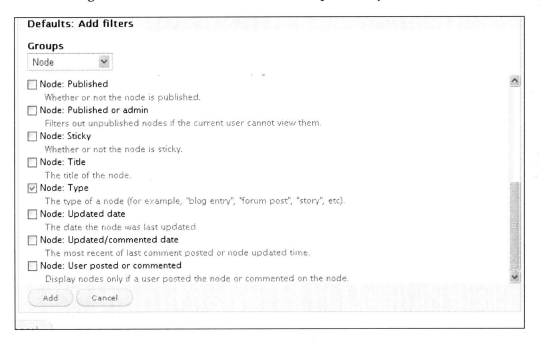

In this case, we need to use the **Node: Type** option so that we can specify **Blog entry**. Check this option, and click on the **Add** button to bring up the following configuration dialog:

Defaults: Configure filter *Node: Type*

This item is currently not exposed. If you **expose** it, users will be able to change the filter as they view it.

Expose

Operator
- ⦿ Is one of
- ○ Is not one of

Node type
- ☑ Blog entry
- ☐ Poll
- ☐ Forum topic
- ☐ Article
- ☐ Book page
- ☐ Basic page
- ☐ Species

Update   Cancel   Remove

Since we know that we want only blogs, we select the **Is one of** option from the **Operator** column and check the **Blog entry** option in the **Node type** column. The English sentence that describes these options is:

Retrieve only those results where the node type is a blog entry

Click on the **Update** button to complete the configuration of this filter. You should now see this filter presented in the **Filter** box, like this:

Note that you only need to click on the option in **Filters** if you wish to edit it again. Now this view will faithfully retrieve any and all content that meets this criterion. However, often this is not sufficiently focused because you'll find that any blog posts, even the ones you have unpublished or that are still in the approval queue, will be returned with the results. This is not really what we want, so we need to add another filter to specify that we only want to see blog posts that are published.

Once again, click on the plus icon in the **Filters** box and select the **Node** group from the select list. Scroll down to **Node: Published** option. Select it and click on the **Add** button. You'll be presented with a single configuration option (should the node be published or not), which is easy enough to decide on. Once that filter is added, we now have a database query equivalent to the English sentence:

Retrieve only those results where the node type is a blog post and the node is published

 The **Node: published** option is very commonly used to avoid returning incomplete or unfit content that is not published to the site.

One might expect to be able to immediately view the results of **Defaults**. However, it is likely that the default display setting uses fields, and we have not yet set any fields. We can control whether or not to use fields or nodes in our **Style settings**, and this will be discussed in the section entitled *Style settings* a bit later in the chapter.

Let's take a look at the **Fields** category.

Fields

Click on the plus icon in the **Fields** box to bring up a list of possible fields that can be shown in the results. From here, we can select any and all the fields that we wish to be returned.

 The **Fields** options will vary depending on which fields are added to which content types. Also, not all fields presented will apply to every node type—a brief glance at the first option **Book: Depth** should suffice to demonstrate this since we are after blog posts, which aren't necessarily part of any book.

We're definitely going to show at least the title of our blog posts in the results, so select the **Node** group from the drop-down list and scroll down to the **Node: title** option. Select it and click on the **Add** button. The field configuration options are fairly comprehensive and can also become quite complex at times. For **Node: title**, we are given the following:

As you can see, the **Label** option is blank since it's a bit redundant to suffix the blog's title with the default text, **Title**. Most of the options are fairly self-explanatory or can easily be tested by selecting them and viewing the results.

Depending on the type of field you are dealing with, some options are more important than others. For example, you might return the teaser of a node, in which case, it may be important to **Trim this field to a maximum length**, so that you avoid untidy results if there happens to be a particularly long teaser.

One of the most useful options appears right at the bottom—**Link this field to its node**. Since most websites link the title (think bookmarking sites) of a post to the post itself, it makes sense for us to choose this option. We're not showing the whole node, only some of its fields so something should link to the full node in case people want to read it, so this might as well be the **Title** field.

Click on the **Update** button once you're done. Views will now automatically build a live preview of this display since it now has a field to output. As expected, we have a list of published blog entry titles linked to their nodes on the site:

Live preview

Display
Defaults

Arguments

Separate arguments with a / as though they were a URL path.

Preview

my first blog post
Worldwide decline in snake populations

Query
```
SELECT node.title AS node_title, node.nid AS nid
FROM
{node} node
WHERE (( (node.type IN (:db_condition_placeholder_0)) ))
LIMIT 10 OFFSET 0
```

We're not quite done yet because our brief called for the "latest blog posts", and as it stands, we haven't done anything to specify the order in which results should be presented. We can't do this using **Filters** or **Fields**, so we need to take a look at **Sort criteria**.

Sort criteria

More often than not, you will want some sort of control over the order in which results are displayed. This doesn't necessarily have to be the most recent to the oldest—in other words, time-based. It could be based on the number of comments each result has—in other words, popularity. There are plenty of different sort criteria to explore, but we are only interested in ordering our results from most recent to oldest for now.

Click on the plus icon in the **Sort criteria** box, and select the **Node** group from the drop-down list. Scroll down to the **Node: Post date** option, select it, and click on the **Add** button:

Defaults: Configure sort criterion *Node: Post date*

This item is currently not exposed. If you **expose** it, users will be able to change the filter as they view it.

[Expose]

○ Sort ascending

◉ Sort descending

Granularity

○ Second

○ Minute

◉ Hour

○ Day

○ Month

○ Year

The granularity is the smallest unit to use when determining whether two dates are the same; for example, if the granularity is "Year" then all dates in 1999, regardless of when they fall in 1999, will be considered the same date.

(Update) (Cancel) (Remove)

The configuration page allows us to specify whether we are sorting in an ascending or descending order and control the granularity of the post date comparison. In other words, should it compare post dates to the nearest second, minute, hour, day, and so on. In our case, we want the latest post first and the oldest last in order to show the most recent posts at the top of the results. So we select the **Sort descending** option.

Incidentally, if we were to **Expose** this option, the result of the view would change to allow users to manually set these criteria, as shown in the next screenshot:

Sort By   **Order**

[Node: Post date ▾]   [Asc ▾]   (Apply)

Latest

Worldwide decline in snake populations

my first blog post

Once you have clicked on **Update**, you should notice that the live preview results now display the results in latest to oldest fashion.

With that setting in place, we have met our aim in terms of retrieving data, and to some extent, displaying it. However, we aren't quite finished because this is only the default display, and while we are perfectly free to use it, it's better to create a specialized page with its own unique settings, so that we can re-use these defaults in another display as and when the need arises.

For the purposes of the next two sections, add a **Page** display by clicking **Add display**.

Basic settings

Basic settings consist of five options, as shown in the following screenshot:

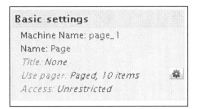

The first two allow you to specify a **Machine Name** and a human-readable **Name** for the display in question. The machine name can become important if you are programmatically referencing a view/display (as we'll see later)—ensure you provide a meaningful name like "latest_blog_posts". It is always worthwhile providing a good name for a display for your own benefit down the line.

> Remember that you are now **Overriding** these settings because they should apply to the new display and not update the **Defaults** display.

If you wish your view to be given a title, then fill out the third option accordingly. For example, we might want something like "Latest blog posts" at the top of the page. Anything you enter here will be used as the title of the view, as seen by people browsing the site.

The fourth option, **Use pager**, is fairly important as it controls how many results to show on a page and whether or not to paginate the results for easy navigation. Note that this option has a small gear icon to its right. The gear icon indicates that there are configuration settings available for this option.

Click on the gear icon to the right of the pager option to bring up the following dialog:

Defaults: Pager options

Items per page

10

The number of items to display per page. Enter 0 for no limit.

Offset

0

The number of items to skip. For example, if this field is 3, the first 3 items will be skipped and not displayed.

Pager ID

0

Unless you're experiencing problems with pagers related to this view, you should leave this at 0. If using multiple pagers on one page you may need to set this number to a higher value so as not to conflict within the ?page= array. Large values will add a lot of commas to your URLs, so avoid if possible.

Number of pages

The total number of pages. Leave empty to show all pages.

EXPOSED OPTIONS

Exposing this options allows users to define their values in a exposed form when view is displayed

☐ Expose items per page

When checked, users can determine how many items per page show in a view

☐ Expose Offset

When checked, users can determine how many items should be skipped at the beginning.

(Update) (Cancel)

From here, it's easy to control how many items to display per page, what the offset should be along with specifying ID, and the number of pages to display in total. In addition, we are also given the option of exposing the offset and items per page to the user.

Of course, these settings could be made redundant depending on the specific pager option you select. Click on the **Use pager** setting link (left of the gear icon) to bring up the list of options:

Defaults: Select which pager, if any, to use for this view

◉ Display a specified number of items
○ Display all items
○ Paged output, full pager
○ Paged output, mini pager

(Update) (Cancel)

From here we can decide whether to show a specified number of results, all results, or select from a full or mini pager. Obviously, if you select one of the first two options, the pager settings no longer apply since we're working in absolute terms that don't require the results to be split up into pages.

The final option, **Access**, allows us to control who should be able to view this display. We can set the restrictions to **None** or control access, based on user permissions or roles. Note that, by default, there are no access restrictions on this display. However, if you set some sort of restriction, the gear icon will appear indicating that you can work with the configuration settings for that option if you need to.

Page settings

Up 'til now, you might have noticed that the live preview persistently complains that:

> Display "*latest blog posts*" *uses a path but the path is undefined.*

The reason for this is that we selected a new **Page** type display for our view and any page in Drupal must have a file path in order for it to be visible on the site. Since our current display returns a list of the latest blog posts, we can click on the **Path** option in **Page** settings and enter something brief and meaningful, such as **latest-blog-posts**, and click on the **Update** button.

The **Menu** option provides a shortcut to adding this display directly to a menu of your choice.

With those settings in place, it is time to **Save** the view. You can now visit the newly defined path (something like `http://localhost/drupal/latest-blog-posts`) directly on the website to see the completed view in action:

Pretty neat. But that's really only the beginning of things. There's far more we can do in terms of isolating and returning the types of content we want, and how we can flesh out the results and control their display.

Creating an advanced View

This section is going to focus on a few examples that highlight how the different categories might be utilized and how they work together. As you'll see, each time we try something new, there will be plenty of configuration options and settings to handle. There's simply not enough space to go into each and every one, so for now, focus more on the broad picture and spend time working out the details by yourself.

 Remember that there are online exercises and quiz questions at site prebuilder (`http://www.siteprebuilder.com`) that will help consolidate and expand on what you learn here.

Arguments

Arguments are really a way to fine-tune or hone the result set more than the standard filters do on their own. More importantly, arguments can be used to make a view dynamic. In other words, the view can return different results, based on a variety of conditions that exist at the time it is being accessed.

For example, you might wish to show a user only the content that they have created. In which case, the argument used would be the current user's ID. John would see one set of results, while Bill would see another because they have unique user IDs, even though they are looking at the same view.

Arguments are most often taken from the URL of a page (though, this is not necessarily always the case). For example, the path `userblogs/3` would indicate to the Views that the number 3 is most likely the user ID to be utilized as an argument for this view. Because of this, setting the correct path for a view becomes an important task because other modules can utilize paths that you might instruct your View to try to use. If this happens, strange things can occur—be aware of this issue and make appropriate changes to your **Path** variable, if needed.

Arguments don't necessarily have to come from an environmental condition, like the current user's ID, it is possible to set them outright too. Not only that, but Views comes with all sorts of facilities to validate arguments (for example, to make sure they are of the proper data type—numeric, text, and so on). You can provide default arguments to use if none are available and also specify what content to display in the event that arguments are missing.

Let's look at a quick example of how to set an argument that will filter the results of our default display to show only the blog posts whose unique Node ID matches the arguments we supply.

To begin with, create a new display based on the **Defaults** display set earlier and call it something like **Arguments**. Click on the **Arguments** category title in the new display and **Override** it. This will help us to avoid accidentally updating the **Defaults** display every time we add a new setting. Your page should look something like the following screenshot:

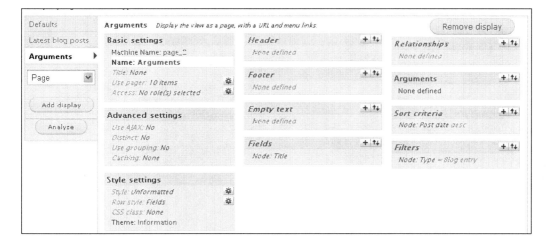

Note that **Arguments** is no longer presented in italics because it is being overridden.

Adding an Argument

Click the plus icon next to **Arguments**, and select the **Node** group from the drop-down list. Scroll down the list until you have located the **Node: Nid** option. Select it and click on **Add**. This will bring up the settings page, as shown in the following screenshot:

Arguments: Configure Argument *Node: Nid*

Status: using overridden values.   Use default

Title

[   ]

The title to use when this argument is present. It will override the title of the view and titles from previous arguments. You can use percent substitution here to replace with argument titles. Use "%1" for the first argument, "%2" for the second, etc.

Breadcrumb

[   ]

The Breadcrumb title to use when this argument is present. If no breadcrumb is set here, default Title values will be used, see "Title" for percent substitutions.

Action to take if argument is not present   **Wildcard**

○ Display all values   [all   ]

○ Hide view / Page not found (404)   If this value is received as an argument, the argument
                                                       will be ignored, i.e, "all values"
◉ Display empty text

○ Summary, sorted ascending   **Wildcard title**

○ Summary, sorted descending   [All   ]

○ Summary, sorted by number of records ascending   The title to use for the wildcard in substitutions
                                                       elsewhere.
○ Summary, sorted by number of records
descending

○ Provide default argument

┌─**Provide default argument options**───────────────────────────────────┐
│   │
│   │
│ **Default argument type**   │
│ ◉ Fixed entry   │
│ ○ Node ID from URL   │
│ ○ PHP Code   │
│ ○ User ID from URL   │
│ ○ User ID from logged in user   │

From here, you can specify a **Title** and **Breadcrumb** (if you want to), but of more immediate concern is **Action to take if the argument is not present**. What do you want Views to display to a user who stumbles across the view and does not add an argument? Let's select the third option, **Display empty text**, for now. We'll come back to what empty text is and how to use it in a while.

To the right of this list of actions are the **Wildcard** settings. Here you can choose a specific argument that covers all your bases and shows all the results (effectively, it nullifies the additional filter any normal argument would provide). You might also wish to specify a title for the wildcard page.

The following section, **Provide default argument options**, allows us to select an appropriate argument default type only if we set **Provide default argument** in the previous section — **Action to take if argument is not present**. Since we are going to be showing some empty text instead, we can safely ignore this option.

The **Validator options** section provides us with the ability to control the type of data that can be considered an argument. Naturally, if we want a node ID, we know that the only type of argument that makes sense would be a numeric argument of some type since node IDs are numbers. If someone tried to access this view using a URL like `argumentblog/five`, it should not validate.

Since we are working specifically in blog posts and numeric arguments, we can make these settings as shown in the following screenshot:

If we wish to provide more than one argument, the following setting, **Argument type**, allows us to specify whether the arguments should be a single ID or a comma (or plus) separated list of IDs (as shown in the preceding screenshot).

The next few settings apply to taxonomy terms or user IDs and so do not directly relate to this specific argument and can be ignored. If you were working with a taxonomy-related argument or a user-related argument, you would work on these settings in the same way we have handled the node-related argument.

The final option, **Action to take if argument does not validate**, can be set to **Display empty text** since this is the action we are taking if no arguments are present at all. You might decide to take different actions based on different scenarios—there's no reason these actions have to be the same as the ones we have used here.

The final two options are fairly important! The first allows us to use multiple values per argument. This is fairly useful because when it comes to specifying a path, it is much neater for us to say something like `argumentblog/%`, knowing that this URL can take a range of arguments, as opposed to taking multiple arguments one at a time with a URL like `advancedblog/%/%/%/%/%/%`.

Finally, we can switch our arguments into reverse by selecting the **Exclude the argument** option. This will show the *negative* side of the current view—in other words, it will show everything except for what is returned by valid arguments. That's not what we want here, but it may come in handy for you some other time.

With our settings in place, we can click on the **Update** button to add the argument to the view.

Setting the Path

We're not done yet because we need a way to pass arguments to the view. In the previous example, we set a static path because the basic view was only meant to show the latest blog posts and not selectively display results based on an argument. The way we pass arguments through a URL is by adding a wildcard character (%) to the **Path** setting.

Go ahead and add something like `argumentblog/%` to the **Path** variable and save the change. This will tell views that the argument is going to be drawn from the URL after `argumentblog` using the wildcard. In other words, if we want to view the blog post with node ID 6, we would go to the path `argumentblog/6`.

It's important to note that you aren't limited to only one argument at a time, you can have as many as you like, and if the arguments are coming out of the URL, then the order in which they appear in the URL is matched to the order in which they are held in the **Arguments** list.

For example, if we have three arguments (arg1, arg2, arg3) in our **Arguments** list, then we might set a **Path** like `argument/%/somethingelse/%/%`, and this would effectively be the same as saying `argument/arg1/somethingelse/arg2/arg3`

Remember that if you change the order of the arguments in the list, it will change the order in which Views looks for the arguments.

With the **Path** set, we can now try out the display.

Testing the arguments with Live preview

Scroll down the page to the **Live preview** and select the **Arguments Display**. In order for this to work, you'll have to have a few blog posts already published on the site, and have a rough idea of what their node IDs are (to find out, try editing one of the blog posts and look at the URL, which will contain the ID). Add a single number (to begin with, any number that does not have an associated blog post—like 100,000) to the **Arguments** textbox, and click on the **Preview** button:

Live preview

Display

Arguments ▾

Arguments

100000

Separate arguments with a / as though they were a URL path.

Preview

```
Query    SELECT node.title AS node_title, node.nid AS nid, node.created AS
         node_created
         FROM
         {node} node
         WHERE (( (node.type IN (:db_condition_placeholder_0)) AND (node.nid =
         :db_condition_placeholder_1) ))
         ORDER BY node_created DESC
         LIMIT 10 OFFSET 0
```

Title

Path   argumentblog/100000

Query build
time   19.69 ms

As you can see, no results are displayed with this query because the number entered into the **Arguments** textbox does not correspond to a blog post, so nothing was returned. This brings us back to the empty text settings we made earlier. Let's assume that we don't want to show a completely blank page, but instead, we would like to add a bit of text to let people know what has happened.

Go up to the **Empty text** category in the **Arguments** display and click on the plus icon. Select the **Global: Text area** option, and click on **Add**. You can now add a brief message before clicking **Override**:

Arguments: Configure Empty text *Global: Text area*

Status: using default values.   Override

Label

Oh dear...

The label for this area that will be displayed only administratively.

We have nothing to show you.

More information about text formats

Text format

Plain text

With that change saved, return to the **Live preview** and re-enter an argument for which there is no corresponding blog post. This time, instead of a blank page, you will be presented with the **Empty text** message just defined.

Notice that a little way down the results, you can see the **Path** at which this particular output would appear and how it relates to the arguments you fed into the **Live preview**:

Live preview

Display

| Arguments ▾ |

Arguments

| 2 |

Separate arguments with a / as though they were a URL path.

(Preview)

my first blog post

| Query | ```
SELECT node.title AS node_title, node.nid AS nid, node.created AS node_created
FROM
{node} node
WHERE (( (node.type IN (:db_condition_placeholder_0)) AND (node.nid =
:db_condition_placeholder_1) ))
ORDER BY node_created DESC
LIMIT 10 OFFSET 0
``` |
|---|---|
| **Title** | |
| **Path** | argumentblog/2 |

Using arguments lends views a more dynamic dimension in that filters can be applied more or less on the fly depending on website environment, users, and practically any other type of condition.

Relationships

Relationships can be used to expand the scope of results to include things that are not necessarily part of the immediate result set, but are related and pertinent in some way to those results. One of the most obvious examples is that any node results you obtain in a view are related to a specific user in that each node has to be *authored* by a user. So there is a relationship between nodes and users in this way.

Since the node-user relationship is given by default in Views, we need to look at something slightly different to highlight how a relationship might work. As you know, it is possible for more than one person to edit and revise any given content—provided they have the permissions to do so.

Let's say, for example, we wanted to show a table of the latest blog posts along with the name of the editor responsible for making the revisions and updates to it (perhaps to check up on the quality of their editing). In this case, we are relating the blog posts not to the original author, but to another user who most likely is not the original author. In order to follow along with this example, you will need to create at least one other user who has sufficient permissions to create and edit the content and work with revisions.
```

Once you have done so, create a few blog posts with one user and then revise those posts with another. With at least a few results to explore, we can now go ahead and create a new display called (something like) **Relationships**. Remember to **Override** the **Relationships** category in this display to avoid modifying **Defaults** by accident.

Adding a relationship

Click on the plus icon in the **Relationships** box, select the **Node revision** group, and scroll down and enable the **Node revision: User** option. In the settings section, change the label to **blog reviewer** for clarity's sake—you'll see why in a moment. Also enable the box **Require this relationship**, as we are only interested in blogs that have been edited—since we are checking up on the quality of our editors in the first place.

We now have a relationship added to the display, but by itself, this means very little since what we really want is to *display the results of this relationship* as it pertains to the original query. In order to do this, go the **Fields** box and add the **User: name** option from the **User** group. Immediately, you will notice an option to select which relationship to use right at the top of the settings page for this new field:

Select **blog reviewer** (recall this is what we labeled the relationship) instead of **Do not use a relationship**. If we did not use the newly created relationship, the **User: name** field would return the name of the user who authored the blog post as per the behind the scenes default node-user relationship mentioned earlier. Also, to make things slightly more understandable, change the **Label** to **Editor**. You might also want to **Link this field to its user** for quick access to the user (editor) profile page—this can be done by checking the second last option—before updating.

Results

With the relationship in place and a field to output the results, we can now turn our attention to the **Live preview**—remember to provide a path for this display, otherwise Views will complain. Assuming you have a couple of blog posts that have been edited by different users, you should be able to view a list of the blog posts along with the name of the user who last revised the blog post (not necessarily the original author), like the following:

While this does show the results we wanted, it's not very exciting and there is much we can do to flesh out this display, reorganize the way it is presented, and generally make things a bit more professional.

Headers and footers

Headers and footers can be used to add content to the top and bottom of any view. For example, you may wish to explain to a user precisely what they are looking at. While it may be clear to you as the creator of a view, it may not be immediately obvious to someone browsing it.

As an exercise, add a header to the current display—since the process for creating **Footer** content is precisely the same, we won't belabor the point by going over that too. **Override** the **Header** category, and then click on the plus icon to add the new text. Remember you aren't limited to plain text here. It is possible to go crazy with **Full HTML** or any other text format that is available, including PHP.

Save the changes and then check the results for yourself.

Style settings

At this point, we have queried the database and retrieved the data we want to show. We are displaying the right information but not really in a useful way. Specifically, looking down the list of results, we can see that each blog post has a corresponding editor, but it would be far more helpful to view the results per editor. In other words, next to or under each editor would appear a list of the blogs he or she has edited. Doing things like this makes the results far more intuitive and user-friendly.

This is where styling can help. Looking at the current settings:

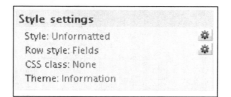

Notice that the first option, **Style**, is set to **Unformatted**. Click on this to see what options are available:

Help Relationships: How should this view be styled

Status: using default values.   Override

○ Grid
○ HTML List
◉ Table
○ Unformatted

If the style you choose has settings, be sure to click the settings button that will appear next to it in the View summary.

You may also adjust the settings for the currently selected style by clicking on the icon.

Update default display   Cancel

Since our proposed method of display would suit a table nicely, select the **Table** option to bring up the following configuration dialog:

This gives us a reasonable amount of control over the layout of the table. For example, we can set certain columns of data to **SORTABLE** (useful if there are going to be long lists of data), we can align content within table cells, and most importantly, set a **Grouping field**. The **Grouping field** is what will allow us to show off the blog post grouped by each editor. Select the **Editor** option from this drop-down list and save the changes.

The preview now shows something like the following screenshot:

That's much better, but there's a bit of redundancy in the format. Notice that the header of each table is denoted by the parent group (in this case, **Editor**), yet we are still showing a column of editors down the right half of the table—this is redundant, since we already know each table pertains to a given editor. How do we go about removing this?

You might have noticed earlier on when we initially added the **User: name** field that there was an option to **Exclude from display**. Go back to the user field, and select this option before saving the changes. Now, even though the username is no longer *displayed* in the results, it is still *available* to Views to use in order to properly group the results.

We now have something like the following in the **Live preview**:

That's much better. Of course, it's still a bit sparse—you might want to consider adding a few more fields such as revision notes or revision date. The point is, by changing the **Style** of the output, we were able to fundamentally improve the usability of this View.

Naturally, **Table** is not the only style we could have used, and very similar results can be obtained using the other options like **List** or **Grid**. While **Table** does not have an associated **Row** style, both **HTML List** and **Grid** do.

Change the **Table** style to **HTML List**, set the **Grouping field**, and then click on the gear icon adjacent to **Row** style. From here, you can decide whether certain fields should be inline (that is, start on the same line instead of a new one) and what the separator between them should be. It is necessary to have slightly more results in your view (we only have one visible result currently) before a separator becomes important.

The next option, **CSS class**, is very useful if you want to individually theme results from a given display. By adding CSS classes to your Views styles, you can control styling more easily, without affecting other aspects of the site. Because of the importance and scope of theming in Views, we're going to discuss this and the **Theme** option in more detail a little later in this chapter (in the section entitled *Theming Views*), so we won't go any further into this at present.

Advanced settings

This section is a mixed bag of settings:

- You can implement AJAX for paginated results (using the **Use AJAX** setting) although this comes with the recommendation only to use this feature for side content (because the view no longer requires a page refresh to display new view content).

- It is also possible to try and enforce only distinct results to be returned. Quite often in views, the way in which an SQL query is constructed can lead to the same record being returned multiple times. This often occurs when there is a need to retrieve data from multiple tables. By setting **Distinct** to **Yes**, duplicate results can be restricted—although using **Distinct** can seriously slow down the query.

- **Use Grouping** causes Views to group and aggregate fields within results. If this is set to **Yes**, then note that **Filters** and **Sort criteria** now have a gear icon next to them allowing you to select whether or not to group or aggregate those results. This is useful for determining information about results as opposed to viewing the results directly.

- **Caching** can be used to reduce processing loads by saving results for a specified amount of time. If, for example, you know that new content comes in once or twice a day, cache the view for six hours. By doing so, Views can calculate results once and serve the page multiple times without incurring additional processing load. Caching can be applied both to **Query results** and **Rendered output**.

Creating an attachment

Before we finish with our advanced view, let's take a look at how to utilize a different type of display—up until now, we have only worked on **Page** displays. We can, for example, further enhance our **arguments** display by adding an attachment. Attachments can be *attached* before or after (or both) to one or more of the other displays in the view. Since an attachment is a fully fledged display in its own right, your imagination is the limit when it comes to how to use them.

Let's say that we want to show off a premiere blog post at the top of our **Arguments** display. This premiere blog post will have a completely different layout and style so as to highlight it against the rest of the results. We're going to morph the original **Arguments** view into one which shows off the blog post specified by the argument, but still displays a list of all the other blog posts below.

Go ahead and add a new **Attachment** by selecting it in the display drop-down list and clicking on **Add display**. The attachment will inherit the default display settings, but since we know that this is only going to show off a single premiere blog post, we can remove empty text or header and footer settings.

To change the way this display is presented, we're going to change from fields to a node-based style. Go to the **Row style** in **Style settings** and change this to **Node**. Configure the options to show only the teaser and no links:

Help **Attachment: Row style options**

Status: using overridden values.   Use default

Build mode
Teaser

☐ Display links

☐ Display node comments

Update   Cancel

The results in the **Live preview** should be similar to the following screenshot:

Live preview

Display
Attachment

Arguments

Separate arguments with a / as though they were a URL path.

Preview

Edit Delete Clone
Latest

- Edit
- Delete

Submitted by admin on Fri, 06/18/2010 – 12:55
Conservation:
Advocacy

Worldwide decline in snake populations

- Edit
- Delete

Submitted by admin on Mon, 06/14/2010 – 13:51
Conservation:
Ecology

Distinct populations of snake species have crashed over the last decade, raising fears that the reptiles may be in global decline, according to a study.

The pattern across the eight species monitored was alarmingly similar despite their geographical isolation, which points to a common cause, say researchers.

That's not precisely what we want because we only want a single blog post (let's say, the latest post) to be presented as the premiere posting at the top of the page. We need to modify the attachment display to show only the blog post specified by a specific argument. We've already seen how this is done in the *Arguments* section earlier—click on the plus icon in **Arguments**, select the **Node** group, and add the **Node: Nid** option.

The only changes to the configuration are that we will select the second option, **Hide view**, in the event that no argument is present, and the second last option, **Allow multiple terms per argument**, can also be selected. With that done, test out the new attachment in the **Live preview** using an existing blog post Nid:

Live preview

Display
Attachment

Arguments
16

Separate arguments with a / as though they were a URL path.

Preview

[Edit] [Ergil] [Kion]
Worldwide decline in snake populations

- Edit
- Delete

Submitted by admin on Mon, 06/14/2010 – 13:51
Conservation:
Ecology

Distinct populations of snake species have crashed over the last decade, raising fears that the reptiles may be in global decline, according to a study.

The pattern across the eight species monitored was alarmingly similar despite their geographical isolation, which points to a common cause, say researchers.

Factors thought to play a role include climate change, habitat loss, pollution, disease, lack of prey and over-exploitation, either for food or trade.

Now that we have the display we want, it's time to attach it to the **Arguments** display. Notice that this attachment display has an additional box entitled **Attachment settings**, in the left-hand settings column:

```
Attachment settings
   Inherit arguments: No
   Inherit exposed filters: No
   Inherit pager: No
   Render pager: Yes
   Position: Before
   Attach to: Arguments
```

These settings control how the attachment relates to the other displays and the view in general. In our case, the first option, **Inherit arguments**, should be set to **No** because we have already taken charge of this. We don't have to worry about **Inherit exposed filters** since we didn't expose anything anyway, but this can be set to **No** to be on the safe side.

The following two options deal with pagers, which are of no concern to us since we are only returning one result with this attachment and so can disregard pagers. Both of these can be set to **No**.

We want this attachment to show at the top of the page, so we can set **Position** to **Before**. If you were providing an attachment with meta-information about a display along with exposed controls, we might want to consider adding the attachment both before and after for completeness.

Finally, we can select which display to attach to from a list of available options in the **Attach to** setting. In this case, select **Arguments**. Now, instead of checking the attachment in the **Live preview**, look at **Arguments** — with and without a valid blog post Nid in the **Arguments** input.

This is close to what we want, except that we have duplicate results because when we supply a valid Nid, both **Arguments** and our attachment display that result. What we want is for the attachment to display the result (as it does now) and for **Arguments** to display the remaining blog posts. Can you guess how this is done?

Go to the **Arguments** display, and in the **Arguments** category, click on the **Node: Nid** setting. Scroll down the configuration settings to the very last option—**Exclude the argument**—and select it before saving. Now, the **Arguments** display shows everything but the premiere blog post, which is displayed by the attachment at the top of the page in **Node** format:

```
Display
[ Arguments        v]


Arguments
[16                                                        ]
Separate arguments with a / as though they were a URL path.


( Preview )
    Edit  Export  Clone
Worldwide decline in snake populations

 • Edit
 • Delete
Submitted by admin on Mon, 06/14/2010 – 13:51
Conservation:
Ecology

Distinct populations of snake species have crashed over the last decade, raising fears that the reptiles may be in global
decline, according to a study.

The pattern across the eight species monitored was alarmingly similar despite their geographical isolation, which points
to a common cause, say researchers.

Factors thought to play a role include climate change, habitat loss, pollution, disease, lack of prey and over-exploitation,
either for food or trade.

Latest
Name: admin
my first blog post
Name: admin

        SELECT node.title AS node_title, node.nid AS nid, users.name AS
        users_name, users.uid AS users_uid, node.created AS node_created
        FROM
```

As you can see from the **Live preview**, we have set up a view that highlights a particular blog post based on the arguments supplied in the URL. The view also displays a list of all the other available blog posts on the site below the highlighted post. It's a nice example of how Views can allow us to create pages that are slightly out of the ordinary.

Theming Views

Views theming relies on a well structured and powerful system of template files that draw upon PHP, HTML, and CSS to control and produce virtually any type of look, feel, and layout for its results. For the majority of everyday formatting needs, Views is well designed enough for you to get by on CSS alone. However, it's worth looking over the template system to get a feel for the broad-based and fine-grained control that can be exerted over results.

Theming Views is a slightly more technical subject than creating and configuring them. In fact, if you are not familiar with theming in Drupal as a whole, I recommend you skip this section until you have gone through *Chapter 9, Drupal Theming*.

This section will take a quick look at how to add and manipulate CSS classes to display results without having to delve into template files. This is followed by a more involved discussion on how the template system is structured and how to use it.

It is recommended that you use the Firefox browser with the Firebug add-on in order to follow along, as we are going to be looking at and analyzing CSS and HTML content throughout this section.

Views CSS

The Views interface comes with a single CSS-related setting that allows us to control the overall look and feel of a given display by assigning it one or more custom CSS classes. To see this in action, create a new CSS class and add it to the appropriate stylesheet (for more information on this, see the following chapter on themes). Here's a class you can add that will give the view a dark blue border and a light blue background:

```
.basicviewstyle{
border: 1px solid #01539b;
background: #dbe9f5;
}
```

With that class saved to your stylesheet, you can now add the basicviewstyle class to a display by clicking on **CSS class** in the **Style settings**. Save the changes, and then use the **Live preview** to view the results:

Editor: Dodge
* Worldwide decline in snake populations

As you can see, the display now has a border and a shaded background — if you don't get this result, check that you have correctly entered the class name and then clear out any caches that may be preventing you from viewing the new CSS class — remember you can always look at the view as it appears on the site by navigating to the pertinent path.

This type of control is useful for broad-based changes, but what if we want to style specific rows or even specific fields in a row? For that, we need to go to the templates.

Views templates

First, let's have a quick overview of how the template system works. The following diagram highlights the hierarchical template file system:

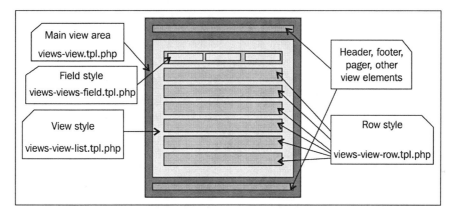

Each and every aspect of a view can be controlled using the various template files assigned to control the output of each part of the view. This modular system is perfect for easy customization because we can dip into and out of various template files without affecting other parts of the display.

Let's put this into practice.

Theme information

Click on the **Information** link next to **Theme** in the **Style** settings of the **latest-blog-posts** page display in your view. This will bring up a list of the currently active template files (highlighted in bold) along with a list of optional template names that can be used to override the default templates, as shown in the following screenshot:

Note that the files are arranged from least specific (templates that affect the entire display) to most specific (templates that affect results at the field level). Furthermore, the optional template filenames often include the **Machine name** and the **Name** provided in the **Basic settings** at the top of the page—as you can see from the presence of template files with names like the following:

- `views-view—latest-blog-posts.tpl.php`.
- `views-view-unformatted—latest-blog-posts.tpl.php`.
- `views-view-fields—latest-blog-posts.tpl.php`, and so on.

While you have a number of options for suitable template names available, it is easiest to keep your naming convention standard and go with the most specific and logical ones available—I generally use the machine name suffixed options. Once you get to the point where there are many views, all with many customized template files, things can get a bit confusing if you haven't stuck to a sound naming convention.

Click on the name of a file to view its contents. For example, the `Field Node` template file looks like this:

```php
<?php
// $Id: views-view-field.tpl.php,v 1.1 2008/05/16 22:22:32
merlinofchaos Exp $
 /**
   * This template is used to print a single field in a view. It is not
   * actually used in default Views, as this is registered as a theme
   * function which has better performance. For single overrides, the
   * template is perfectly okay.
   *
   * Variables available:
   * - $view: The view object
   * - $field: The field handler object that can process the input
   * - $row: The raw SQL result that can be used
   * - $output: The processed output that will normally be used.
   *
   * When fetching output from the $row, this construct should be used:
   * $data = $row->{$field->field_alias}
   *
   * The above will guarantee that you'll always get the correct data,
   * regardless of any changes in the aliasing that might happen if
   * the view is modified.
   */
?>
<?php print $output; ?>
```

While the preponderance of this file is commented information on how to use the template file, it does show several important things:

1. The template files are themselves a source of helpful information on how to manipulate Views themes.

2. We have direct access to the PHP variables that contain the data, and we are told which ones are available to this template file.

3. There are recommended ways of accessing this information to protect against broken code if changes are instituted at a later date.

4. The actual output of the file is very simple—`print $output;`

Creating a custom template file

Using the standard Drupal method for adding custom theme files, we can open up a file for editing, copy and paste the contents of the default `Field Node` template file into a new file, and save it with the **latest-blog-posts** addition (plus the name of the field since we are working at the field level) directly to our active theme folder. In this case, I have saved the text in a file, and I have saved this file as `views-view-field-latest-blog-posts--title.tpl.php` in the main theme folder.

Views won't automatically start using this new template file because:

 You have to rescan the template files in order for Views to pick up any new files.

Once the file is saved to your theme directory, click the **Rescan template files** button. The new template file should be picked up and highlighted in bold to indicate it is now the active template file. If it's not picked up, make sure you have properly named the file—remember, you can only use filenames that are provided in the **Theme information** list.

With the new template file being picked up by Views, we can start having some fun with it…

Modifying the custom template file

Let's start off with a fairly crude change, simply to demonstrate that the changes we make do in fact affect the display. Comment out the `print` statement at the bottom of the file, like the following:

```
<?php // print $output; ?>
```

Save this change, and then test the **Live preview** of the **basic** display. You should find that the results are blank (or at least lacking the **Title** field)—this is because this specific field is governed by the new template file, and we just commented out the only statement being used to print the results to the screen.

Undo the changes and modify the last line so that it looks like the following:

```
<div style="float: right;"><?php print $output; ?></div>
```

Save the changes, and then refresh the **Live preview** to see the results. You should find that the **Title** field floats to the right of the display instead of being left aligned.

We have now used PHP and HTML to modify the output, so let's take a quick look at one last example that will use CSS. Modify the last line again, adding in a new CSS class declaration like:

```
<div class="latestblogposttitle" style="float: right;"><?php print
$output; ?></div>
```

Now, save the file and then add the new `latestblogposttitle` class:

```
.latestblogposttitle{
font-size: 1.3em;
font-weight: bold;
color: red;
}
```

to your stylesheet; flush any caches, if necessary, and view the results. You should now be able to view the floating, right aligned titles with new coloring and formatting. In the same way, each aspect of every display can be carefully manipulated and controlled using PHP, HTML, and CSS.

Importing, exporting, and cloning views

The ability to clone a view is supremely useful—as is the ability to import and export. For a variety of reasons, you might find yourself wanting to create a new view based on a current one or even based on one from another website.

If you are looking to duplicate a current view, then doing so is as easy as clicking on the **Clone** link at the top of the page. This will bring up a settings page that allows you to enter a different unique view name and description—obviously, you can't keep the current name as each view name must be unique:

Clicking on **Next** brings you to the editing interface for the new, cloned view and away you go. You might consider using this feature to work on an established view that you don't want to risk inadvertently mangling—it has happened.

Exporting is even easier. Click on the **Export** link to bring up the View creation code:

```
latest_blog_posts

$view = new view;
$view->name = 'latest_blog_posts';
$view->description = 'Returns a list of the latest blog postings';
$view->tag = '';
$view->view_php = '';
$view->base_table = 'node';
$view->is_cacheable = FALSE;
$view->api_version = 3.0-alpha1;
$view->disabled = FALSE; /* Edit this to true to make a default view disabled initially */


/* Display: Defaults */
$handler = $view->new_display('default', 'Defaults', 'default');
$handler->display->display_options['css_class'] = 'basicviewstyle';
$handler->display->display_options['access']['type'] = 'role';
$handler->display->display_options['cache']['type'] = 'none';
$handler->display->display_options['exposed_form']['type'] = 'basic';
$handler->display->display_options['pager']['type'] = 'some';
$handler->display->display_options['pager']['options']['items_per_page'] = '10';
$handler->display->display_options['pager']['options']['offset'] = '0';
$handler->display->display_options['style_plugin'] = 'default';
$handler->display->display_options['row_plugin'] = 'fields';
/* Relationship: Node revision: User */
$handler->display->display_options['relationships']['uid']['id'] = 'uid';
$handler->display->display_options['relationships']['uid']['table'] = 'node_revision';
```

Copy and paste this code into a file and save it to a removable storage device in order to keep secure backups of all your hard work. Alternatively, copy and paste the code, and send it to a friend to use on their website—remember though, a view is only useful on another site, if that site has the same fields and functionality.

To import a view, simply click on the **IMPORT** tab, enter a unique name, and paste the exported view's code into the space provided:

Clicking on the **Import** button will take you directly to the newly imported Views interface, so you can begin working on it immediately. Remember that the imported view isn't permanently saved to the site until you click on the **Save** button.

Summary

Views are an integral part of any Drupal-based website that has more than the most basic requirements. This chapter focused on providing a comprehensive and practical overview of how Views can be used to present different types of content. It's important to remember that content is not the only thing that Views can work on; comments, files, users, and more, all fall within the remit of Views.

The section on creating a basic view provided an insight into the most commonly used features of a view, and it is likely that most Views you ever create will make use of much of what you learned here. In particular, filters and fields form the core of almost all views you will create.

The advanced section explored the arguments and relationships categories and showed how they can be used to create more dynamic views based on the context in which a View is being seen. Furthermore, relationships hinted at how Views allows us to create more complex queries that can span multiple disparate bits of data from within the Drupal database.

Finally, we discussed theming and the template system, which are essential for managing the look and feel of the data returned by Views. In particular, our first foray into how template files are handled within Drupal highlighted the power and flexibility of Drupal's modular template system in general. You'll gain a better understanding of this in the upcoming chapter on *Drupal Theming*.

Mastery of Drupal Views is one the cornerstones of being a competent Drupal user. While achieving this can be a lot of work, hopefully you are excited about the prospect of being able to create some really innovative and powerful features for your website.

9
Drupal Theming

Working on a site's interface to make it distinctive and attractive not only requires some technical know-how, but just like any other design-related task, it also needs some creativity. Your site, at the moment, is fully functional and doesn't look awful—it's a bit plain, but it will get the job done. With a bit of effort, creating something entirely new can be fun and rewarding, and Drupal comes with a host of features to make our lives easier.

If, like me, you enjoy working on the more creative aspects of a website, then this is really the chapter you have been waiting for. It's time to design, plan, and implement the visual environment in which your website's users will be immersed.

This chapter will discuss the following:

- Planning a web-based interface
- CSS
- Themes

When considering the look and feel of your new website, take some time to look at what is already out there. Many issues that you will encounter while designing a site have already been successfully dealt with by others, and not only by Drupal users of course. Also, don't be scared to treat your design as an ongoing process. While it is never really good to drastically change sites on a weekly basis, regular tweaking or upgrading of the interface can keep it modern and fresh.

Planning a web-based interface

The tenet, *form follows function* is widely applied in many spheres of human knowledge. It is a well understood concept that states that the way something is built or made must reflect the purpose it was made for. This is an exceptionally sensible thought, and applying it to the design of your site will provide a yardstick to measure how well you have designed it.

That's not to say one site should look like every other site that performs the same function. In fact, if anything, you want to make it as distinctive as possible, without stepping over the bounds of what the target user will consider good taste or common sense.

How do you do that? The trick is to relate what you have and what you need to do for a website with a specific target audience. Providing content that has appeal to both genders, all ages, and all nationalities, races, or religions implies that you should go with something that everyone can use. If anything, this might be a slightly flavorless site because you wouldn't want to marginalize any group of users by explicitly making the site biased towards another group. Luckily though, to some extent, your target audience will be slightly easier to define than this; so you can generally make some concessions for a particular type of user.

Visual design

There's no beating about the bush on this issue. Make the site appear as visually appealing as possible without hiding or obscuring any critical or useful information. By this, I mean don't be afraid to leave a fairly large list of items on a page—if all the items on that list are useful and will be (or are) used frequently. Hiding an important thing from users—no matter how easy it appears to be to find it on other pages—will frustrate them; and the site's popularity might suffer.

How a site looks can also have a big impact on how users understand it. For example, if several different fonts apply to different links, then it is entirely likely that users will not think of clicking on one type of link or another because of the different font styles. Think about this yourself for a moment, and visualize whether or not you would spend time hovering the pointer over each and every font type in the hope that it was a link.

This can be summed up as:

 Make sure your site is visually consistent and that there are no style discrepancies from one page to the next.

By the same token, reading a page of text where the links are given in the same font and style as the writing would effectively hide that functionality.

There are quite a few so-called *rules of visual design*, which can be applied to the design of any site. Some that might interest you are: the rule of thirds, which states that things divided up into thirds—either vertically or horizontally—are more visually appealing than other designs; or the visual center rule, which states that the visual center of the page (where the eye is most attracted to) is just above and to the right of the actual center of the page.

You may wish to visit the website A List Apart at `http://www.alistapart.com/` that has plenty of useful articles on design for the Web or try searching on Google for more information.

Language

Now this is a truly interesting part of a site's design, and the art of writing for the Web is a lot more subtle than just saying what you mean. The reason for this is that you are no longer writing simply for human consumption, but also for consumption by machines. Because machines can only follow a certain number of rules when interpreting a page, concessions on the language used must be made by the writers (if they want their sites to feature highly on search engines).

Before making your site's text highly optimized for searching, there are a few more fundamental things that are important to consider. First off, make sure your language is clear and concise. This is most important; rather sacrifice racy, stylized copy for more mundane text if the mundane text is going to elucidate important points better. People have very short attention spans when it comes to reading web copy; so keep things to the point.

Apart from the actual content of your language, the visual and structural appearance of the copy is also important. Use bold or larger fonts to emphasize headings or important points, and ensure that text is spaced out nicely to make the page easier on the eye, and therefore easier to read and understand.

Images

Working with images for the Web is very much an art. I don't mean this in the sense that generally one should be quite artistic in order to make nice pictures. I mean that actually managing and dealing with image files is itself an art. There is a lot of work to be done for the aspiring website owner with respect to attaining a pleasing and meaningful visual environment. This is because the Web is an environment that is most reliant on visual images to have an effect on users—because sight and sound are the only two senses that are targeted by the Internet (for now).

In order to have the freedom to manipulate images, you need to use a reasonably powerful image editor.

 In this case, we are talking about images that form part of the site design. Drupal 7 has comprehensive image handling support for images that form part of the site's content, as discussed in *Chapter 7, Multimedia*.

Gimp (`http://www.gimp.org/`) is an example of a good image-editing environment, but anything that allows you to save files in a variety of different formats and provides resizing capabilities, should be sufficient.

There are several areas of concern when working with images, all of which need to be closely scrutinized in order to produce an integrated and pleasing visual environment:

- One of the biggest problems with images is that they take up a lot more space and bandwidth than text or code. For this reason, having an effective method for dealing with large images is required—for example, you might use CSS to repeat small background images on the X or Y axis instead of using large images

- Deciding what type of image you actually want to use from the available variety can also be a bit of an issue because some image types take up more space than others, and some may not even be rendered properly in a browser. By and large, there are really only three image types that are most commonly used—GIF, PNG, and JPG

- The intended use of an image can also be a big factor when deciding upon how to create, size, and format the file. For example, icons and logos should really be saved as PNG or GIF files, whereas photos and large or complex images should be saved in the JPG format because of the efficiency with which JPG handles complex images

Let's take a quick look at those here.

GIF (Graphics Interchange Format) is known for its compression and the fact that it can store and display multiple images. The major drawback to GIF is that images can only display up to 256 distinct colors. For photographic-quality images, this is a significant obstacle. However, you should use GIFs for:

- Images with a transparent background
- Animated graphics
- Smaller, less complex images requiring no more than 256 colors

PNG (Portable Network Graphics) is actually designed as a replacement for GIF files. In general, it can achieve greater file compression; gives a wider range of color depth, and quite a bit more. PNG, unlike GIF files, does not support animations. You can use PNG files for anything that you would otherwise use GIFs for, with the exception of animations.

> Internet Explorer does not render many PNG images correctly, so be aware that this may affect what people think about your site—having ugly-shaded regions around images can make your site appear to be of poor quality.
>
> The issue can, most often, be resolved by **stripping gAMA information** from the PNG file using something like TweakPNG (http://entropymine.com/jason/tweakpng/).

Incidentally, there is also an MNG format that allows for animations—you might want to check that out as an alternative to animated GIFs.

JPG, or **JPEG** (Joint Photographic Experts Group), should be used when presenting photo-realistic images. JPG can compress large images while retaining the overall photographic quality. JPG files can use any number of colors, and so it's a very convenient format for images that require a lot of color. JPG should be used for:

- Photographs
- Larger, complex images requiring more than 256 colors to display with high accuracy

Be aware that JPG uses lossy compression, which means that in order to handle images efficiently, the compression process loses quality.

Before we begin an in-depth look at themes that are responsible for just about everything when it comes to our site's look and feel, we still need to briefly cover one last vital component technology—CSS. If you are already familiar with CSS, feel free to skip this section and go straight to the *Themes* section.

CSS

The pages in a Drupal site obtain their style-related information from the associated stylesheets that are held in their respective theme or module folders. Using stylesheets gives designers excellent, fine-grained control over the appearance of web pages and its various elements, and can produce some great effects. The appearance of pretty much every aspect of the site can be controlled from CSS within a (good) theme, and all that is needed is a little knowledge of fonts, colors, and stylesheet syntax.

It will make life easier if you have a readymade list of the type of things you should look at setting using the stylesheet. Here are the most common areas (defined by HTML elements) where stylesheets can be used to determine the look and feel of a site.

- Background
- Text
- Font
- Color
- Images
- Border
- Margin
- Padding
- Lists

Besides being able to change all these aspects of HTML, different effects can be applied, depending on whether certain conditions, like a mouse hovering over the specified area, are met — this will be demonstrated a little later on. You can also specify attributes for certain HTML tags that can then be used to apply styles to those specific tags instead of creating application-wide changes. For example, imagine one paragraph style with a class attribute set, like this:

```
<p class="signature"></p>
```

You could reference this type of paragraph in a stylesheet explicitly by saying something like:

```
p.signature {
    color: green;
}
```

Analyzing this line highlights the structure of the standard stylesheet code block in the form of a:

- **Selector**: In this case, p.signature
- **Property**: In this case, color
- **Delimiter**: This is always :
- **Value**: In this case, green

Note that all the property/value pairs are contained within curly braces and each is ended with a semicolon. It is possible to specify many properties for each selector, and indeed, we are able to specify several selectors to have the same properties. For example, the following block is taken from the **garland** stylesheet, `style.css`, and is used to provide all the header text within the theme with a similar look-and-feel, by giving them all the same properties:

```
h1, h2, h3, h4, h5, h6 {
   margin: 0;
   padding: 0;
   font-weight: normal;
   font-family: Helvetica, Arial, sans-serif;
}
```

In this instance, multiple selectors have been specified in a comma delimited list, with each selector given four properties to control the `margin`, `padding`, `font-weight`, and `font-family` of the header tags.

It is also important to realize that tags can be referenced using either the `class` attribute, or the `id` attribute, or both. For example, the following HTML:

```
<p class="signature" id="unique-signature"></p>
```

makes it possible for this tag to be referenced both as part of a class of tags all with the same property or specifically by its unique **id** attribute. The distinction between the two is important because **class** gives broad sweeping powers to make changes to all tags within that class, and **id** gives fine-grained control over a tag with that unique ID.

This introduction to CSS has been very brief, and there are plenty of excellent resources available. If you would like to learn more about CSS, and it is highly recommended, then a quick search on Google will turn up plenty of resources.

Themes

The use of themes makes Drupal exceptionally flexible when it comes to working with the site's interface. Because the functionality of the site is by and large decoupled from the presentation of the site, it is quite easy to chop and change the look, without having to worry about affecting the functionality. This is obviously a very useful feature because it frees you up to experiment, knowing that if worst comes to worst, you can reset the default settings and start from scratch.

You can think of a theme as a mask for your site that can be modified in order to achieve virtually any design criteria. Of course, different themes have widely varying attributes, so it is important to find the theme that most closely resembles what you are looking for in order to reduce the amount of work needed to match it to your envisaged design.

> It is also important to understand that not all downloadable themes are of the same quality. Some are designed better than others. This chapter utilizes Zen, which is one of the cleanest and most flexible around.

Different themes are implemented differently. Some themes use fixed layouts with tables (avoid these because web design should not rely on tables), while others use `div` tags and CSS (favor these as they are far more flexible and powerful)—you should play around with a variety of themes in order to familiarize yourself with a few different ways of creating a web page. As mentioned, we only have space to cover Zen here, but the lessons learned are easily transferred to other themes with a bit of time and practice.

Before we go ahead and look at an actual example, it is important to get an overview of how themes are put together in general.

Theme anatomy

Drupal themes consist of a set of files that define and control the features of Drupal's web pages (ranging from what functionality to include within a page to how individual page elements will be presented) using PHP, HTML, CSS, and images.

Different Drupal 7 template files control different regions of a page, as shown in the following diagram:

Looking at how theme files are set up within Drupal hints at the overall process and structure of that theme. Bear in mind that there are several ways to create a working theme, and not all themes make use of template files. However, in the case of the Drupal's default theme setup, we have the following:

The left-hand column shows the folders contained within the **themes** directory. There are a number of standard themes, accompanied by the **engines** folder that houses a `phptemplate.engine` file, to handle the integration of templates into Drupal's theming system.

Looking at the files present in the **garland** folder, notice that there are a number of PHP Template files suffixed by **tpl.php**. These files make use of HTML and PHP code to modify Drupal's appearance. The default versions of these files, which are the ones that would be used in the event a theme had not implemented on its own, can be found in the relevant **modules** directory. For example, the default **comment. tpl.php** file is found in **modules | comment**, and the default **page.tpl.php** file is located, along with others, in the **modules | system** folder.

Each template file focuses on its specific page element or page, with the noted exception of **template.php** that is used to override non-standard theme functions—that is, not block, box, comment, node, or page.

The **themes** folder also houses the stylesheets along with images, and in the case of the default theme, colors. Of special interest is the .info file that contains information about the theme to allow Drupal to find and set a host of different parameters.

 A theme's .info file holds the basic information about a theme that Drupal needs to know, namely, its name, description, features, template regions, CSS files, and JavaScript.

Here's Garland's .info file:

```
; $Id: garland.info,v 1.9 2009/12/01 15:57:40 webchick Exp $
name = Garland
description = A multi-column theme which can be configured to modify
colors and switch between fixed and fluid width layouts.
package = Core
version = VERSION
core = 7.x
engine = phptemplate
stylesheets[all][] = style.css
stylesheets[print][] = print.css
settings[garland_width] = fluid

; Information added by drupal.org packaging script on 2010-05-23
version = "7.0-alpha5"
project = "drupal"
datestamp = "1274628610"
```

Note that this file holds, amongst other things:

- Name — A human-readable theme name
- Description — A description of the theme
- Core — The major version of Drupal that the theme is compatible with
- Stylesheets — Stipulate which stylesheets are to be used by the theme

These are not the only types of information that can be held by .info files. As we'll see a bit later on, when it's time to add scripts to a theme, they can be added to the .info file too.

To quickly see one way in which .info files can be put to work, look closely at the .info file in the update_test_subtheme theme folder in tests (Below garland):

```
; $Id: update_test_subtheme.info,v 1.1 2009/10/08 15:40:34 dries Exp $
name = Update test subtheme
description = Test theme which uses update_test_basetheme as the base
theme.
core = 7.x
engine = phptemplate
base theme = update_test_basetheme
hidden = TRUE

; Information added by drupal.org packaging script on 2010-05-23
version = "7.0-alpha5"
project = "drupal"
datestamp = "1274628610"
```

Notice that this contains a base theme directive that is used to specify the parent, or base, theme.

> A sub-theme shares its parents' code, but modifies parts of it to produce a new look, new functionality, or both.

Drupal allows us to create new sub-themes by creating a new folder within the themes directory and specifying the base theme directive in the new theme's .info file—just as we saw in update_test_subtheme.

In a nutshell, Drupal provides a range of default themeable functions that expose Drupal's underlying data: such as content and information about that content. Themes can pick and choose which snippets of rendered content they want to override—the most popular method being through the use of PHP template files in conjunction with stylesheets and a .info file. Themes and sub-themes are easily created and modified, provided that you have some knowledge of CSS and HTML—PHP helps if you want to do something more complicated.

I should make it clear that this system makes building a new theme fairly easy, provided one knows a bit about PHP. Here's the process:

- Create a new `themes` folder in the `sites|all` folder, and add your new theme folder in there—call it whatever you want (provided it is a unique name)
- Copy the default template files (or files from any other theme you want to modify) across to the new theme directory, along with any other files that are applicable (such as `CSS` files)
- Rewrite the `.info` file to reflect the attributes and requirements of the new theme, including specifying the `base theme` directive
- Modify the layout (this is where your PHP and HTML skills come in handy) and add some flavor with your own stylesheet (included into the new theme through the `.info` file)

Before moving on, there's one small issue of practicality that must be addressed. When it is time for you to begin doing a bit of theme development, bear in mind that there are many types of browser and not all of them are created equal. What this means is that a page that is rendered nicely on one browser might look bad, or worse, not even function properly on another. For this reason, you should:

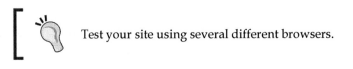

Test your site using several different browsers.

The Drupal help site has this to say about browsers:

It is recommended you use the Firefox browser with a developer toolbar and view the formatted sources' extensions.

I wholeheartedly agree. You can obtain a copy of the Firefox browser at `http://www.mozilla.com/firefox/`. Firefox **should** also be extended with Firebug, which is an extremely useful tool for client-side web debugging: `https://addons.mozilla.org/en-US/firefox/addon/1843/`.

Choosing a base theme

As discussed, Drupal ships with a few default themes, and there are quite a few more available in the **Downloads** section of the Drupal site. Looking at how Drupal presents its core **Themes** page under **Appearance** in the toolbar menu, we can see the following:

Any new themes that are added to the site will be used to enable, disable, configure, or set as a default from this page.

> Be aware that some themes might not implement functionality that is important to your site. Ensure that you test each theme thoroughly before allowing users to select it.

Enabling the **Stark** theme, and setting it as the default theme, causes the site, which has been presented in the standard **Garland** theme up until now, to look something like this:

This is a vast change from the previous look. Notice too that the entire layout of the site has changed—there are no well defined columns, no visually defined header section, and so on. In addition, the previous fonts and colors have also been demolished.

> Take the time to view each theme that is available by default in order to get a feel for how different themes can produce wildly differing looks and layouts.

That is not the end of the story, because the Drupal site also has a whole bunch of themes for us to explore. So head on over to the themes page at http://drupal.org/project/themes and select the relevant version tab to bring up the themes that are available.

You have already seen how to download and install other modules, and the process for installing themes is no different—download and extract the contents of the desired theme to the `themes` folder in **sites | default** or **sites | all**. For example, the **Zen** theme was downloaded and extracted, and provides us with a new option in the list of themes (some downloads will provide a number of sub-themes too), as shown in the following screenshot:

Enable and set default causes the site to look like the next screenshot:

Notice that while the color scheme is effectively non-existent, the page has retained its overall structure in that it has defined sidebars, a header region, and a central content region. Before we begin customizing this, let's take a look at the configuration settings for this theme.

Theme settings

Clicking on the **Settings** tab at the top of the **Appearance** overlay brings up the global theme options that will influence each theme, regardless of which one is being used. This is useful if you always want certain features enabled (it's also easy enough to navigate between global and theme-specific settings using the links given at the top of the page):

The **Global settings** page is fairly representative of all the theme configuration pages. Note that the settings made here can be overridden by the **Settings** of each specific theme.

Along with a selection of page elements to be hidden or displayed, each individual theme might provide a number of different options. In the case of the **Garland** theme, we are able to set the **Color scheme** and **Content width** options, as shown in the following screenshot:

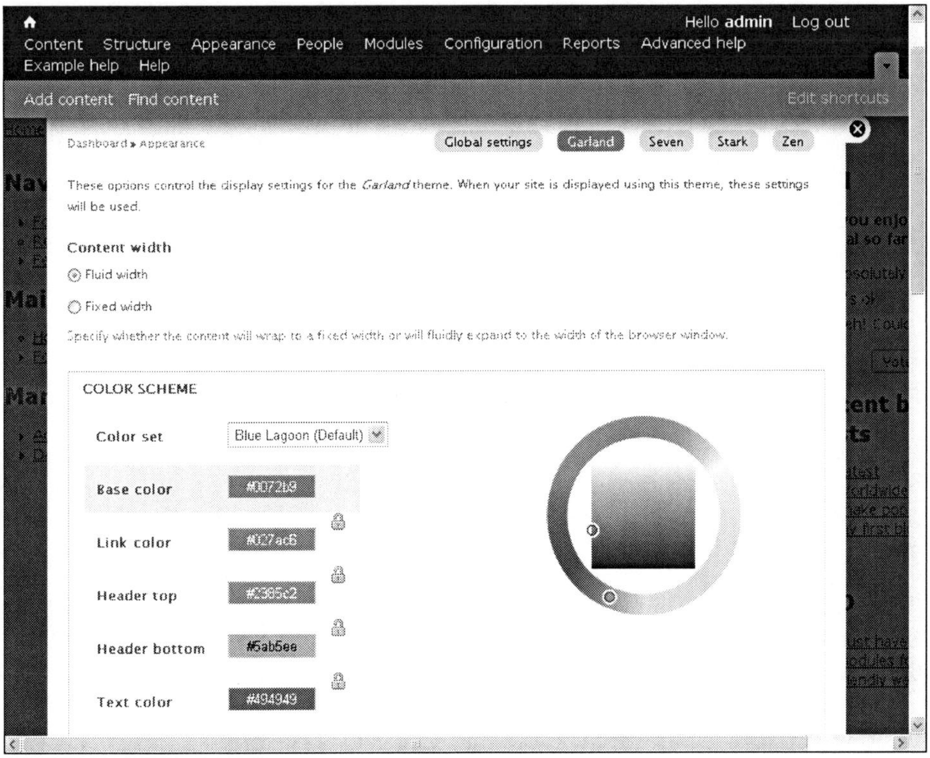

Next, we can specify which page elements should or shouldn't be displayed in the **TOGGLE DISPLAY** section.

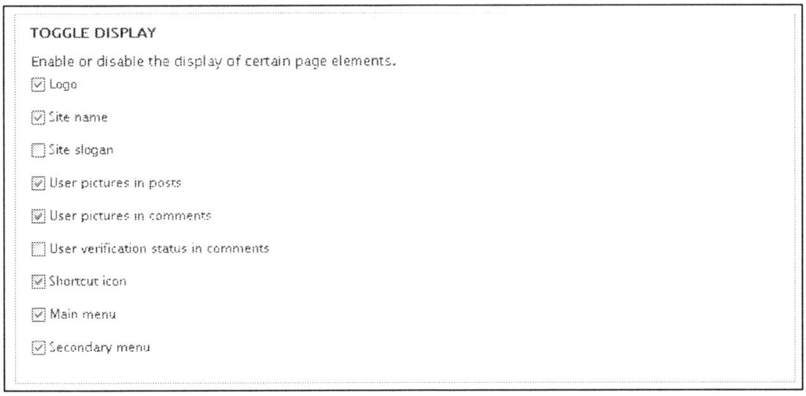

Then, we can either use the default logo supplied with the theme, or alternatively, specify a path to another logo or upload a new logo to the site, as shown below.

```
LOGO IMAGE SETTINGS
If toggled on, the following logo will be displayed.
☐ Use the default logo
    Check here if you want the theme to use the logo supplied with it.

Path to custom logo
[                                              ]
The path to the file you would like to use as your logo file instead of the default logo.

Upload logo image
[C:\Documents and Settings\user\My Documents\Downloads\iS|c] [ Browse… ]
If you don't have direct file access to the server, use this field to upload your logo.
```

In the case of the demo site, we will be making use of a background image to display the logo and name, so this option can be unchecked. If you have a site logo, or plan to have one, then this is where you'll come (for whichever theme you are using—most likely a Zen sub-theme).

The final section deals with favicons (an icon that will be displayed in the site's address bar and in any bookmarks). Once again, what you use here is really up to you, but favicons can be a bit of a pain to create. Internet Explorer looks for icons in the ICO format, whereas Firefox will happily include .png files. There are a couple of online icon creation websites that can make or convert favicons—http://www.html-kit.com/favicon/ is one such example.

Customizing themes

Up until now, any settings or changes made have been fairly generic. Things are about to change as we begin to implement some more radical modifications that will require amendments to the stylesheet in order to get things just right. In the case of the demo site, I have chosen to work with the **Zen** theme, as it is clean and well designed and demonstrates the use of sub-themes really nicely.

> If you haven't already, now is the time to find a fairly good code editor, as you will be looking at code files of one sort or another from here on out.

Sub-themes

Zen is designed to work through sub-themes—we don't want to modify the base theme at all. This should make sense because we would have a hard time upgrading the theme if we spent all our time working on it directly. Follow this process to create your new Zen sub-theme:

1. Copy the STARTERKIT folder to your `themes` directory and give it a name (lowercase, no special characters). For this example, I am using `drupalbook`.

2. Open the new `drupalbook` sub-theme directory and rename STARTERKIT. `info.txt` to `drupalbook.info`. The `.info` file should always have the same name as its theme.

3. Open the `drupalbook.info` file and change the name and description fields to something more suitable such as:
   name = **drupalbook**
   description = **This is the Drupal 7 book's Zen subtheme.**

4. Edit `template.php` and `theme-settings.php` by doing a search for all occurrences of STARTERKIT and replacing it with the name of the sub-theme—`drupalbook`. Save the changes.

That's it. You can now access and use this new sub-theme just like any other theme on the Drupal site. Go to the **Appearance** overlay:

and enable and set this new sub-theme as the default. Note that the name and description information that we supplied to the `drupalbook.info` file is displayed with the theme. Once this is done, you should notice that your site looks exactly the same as it did when we enabled the Zen theme itself. That's because they are exactly the same.

> The Zen theme is a starting point from which we can create any type of look we want through sub-themes.

If you have any trouble, refer to the README.txt file that comes in the STARTERKIT folder within the Zen theme.

Working with the Sub-theme

Now that we have a fully operational **drupalbook** theme, it's time to start making changes. You are completely free to change anything you want in any way you can imagine—there are literally limitless possibilities. The important thing to know is how everything is organized within this theme so that you understand where changes need to be made in order to achieve your theming requirements.

The drupalbook sub-theme has the following structure:

By and large, the vast majority of changes you will implement will be carried out in the css files contained in the css folder. We've already had a brief overview of how CSS works, and looking at the contents of the css folder, we can see that each CSS file pertains to specific elements of the page:

This is fantastic, because it means that everything is really logically and intuitively organized and this will save you a lot of time. In lesser themes, combing through large CSS files or trying to locate the correct files to modify can be an ever present source of irritation.

Open the blocks.css file for editing and modify the following:

```
.block /* Block wrapper */ {
  margin-bottom: 1em;
}
```

By adding a background attribute, as shown here:

```
.block /* Block wrapper */ {
  margin-bottom: 1em;
  background: #C00000;
}
```

Save the changes, and refresh your browser. You should now see that all the block regions on the site have a healthy red glow about them:

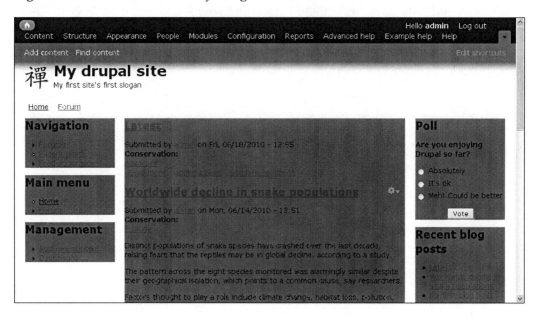

All the block settings you could want to make, are sitting in the `blocks.css` file. Note that, by default, the CSS declarations are mostly empty, which is why the site currently looks so plain. Your job is to make changes to the regions and classes in order to get things looking the way you want them to.

In the same way, you can work on styling pages, nodes, comments, and forms and anything else you can think of—it's all there, nicely organized, and waiting for you. It might seem like a huge amount of work, but you'll be surprised by how much you can get done in a relatively short amount of time. For example, adding a nice background image to the body tag and setting the fonts goes a long way in giving the site an identity and that's only two small changes.

Moving down the list, the next folder, `images`, houses any and all images that you use as part of your theme. Save them here and reference them from your CSS files—nothing too complicated, and we have already discussed images earlier in this chapter.

The `js` directory holds any additional script files that you might need in order for your site to function. We'll be discussing how to incorporate third-party scripts into our site in the following chapter, so we won't look at how to add a script file to Drupal here.

Finally, the `templates` folder holds any and all template files that we wish to override ourselves. Even if you are not familiar with PHP, Drupal's modular design and template system makes it really easy to fiddle around with the internals of Drupal. Let's take a look at the process of overriding a template file.

Zen gives us a head start in the form of the `README.txt` file that is included in the templates directory. Here's a snippet:

```
TEMPLATES
---------


Drupal 6 contains the following template files which you can override
and modify by copying them to your sub-theme. The Zen theme overrides
a handful of Drupal's templates. In order to override those templates,
you should copy them from the zen/templates folder to your sub-theme's
templates folder.

As always, when adding a new template file to your sub-theme, you will
need to rebuild the "theme registry" in order for Drupal to see it.
For more info, see:   http://drupal.org/node/173880#theme-registry

Located in zen/templates:
  page.tpl.php
  maintenance-page.tpl.php
  node.tpl.php
  block.tpl.php
  comment-wrapper.tpl.php
  comment.tpl.php


Located in /modules/aggregator:
  aggregator-feed-source.tpl.php
  aggregator-item.tpl.php
  aggregator-summary-item.tpl.php
  aggregator-summary-items.tpl.php
  aggregator-wrapper.tpl.php


Located in /modules/block:
  block-admin-display-form.tpl.php
```

This code directs us to the location of the template files that we can use to override specific aspects of the site. In particular, notice that I have highlighted the Zen template files in the previous snippet that are available for us to override. There is also a sentence in the comments that is very important:

> When overriding a file, the theme registry has to be rebuilt before Drupal will pick up the changes.

Before we try overriding a template file, head over to the **Settings** page for **drupalbook**, and ensure that the **Theme registry** setting is checked:

THEME DEVELOPMENT SETTINGS

Theme registry: ☑ Rebuild theme registry on every page.

During theme development, it can be very useful to continuously rebuild the theme registry. WARNING: this is a huge performance penalty and must be turned off on production websites.

Wireframes: ☐ Display borders around main layout elements

Wireframes are useful when prototyping a website.

This causes the theme registry to be rebuilt every time we refresh the page. It's great for development, but you **must** switch it off for production sites as it is very costly in terms of performance. With that setting saved, we can be sure that any changes we make to the template files will be picked up each time a new page is loaded.

To override a template file:

1. Copy the default file to the `templates` directory in the sub-theme. For example, you might want to copy `block.tpl.php` from **zen | templates** to **drupalbook | templates**.
2. Open the file for editing, implement and save the changes.
3. Refresh your browser page to view the results.

By way of example, I made a trivial, but visible, change to the `block.tpl.php` file saved to the sub-theme's `templates` folder:

```
<div class="content"<?php print $content_attributes; ?>>
    <?php
print 'you can see this change in every block in the drupalbook
theme';
print $content;
?>
  </div>
```

While this is not a particularly useful change—it does serve to demonstrate the fact that changes to this template file do affect the way in which the theme displays the relevant element on the site, as evidenced by refreshing the page:

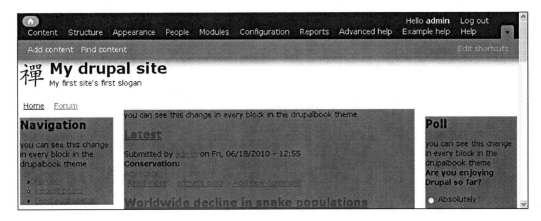

As expected, each block now displays the additional message before it prints out the block content. While this example is fairly trivial, users who have experience with Drupal can make more complex and fundamental changes by accessing the underlying PHP data. Each template file helps developers out in this regard by telling them what is and isn't available in the comments at the top of each template page.

Knowing how to combine CSS with PHP and HTML templating puts you in complete control over the look and feel of your website. You can use any combination of CSS, HTML, JavaScript, or PHP to implement any and all changes you like.

Summary

From learning about what considerations must be taken into account when planning a website's look-and-feel, to making changes to the code, this chapter has provided a firm grounding in the fundamentals of working with Drupal themes.

One of the most important aspects of customizing a site's look is understanding how Drupal is set up, in order to leverage the power of themes. As we saw, themes provide a kind of template from which you can work to create your own unique site. This saves a lot of time and effort because we no longer need to work from scratch.

With respect to building your site's interface, experience is very important. There are three main technologies that you need to spend some time working with, namely, HTML, CSS, and PHP. In this chapter, we looked at CSS in some detail, as you should be able to achieve most of your theming requirements using this alone.

10
Advanced Features

We are going to start out by looking at a grab-bag of topics that showcase some of the more advanced or interesting features in Drupal in order to give you the opportunity to add that *something special*. We're also going to try our hand at integrating third-party code into Drupal in order to provide some cool functionality that is not currently available.

Remember though that if this chapter does not quite cover exactly what you are after, you are not totally out of luck. The chances are that someone else in the community has had to do something similar before, so making inquiries in the Drupal forums should yield some positive results. If, at some point, you do manage to create something utterly fantastic, please give back to the community by sharing your work with others.

This chapter will look at the following topics:

- Panels
- Additional theming

It is often important to be able to make your own additions to a site in order to get it just right. Accordingly, we will also look at how to apply some lateral thinking and judicious use of what we have already learned in this and the previous chapters to create some entirely new features for your website in the section entitled *Customized content reviews*.

One final thing to remember before we begin is that you *must, must, must* make frequent and regular backups of the whole site, including the database (preferably before adding a new feature). The topic of making backups is discussed in the following chapter—I mention this just in case you feel it is time to make a backup of what you have now, before making any further changes.

Introduction to Panels

Panels are a powerful and convenient way to create dynamic and complex web pages. Up until now, a given posting was just a single node being displayed on a page. Views allow us to build lists of content, which is a step up on single nodes, but Panels completes the picture by providing a mechanism for combining nodes and views and all sorts of other content and features into a single page.

One of the most common uses of Panels is for the landing or the front page of a website. Often, a simple list or single page of content is not really sufficient to show off the full scope of a site. For example, a news website may wish to show the latest headlines from a range of important topics such as business, world news, sports, and so on. Clearly one big list of the headlines is not really suitable in this instance, so panels can be used to separate different, focused views into different parts of the page.

The site prebuilder home page (`http://www.siteprebuilder.com`) is a good example of using panels on a page. From this, you can see clearly defined *panes* of content highlighting different aspects of the site.

 At the time of writing, no stable release of *Panels* exists for Drupal 7. However, given the importance of this topic, it still warrants coverage. Be aware that slight differences might occur between this text and the module as you view it as a result.

Head on over to the Drupal website and download and install the `Panels` module—it depends on `Chaos tools` in order to function, so make sure that you also get the latest stable copy of that module. Note that for the purposes of our discussion, you will need to enable the `Page manager` module in `Chaos tools` in addition to the default `Panels` and `Chaos tools` module in the **Modules** section.

Before we begin, take special note of the fact that this section is intended as an introduction to Panels. It's a huge subject, so we don't have room to go into everything, but after reading this, you will be able to create some really cool, dynamic pages that integrate with a number of other website features and modules—most importantly, Views.

A basic Panels page

Once the `Panels` module is installed and enabled, it's time to create our first page. Click on **Panels**, under **Structure**, to bring up the following overlay:

Panels

Dashboard Settings

Create new...

Panel page
Panel pages can be used as landing pages. They have a URL path, accept arguments and can have menu entries.
Panel node
Panel nodes are node content and appear in your searches, but are more limited than panel pages.
Mini panel
You must activate the Mini panels module for this functionality.
Mini panels are small content areas exposed as blocks, for when you need to have complex block layouts or layouts within layouts.

Manage mini panels...

You must install and activate the Mini Panels module to manage them.

Manage pages...

Site contact page	Edit	Enable
User contact	Edit	Enable
Node add/edit form	Edit	Enable
Node template	Edit	Enable
Landing page	Edit	Disable
Content	Edit	Enable
Users	Edit	Enable
Taxonomy term template	Edit	Enable
User profile template	Edit	Enable

Go to list

As you can see, there are a few default panels provided already. Any new panels you create will be listed here for convenient moderation. There is also a **Settings** tab that allows you to access the **Panels** configuration, but this doesn't warrant much coverage. The default settings are absolutely fine for practically all of your needs, but feel free to take a quick gaze over them for curiosity's sake.

Now, click on the **Panel page** link in order to start the process of creating a new panel page:

Pages

| List | **Add custom page** | Import page |

Administrative title:

Landing page

The name of this page. This will appear in the administrative interface to easily identify it.

Machine name:

landing

The machine readable name of this page. It must be unique, and it must contain only alphanumeric characters and underscores. Once created, you will not be able to change this value!

Administrative description:

A description of what this page is, does or is for, for administrative use.

Path:

http://localhost/topulous/ index

The URL path to get to this page. You may create named placeholders for variable parts of the path by using %name for required elements and !name for optional elements. For example: "node/%node/foo", "forum/%forum" or "dashboard/!input". These named placeholders can be turned into contexts on the arguments form.

Provide a meaningful **Administrative title** (something that will help you locate this particular panel in the event you end up having a really large list of them) and **Machine name**. It's important to choose a *unique* and *meaningful* **Path** name too. Remember that search engines take a URL into account when ranking a page's keyword importance, so pick something relevant to the panel's content.

If you want the current panel to become the site's home page, enable the **Make this site your home page** box. This will override other settings you might have made in **Site configuration** earlier. The remaining options, **Variant type** and **Optional features**, are not currently relevant and you can always modify them at a later stage, if needed.

Click on the **Continue** button to bring up the layout selection page:

Each option shows how a given page will be divided into the various panes. Remember that this is the macro structure of the page and you will easily be able to add as many or as few pieces of content within each section. Select an option that most closely matches what you have in mind for your content. If, for example, you wanted to show a series of different teasers by topic, then three columns might be suitable. This would display as many bits of content as you like, separated into three columns.

This fundamental layout is important, but it can be edited later on using the full panel page interface. For this example, we are going to be using the first option, **Two column stacked**. Go ahead and make a selection and then click on the **Continue** button. This brings up the **Display settings** editor, as shown in the following screenshot:

From here, we can decide on a **Title** for the page (or no title if you wish) and have an AJAX representation of the layout, as selected in the previous step. As you can see from the preceding screenshot, we have a **Top**, **Left side**, **Right side**, and **Bottom** region to work with content and features. Using this interface allows us to add content and drag it around the page to reorder or place it anywhere we wish within the overall defined layout.

To add content to a pane, click on the gear icon at the top-left of a pane and click on **Add content**, as shown in the following screenshot:

This brings up the content addition overlay that presents options in a nicely categorized list. The default options are as follows:

- **Activity** — adds recent blog posts, comments, who's online, and so on
- **Menus** — allows for insertion of any available menus on the site
- **Miscellaneous** — grab-bag on content, but important because available views can be selected
- **Page elements** — add standard site elements such as mission, status messages, page title, and so on
- **Widgets** — adds elements such as contact forms, user login, and searches
- **Existing node** — directly insert an existing node by referencing its node ID
- **New custom content** — manually insert content or code

To get our first example underway, select the **New custom content** and fill out the page, as shown in the following screenshot:

Administrative title:

Hello world

This title will be used administratively to identify this pane. If blank, the regular title will be used.

Title:

Body:

<h3>Hello world</h3>

▾ Input format

○ Filtered HTML
- Web page addresses and e-mail addresses turn into links automatically.
- Allowed HTML tags: <a> <em> <strong> <cite> <code> <ul> <ol> <li> <dl> <dt> <dd>
- Lines and paragraphs break automatically.

◉ Full HTML
- Web page addresses and e-mail addresses turn into links automatically.
- Lines and paragraphs break automatically.

○ PHP code
- You may post PHP code. You should include <?php ?> tags.

More information about formatting options

Finish

Be sure to select the **Full HTML** text format before clicking on the **Finish** button. This takes us back to the layout builder, with one important difference. The new custom content is now available as a draggable pane in the **Top** region of the page (or in whichever region you have added it):

Pages

| List | **Add custom page** | Import page |

Basic settings » Choose layout » **Panel content**
▼ Display settings

Title type:
Manually set ▾

Title:

The title of this panel. If left blank, a default title may be used. Set to No Title if you want the title to actually be blank.

⚙	Top	
Custom: Hello world *		⚙
▶ No title		
status: changes not saved		

| ⚙ | Left side | | ⚙ | Right side |

| ⚙ | Bottom |

| Back | Finish |

Clicking on the small arrow displayed within the pane displays the content of that pane (if possible). This saves you from having to persistently save and browse the panel each time you want to view the content.

Note that it currently has a warning displayed in red:

Status: changes not saved

Until you click on the **Finish** button and actually save the panel page, nothing is permanently stored. Be wary of this because it is easy to fill out the entire panel page and forget to click on the **Finish** button and go on to save everything.

Left-click on the header bar of the new block and drag into one of the other sections. Any and all the content can be moved around the page in exactly the same way. Return the custom content to the **Top** pane and click on the **Finish** button.

Finally, the full panel page interface is displayed and we now have access not only to the content but also to other settings like **Access**, **Menu**, and **Variants**, as well as **Clone** and **Export** facilities. We'll look at how to utilize many of these features in the following section. For now, click on the **Update and Save** button.

The new panel page is now available at the URL specified at the start of the process—or at the home page, if specified. Navigating to this URL gives us our **Hello world** message (Click on **Summary** at the top of the left-hand column of the panel page interface and then click on the URL link provided in the summary page for quick access).

You should be able to see the simple **Hello world** message on the page. It may not look like much now, but the procedure outlined here is the basis for creating any and all types of panel pages, no matter how complex. Let's take a look at how to create a more interesting panel page by including views and other content, as well as working with some of the native style features.

A more advanced Panels page

Open up the content view of your panel page and remove the **Hello world** block by clicking on the block's gear icon and selecting **Remove** from the bottom of the list:

Let's assume that, for the sake of this example, we wish to create a super cool resources page that will provide a site search form, list some of the FAQs, show a selection of forum postings, and provide a contact form (in case the visitor still can't solve their problem). In order to get a good idea of what this page is going to look like, you will need to quickly do the following before continuing with this example:

- Create a new **FAQ** content type and add a bunch of dummy postings (so that our list of FAQs in the resources panel page has something to display)

- Enable the `Forum` module (if not already) and add a container with some posts (so that our selection of helpful forum postings in the resource panel has something to display)

- Create a basic **FAQ** view that displays a list of titles of the FAQs linked to their nodes (Hint: Filter by **Node Type** and select **FAQ**)

- Create a basic **Forum** view that displays a list of title/teasers of any forum postings (Hint: Filter by **Node: Type** and select **Forum topic**)

With our **FAQ** and **Forum** views saved, they are automatically available to Panels. Go back to the panel page and select **Add content** in the **Top** region, select **Widgets**, and add the **Search form**.

However, one important thing to note is that not all users will initially have sufficient permissions to use this form, so be aware of this if you intend to make something like this available for general use.

Once the changes are saved, click on **Add content** on the **Left side** and then add the **FAQ** view from the **Miscellaneous** category. Do the same for the **Forum** view on the right-hand side of the page. Finally, in the **Bottom** region, add a **Contact form** using the **Widgets** section, so that your page now looks like the following screenshot:

Title type:

Manually set ⌄

Title:

The title of this panel. If left blank, a default title may be used. Set to No Title if you want the title to actually be blank.

Top

Search form ⚙

▶ Search

Left side

teset: FAQ ⚙

▶ No info

Right side

teset: Forum ⚙

▶ No info

Bottom

Contact form ⚙

▶ No info

[Update] [Update and save] [Update and preview]

 Note that it is possible to cause a bit of erratic behavior in Panels if you don't take the time to ensure your administrative titles are filled in and are unique.

Click on the **Update and save** button to finalize the changes and browse to the page. You should now see something like the following when viewing the panel on the site:

Search

[   ] [Search]

Where am I?   You are here
How did I get here?   You walked
Who am I?   On the Internet
Where are we?   You are a Drupal 7 learner

Contact

You can leave a message using the contact form below.

Your name: *

[admin   ]

Your e-mail address: *

[staff@ranktracer.com   ]

Subject: *

[   ]

Message: *

[   ]

☐ Send yourself a copy.

[Send e-mail]

This is a far more dynamic page than any of our previous efforts. The two middle sections will automatically keep themselves up-to-date, because they are part of the views. In the same way, any panel page you add can integrate nicely with any view you can imagine. Think along the lines of presenting dynamic grids of new user profile pictures in a section of the landing page, or the latest blog posts and comments.

As it stands, we have some nice content, but we haven't done much to format it. While individual views can be themed in a variety of ways, Panels also provides us with a number of display features, among other things. Let's take a look at how to enhance this panel page using some of Panels' other features and settings.

Important Panels features and settings

I'm sure you noticed that there is a **Region style: default** link available just beneath the **Add content** link, whenever you click on the gear icon at the top left of a given region. Clicking on this link brings up the following formatting configuration page:

Style:

- ○ List
- ○ No style
- ○ Rounded corners
- ◉ Use display default style

[Next]

Play around with each of these to see the effect they have on the overall region. For example, selecting **Rounded corners** for the **Bottom** region (with the **Box around** config option set to **Each region**) makes the **Contact form** stand out a bit more:

Search

[   ] [Search]

Where am I?   You are here
How did I get here?   You walked
Who am I?   On the Internet
Where are we?   You are a Drupal 7 learner

Contact

You can leave a message using the contact form below.

Your name: *

[admin   ]

Your e-mail address: *

[staff@ranktracer.com   ]

Subject: *

[   ]

Message: *

[   ]
[   ]
[   ]

☐ Send yourself a copy.

[Send e-mail]

In the same way as regions can have basic styles applied, each pane within a region also comes with a set of options, not limited solely to style. Each has a number of categorized options, as shown in the next screenshot:

From here, you can:

- **Disable this pane** — make it unavailable to viewers but not deleted from the panel
- **Settings** — edit the content and other basic settings
- **CSS properties** — apply a CSS class and ID to the pane so that it can be individually styled, or styled as part of a group
- **Style/Change** — apply a basic style in the same way as region styles are applied
- **Visibility rules/Add new rule** — control access to the content by using:
    - **Context exists**
    - **PHP Code**
    - **User: permission**
    - **User: role**
- **Visibility rules/Settings** — specify how the rules applied in the previous option should be implemented:
    - **All criteria must pass.**
    - **Only one criteria must pass.**

- **Caching/Change** — control whether the content presented within this pane should be cached:
  - ° **No caching**
  - ° **Simple cache**

Of particular interest in this list are the last two options — **Visibility rules** and the **Caching**. The **Visibility rules** option makes it possible to control who can access the content of a pane depending on their permissions or more importantly, their role. For example, you might have a **premium members** role that can access a block of content, while any other users may not.

Caching has important performance-related ramifications, so it's a good idea to cache any content that is resource-intensive to prevent Panels from putting undue load on the server.

There is a lot more to panels than what we have covered so far. However, it is easily possible to create some very powerful and dynamic pages using the directions provided in this introduction. It is highly recommended that you continue to play around with the layout builder in order to get a feel for what is available.

Remember that it is also possible to **Clone**, **Export**, **Disable**, and **Delete** panels using the options along the top of the page, and although not discussed here, it's worth exploring the contexts and variants for more advanced usage of panels. For more information, view the documentation provided on the `Panels` module page on the Drupal site.

Additional theming

Recall from the previous two chapters that it is possible to override the default template files in favor of our own template files. In views, we used the theme information to tell us which template filenames the Views system would work on and we then modified one of those. In the theme chapter, we modified the block template file by copying it to our subtheme and making changes.

In this section, we are going to look at how to override the template file for an entire content type. This allows us to create an entirely unique look and feel for any content type we choose. To compliment this theme-related task, we'll follow up with a more detailed example of theming a view.

The goal of this section is to provide the basic features that will be used in the final section of this chapter when we create a unique content review system that relies heavily on views and theming and one or two other neat little tricks.

Theming nodes

Like many things in life and in programming, taking full control over the specific look and feel of any given content type is a breeze, but *only once you know how*. Overriding a content type is a case of saving a suffixed node template file to your `themes` folder.

Before we begin though, we are going to need to do the following:

- Create a new **Review** content type
- Give the **Review** type a mandatory new **Rating** field (you can either use the **Integer** type and configure the minimum to 0 and maximum to 10, or for the more adventurous, try the `Fivestar` (or something similar) module)
- Give the **Review** type a mandatory **Node reference** field, and give it the label **Which article are you reviewing?** *Note that you will have to download the Drupal 7 version of the* **CCK** *module and enable the* **Node reference** *option that comes with the package*
- Specify **Article** in the **Content types that can be referenced Field Setting**, and save the changes

Once you are done, the new content type should look like the following screenshot:

Now that we have a new **Review** content type, navigate to your themes folder and perform the following tasks:

- Make a copy of the node.tpl.php template file in your subtheme's templates folder

- Rename the copy as node--review.tpl.php

Et voila! You have overridden the **Review** content type. Of course, since node--review.tpl.php has not been modified in any way, it doesn't really count.

It's worth re-iterating that this method of modular template files makes for easy development because any changes you make to the new template file are limited only to that particular node type. Also, when it comes time to update a theme, none of the customized template files are affected by a direct extraction of the new theme files to the themes folder.

The limiting factor in terms of what can be accomplished with an overridden template file is your level of experience and skill with PHP, HTML, and CSS. As we have seen before, Drupal template files, in anticipation of being overridden, often present plenty of useful information in the file itself. The node.tpl.php file for the zen theme has this to say (abridged):

```
/**
 * @file
 * Theme implementation to display a node.
 *
 * Available variables:
 * - $title: the (sanitized) title of the node.
 * - $content: An array of node items. Use render($content) to print
     them all,
 *   or print a subset such as render($content['field_example']). Use
 *    hide($content['field_example']) to temporarily suppress the
      printing of a
 *   given element.
 * - $user_picture: The node author's picture from
     user-picture.tpl.php.
 * - $date: Formatted creation date. Preprocess functions can reformat
     it by
 *   calling format_date() with the desired parameters on the $created
     variable.
```

```
* - $name: Themed username of node author output from
*   theme_username().
* - $node_url: Direct url of the current node.
* - $terms: the themed list of taxonomy term links output from
*   theme_links().
* - $display_submitted: whether submission information should be
*   displayed.
* - $classes: String of classes that can be used to style
*   contextually through
*   CSS. It can be manipulated through the variable
*   $classes_array from
*   preprocess functions. The default values can be one or more of the
*   following:
*   - node: The current template type, i.e., "theming hook".
*   - node-[type]: The current node type. For example, if the node is
*     a
*     "Blog entry" it would result in "node-blog". Note that the
*     machine
*     name will often be in a short form of the human readable label.
*   - node-teaser: Nodes in teaser form.
*   - node-preview: Nodes in preview mode.
*   The following are controlled through the node publishing options.
*   - node-promoted: Nodes promoted to the front page.
*   - node-sticky: Nodes ordered above other non-sticky nodes in
*     teaser
*     listings.
```

If you have experience in PHP, then it's worth trying your hand at adding and removing content using the available variables.

For the purposes of this example, we are going to strip down the node template file so that only the title, rating, and review show up. Everything else will be removed. We're doing this because we are going to display the reviews in shadowbox overlays that can be accessed from a node (about which there are reviews) and so don't want to display sidebars and navigation in the overlay page.

To start with, the code (not counting the commented out instructions at the top of the page) in node--review.tpl.php looks like the following (note that this code may differ depending on which theme you are working with):

```php
<div id="node-<?php print $node->nid; ?>" class="<?php print $classes;
?> clearfix"<?php print $attributes; ?>>

  <?php print $user_picture; ?>

  <?php print render($title_prefix); ?>
  <?php if (!$page): ?>
    <h2<?php print $title_attributes; ?>><a href="<?php print $node_
url;
    ?>"><?php print $title; ?></a></h2>
  <?php endif; ?>
  <?php print render($title_suffix); ?>

  <?php if ($unpublished): ?>
    <div class="unpublished"><?php print t('Unpublished'); ?></div>
  <?php endif; ?>

  <?php if ($display_submitted || !empty($content['links']['terms'])):
    ?>
    <div class="meta">
      <?php if ($display_submitted): ?>
        <span class="submitted">
          <?php
            print t('Submitted by !username on !datetime',
              array('!username' => $name, '!datetime' => $date));
          ?>
        </span>
      <?php endif; ?>

      <?php if (!empty($content['links']['terms'])): ?>
        <div class="terms terms-inline"><?php print rend
        er($content['links']['terms']); ?></div>
      <?php endif; ?>
    </div>
  <?php endif; ?>

  <div class="content"<?php print $content_attributes; ?>>
    <?php
```

```
        // We hide the comments and links now so that we can render them
    later.
        hide($content['comments']);
        hide($content['links']);
        print render($content);
    ?>
  </div>

  <?php print render($content['links']); ?>

  <?php print render($content['comments']); ?>

</div>
```

The highlighted `print` statements in the preceding code are responsible for giving us the title and author of the node and the content.

Post a new review using the **Review** content type and view the new page as it stands (remember, you'll need an article posting already on the site in order for it to be referenced in the **Which article are you reviewing** field):

Apart from the highlighted lines in the preceding code, nothing else is really necessary for our purposes—we don't need to show links, comments, or a user picture, so we can comment out the lines responsible for that, like this:

```
<div id="node-<?php print $node->nid; ?>" class="<?php print $classes;
?> clearfix"<?php print $attributes; ?>>

  <?php // print $user_picture; ?>

  <?php print render($title_prefix); ?>
  <?php if (!$page): ?>
    <h2<?php print $title_attributes; ?>><a href="<?php print $node_
url;
    ?>"><?php print $title; ?></a></h2>
  <?php endif; ?>
  <?php print render($title_suffix); ?>

  <?php if ($unpublished): ?>
    <div class="unpublished"><?php print t('Unpublished'); ?></div>
  <?php endif; ?>

  <?php if ($display_submitted || !empty($content['links']['terms'])):
?>
    <div class="meta">
      <?php if ($display_submitted): ?>
        <span class="submitted">
          <?php
            print t('Submitted by !username on !datetime',
              array('!username' => $name, '!datetime' => $date));
          ?>
        </span>
      <?php endif; ?>

      <?php if (!empty($content['links']['terms'])): ?>
        <div class="terms terms-inline"><?php print rend
        er($content['links']['terms']); ?></div>
      <?php endif; ?>
    </div>
  <?php endif; ?>

  <div class="content"<?php print $content_attributes; ?>>
    <?php
```

```
      // We hide the comments and links now so that we can render them
        later.
      hide($content['comments']);
      hide($content['links']);
      print render($content);
    ?>
  </div>

  <?php // print render($content['links']); ?>

  <?php // print render($content['comments']); ?>

</div>
```

After saving these changes, refresh the review page. You should now see something like the following screenshot:

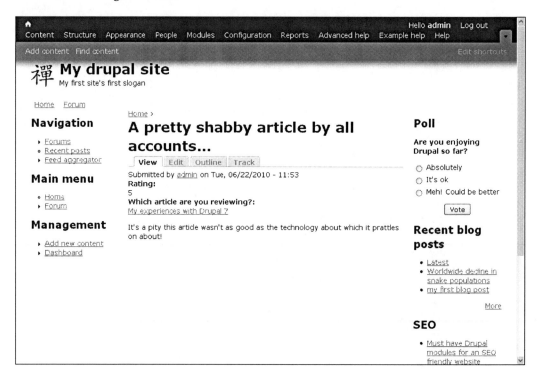

Note that the node-related content below the body of the posting has all vanished as expected—there are no links or comments. If you cannot see any changes, ensure that you have correctly named the template file. You must suffix the node part with the **Machine name** (not the human-readable name of the new content type). The **Machine name** is shown next to the human-readable name in the **Content types** list under **Structure**.

 Remember to rebuild the theme registry before trying to see the changes. You can also disable and re-enable the module just to be certain.

If there is still no change, then clear out your caches (in the **Performance** section of **Configuration**) and retry.

Theming pages

Now for the far more drastic changes! Using the same process for the page template as we did for the node template, make a copy of the `page.tpl.php` file and save it to `page--node--review.tpl.php` in the subtheme's `templates` folder. Then open it up. It should look similar to the following (abridged):

```
<div id="page-wrapper"><div id="page">

  <div id="header"><div class="section clearfix">

    <?php if ($logo): ?>
      <a href="<?php print $front_page; ?>" title="<?php print
t('Home');
        ?>" rel="home" id="logo"><img src="<?php print $logo; ?>"
        alt="<?php print t('Home'); ?>" /></a>
    <?php endif; ?>

    <?php if ($site_name || $site_slogan): ?>
      <div id="name-and-slogan">
        <?php if ($site_name): ?>
          <?php if ($title): ?>
            <div id="site-name"><strong>
              <a href="<?php print $front_page; ?>" title="<?php print
              t('Home'); ?>" rel="home"><span><?php print $site_name;
              ?></span></a>
            </strong></div>
          <?php else: /* Use h1 when the content title is empty */ ?>
```

```
            <h1 id="site-name">
              <a href="<?php print $front_page; ?>" title="<?php print
              t('Home'); ?>" rel="home"><span><?php print $site_name;
              ?></span></a>
            </h1>
          <?php endif; ?>
        <?php endif; ?>

        <?php if ($site_slogan): ?>
          <div id="site-slogan"><?php print $site_slogan; ?></div>
        <?php endif; ?>
      </div> <!-- /#name-and-slogan -->
    <?php endif; ?>

    <?php print render($page['header']); ?>

  </div></div> <!-- /.section, /#header -->

  <div id="main-wrapper"><div id="main" class="clearfix<?php if
($main_menu || $page['navigation']) { print ' with-navigation'; } ?>">

    <div id="content" class="column"><div class="section">
      <?php print render($page['highlight']); ?>
      <?php print $breadcrumb; ?>
      <a name="main-content" id="main-content"></a>
      <?php print render($title_prefix); ?>
      <?php if ($title): ?>
        <h1 class="title" id="page-title"><?php print $title; ?></h1>
      <?php endif; ?>
      <?php print render($title_suffix); ?>
      <?php print $messages; ?>
      <?php if ($tabs): ?>
        <div class="tabs"><?php print render($tabs); ?></div>
      <?php endif; ?>
      <?php print render($page['help']); ?>
      <?php if ($action_links): ?>
        <ul class="action-links"><?php print render($action_links);
        ?></ul>
      <?php endif; ?>
      <?php print render($page['content']); ?>
      <?php print $feed_icons; ?>
    </div></div> <!-- /.section, /#content -->
```

This template file is responsible for adding all the sidebars, navigation, feed icons, and so on. We're going to cut most of it out and present only the title, author, and content of the node. Doing so gives us a file like the following:

```
<div id="page-wrapper"><div id="page">

  <div id="main-wrapper"><div id="main" class="clearfix<?php if
($main_menu || $page['navigation']) { print ' with-navigation'; } ?>">

    <div id="content" class="column"><div class="section">

      <a name="main-content" id="main-content"></a>
      <?php print render($title_prefix); ?>
      <?php if ($title): ?>
        <h1 class="title" id="page-title"><?php print $title; ?></h1>
      <?php endif; ?>
      <?php print render($title_suffix); ?>

      <?php print render($page['content']); ?>

    </div></div> <!-- /.section, /#content -->

  </div></div> <!-- /#main, /#main-wrapper -->

</div></div> <!-- /#page, /#page-wrapper -->
```

As you can see, pretty much everything other than the title and page content `print` functions have been taken out. This is going to give us a pretty sparse page, which is perfect for its intended usage later on:

Again, if you have any trouble viewing the changes, check if the filenames are correct and clear the cache. With the node and page displays for the **Review** content type stripped down, we are ready to put everything together.

Customized content reviews

We're finally ready to start working on a more real-world example that incorporates a range of different skills, features, and modules into one new feature. This example has practical applications for real websites, as it can easily be modified to allow Amazon-style reviews for people setting up e-commerce sites, among other things. In particular, I am referring to the ability to restrict reviews to a specific group of people (for example, only people who have purchased a given product may review it).

This particular functionality does not currently exist in Drupal core or as a contribution, although some of what we create here has overlapping features with the FiveStar voting module.

Here's our brief:
Create a review system that allows people to write a review and rate a given piece of content.

For argument's sake, let's say the **Article** content type is the one that will be reviewed. You could easily modify this to apply to a product or blog. The following is what we have to do in order to achieve it:

- Create a view that displays all the reviews of the current node (assuming it is an article).
- Embed this view into the **article** node. Anyone viewing the article can then browse a list of the reviews that apply to the currently viewed article.
- Theme the view so that the review title links to a shadowbox overlay that displays the themed **Review** content type (which is why we spent so much time stripping out sidebars, headers, and so on in the previous section).

Now, as mentioned, Fivestar can do some of this already. However, this example demonstrates another useful lesson—while there are generally modules available that can do what you need (more or less), it's often possible to get a more flexible and powerful solution by using the basics—panels, views, imagecache, theming, and core features. Because we have the power of views at our fingertips, this example can be modified to restrict reviews in a way that Fivestar can't.

Integrating Shadowbox

It's important to realize that, at the time of writing, no modules existed that could provide us with an out of the box solution to easily create overlaid pages of content. By the time you read this, those modules may well be up and running and you should check the Drupal modules for projects like Shadowbox, Thickbox, Colorbox, and so on.

In many respects, doing things the way we have is a great way to get a bit of additional practice at modifying themes, playing around with new technologies, and drawing on a variety of different software and functionality to achieve our goal. This is great practical experience, even if there may be quicker (but probably less flexible) ways to accomplish the same thing in due course.

To get started, do the following:

- Download the `shadowbox` package from
  `http://www.shadowbox-js.com/download.html`
- Select the standalone option and ensure that the first three checkboxes are selected, as shown in the following screenshot:

- Extract the shadowbox download to your subtheme's `script` folder (`js`)

With these steps complete, we are ready to tell Drupal to include the relevant `.js` file. To do this, open up your theme's `.info` file and reference the `shadowbox.js` file. Depending on which theme you're using, the file will look something like the following:

```
; stylesheets[only screen and (max-device-width: 480px)][] = css/
iphone.css

  ; Set the conditional stylesheets that are processed by IE.
conditional-stylesheets[if IE][all][]        = css/ie.css
conditional-stylesheets[if lte IE 6][all][] = css/ie6.css

  ; Optionally add some JavaScripts to your theme.
; scripts[] = js/script.js

scripts[] = js/shadowbox-3.0.3/shadowbox.js

  ; The regions defined in Zen's default page.tpl.php file.  The name
in
  ; brackets is the name of the variable in the page.tpl.php file,
(e.g.
  ; "[content_top]" in the .info file means there should be a
$content_top
  ; variable in the page.tpl.php file.) The text after the equals sign
is a
  ; descriptive text used on the admin/build/blocks page.
```

Remember to correctly enter the path as it appears on your setup. Before finishing here, it's important to note that, in order for shadowbox to function, it needs to be initialized. To do so, create a new file called `sb-init.js` and include the following line:

```
Shadowbox.init();
```

Save this file to the `js` script directory and reference it from the `.info` file too:

```
scripts[] = js/shadowbox-3.0.3/shadowbox.js
scripts[] = js/sb-init.js
```

Once the changes are saved, the shadowbox functionality is now available to Drupal. Remember to clear out all your caches; otherwise the theme might not pick up the changes for some time. You can confirm that the file is correctly included by looking at the <HEAD> section of your page:

```
⊞ <script src="http://localhost/drupal/modules/contextual
   /contextual.js?v=1.0" type="text/javascript">
⊞ <script src="http://localhost/drupal
   /misc/jquery.cookie.js?l4esor" type="text/javascript">
⊞ <script src="http://localhost/drupal/modules/toolbar
   /toolbar.js?l4esor" type="text/javascript">
⊞ <script src="http://localhost/drupal/sites/all/themes/drupalbook
   /js/shadowbox-3.0.3/shadowbox.js?l4esor" type="text/javascript">
⊟ <script src="http://localhost/drupal/sites/all/themes/drupalbook/js/sb-
   init.js?l4esor" type="text/javascript">
     1   Shadowbox.init();
   </script>
⊞ <script type="text/javascript">
</head>
```

That's all there is to it. We can now turn our attention to building and theming the view that will present the lists of reviews with the shadowbox enhancement.

Creating the article reviews view

Recall that during the creation of our **Review** content type, we added a mandatory node reference field called **Which article are you reviewing**. This field is going to play a critical role in how we display only the reviews that apply to the current article and will also be a great demonstration of how to use relationships and arguments (well, default arguments anyway).

If you haven't already, create a few dummy articles and then write a few dummy reviews about them, just so that the view will have something to display. If you don't do this, there's no way you can test whether or not the review is working correctly, since there will be no reviews to return in the first place.

Let's begin:

1. Create an **Article_reviews** view

2. In the default view, add a **Filter** by **Node: Type** and select **Review**:

3. Add **Node: Title** (don't link the title to its node, we are going to do this by modifying the template files) and **Fields: field_rating**

4. Add the **Node: path** field but exclude it from the display—we are simply going to make use of this data, but we don't want users to be able to see it. Check the final option—**Use absolute link**

5. Add the **Which article are you reviewing** relationship in the **Relationships category**

6. Set a **Node: ID Argument** and specify the newly created relationship

7. Select the **Provide default argument option** and set the **Default argument type** to **Node ID from URL**:

○ Summary, sorted by number of records ascending
○ Summary, sorted by number of records descending
◉ Provide default argument

Provide default argument options

Default argument type
○ Fixed entry
◉ Node ID from URL
○ PHP Code
○ User ID from URL
○ User ID from logged in user

8. Add a new **Page** display called **Article reviews** and give it the path **article-reviews**

We have told Views to go look for reviews that relate to the node ID of the current page using the **Which article are you reviewing** relationship. In effect, we are settings things up so that when a visitor looks at an article, the view will return all the associated reviews by getting the Node ID from the URL and working back using the specified relationship.

To prevent unforeseen problems, it's also a good idea to do a bit of validation. In this case, we want the validator to ensure that we are looking at an article node type (because reviews only apply to articles). Go back to the **Node: Nid** argument and change the **Validator** settings, as shown in the following screenshot:

If the validation fails (in other words, if the visitor is not looking at an article node), we should simply hide the view (in the section entitled **Action to take if argument does not validate** further down the page) as it wouldn't return anything anyway. You might think this is redundant as the view will only be embedded within the article node anyway. That's not quite true, because article nodes can get returned as a part of taxonomy lists (among other things), causing the **Node ID** argument to fail.

You might want to do a bit of formatting work, but the meat of the work is done now. Save the changes and then let's move on to the real magic.

Theming the view

As you know, it is quite possible to theme pretty much any part of a view. In this particular case, we need to modify the view so that each review title from the list of results presents a shadowbox-enhanced link to the review itself. This is one of those cases where it's simply not possible to rely on CSS and HTML alone. We've actually got to gain access to the underlying PHP data.

In the **Article review** display, click on **Theme: Information** and go the **Row style output** section (make sure you change the theme to the one you are using):

Help Article reviews: Theming information

This section lists all possible templates for the display plugin and for the style plugins, ordered roughly from the least specific to the most specific. The active template for each plugin -- which is the most specific template found on the system -- is highlighted in bold.

drupalbook   [Change theme]

- Display output: **views-view.tpl.php**, views-view--article-reviews.tpl.php, views-view--page.tpl.php, views-view--article-reviews--page.tpl.php, views-view--.tpl.php, views-view--page-1.tpl.php, views-view--article-reviews--page-1.tpl.php
- Style output: **views-view-unformatted.tpl.php**, views-view-unformatted--article-reviews.tpl.php, views-view-unformatted--page.tpl.php, views-view-unformatted--article-reviews--page.tpl.php, views-view-unformatted--.tpl.php, views-view-unformatted--page-1.tpl.php, views-view-unformatted--article-reviews--page-1.tpl.php
- Row style output: **views-view-fields.tpl.php**, views-view-fields--article-reviews.tpl.php, views-view-fields--page.tpl.php, views-view-fields--article-reviews--page.tpl.php, views-view-fields--.tpl.php, views-view-fields--page-1.tpl.php, views-view-fields--article-reviews--page-1.tpl.php
- Field Node: Title (ID: title): **views-view-field.tpl.php**, views-view-field--title.tpl.php, views-view-field--article-reviews.tpl.php, views-view-field--article-reviews--title.tpl.php, views-view-field--page.tpl.php, views-view-field--page--title.tpl.php, views-view-field--article-reviews--page.tpl.php, views-view-field--article-reviews--page--title.tpl.php, views-view-field--page-1.tpl.php, views-view-field--page-1--title.tpl.php, views-view-field--article-reviews--page-1.tpl.php, views-view-field--article-reviews--page-1--title.tpl.php

---

Currently, `views-view-fields.tpl.php` is being used, so we need to copy that file from the `views/theme` folder to our `templates` directory and rename it to one of the other available names—`views-view-fields--article-reviews.tpl.php` is perfect for our purposes.

Open the file for editing; you should have something like the following:

```php
<?php foreach ($fields as $id => $field): ?>
  <?php if (!empty($field->separator)): ?>
    <?php print $field->separator; ?>
  <?php endif; ?>

  <<?php print $field->inline_html;?> class="views-field-<?php print $field->class; ?>">
    <?php if ($field->label): ?>
      <label class="views-label-<?php print $field->class; ?>">
        <?php print $field->label; ?>:
      </label>
    <?php endif; ?>
```

```
<?php
// $field->element_type is either SPAN or DIV depending upon
   whether  or not
// the field is a 'block' element type or 'inline' element type.
?>
<<?php print $field->element_type; ?> class="field-
content"><?php
     print $field->content; ?></<?php print $field->element_type;
?>>
  </<?php print $field->inline_html;?>>
<?php endforeach; ?>
```

The part that really interests us is right at the bottom where the content of each field is printed out:

```
<?php print $field->content; ?>
```

We need to determine when the **Title** field is being printed out and wrap it within a shadowbox link (using the **Path** field that we included in our results). So, instead of the normal title output looking like this:

```
<div class="views-field-title">
  <span class="field-content">this is my review</span>
</div>
```

We want it to look like the following:

```
<div class="views-field-title">
  <span class="field-content">
<a href="path/to/node" rel="shadowbox[Mixed];width=800;height=600"
>this is my review</a>
  </span>
</div>
```

By adding the `rel` attribute and specifying `shadowbox[Mixed];width=800;height` `=600` in the link, we are instructing shadowbox to act on it by creating an overlay 800 px by 600 px in dimension.

In order to correctly inject this link, we need to use a bit of PHP to decide when to add the shadowbox link and which path to use for that link. We can work out how to do this by analyzing how the template file works in the first place. In particular, the first line:

```
foreach ($fields as $id => $field)
```

tells us that it is iterating through each field one at a time in order to display them. Using this knowledge, and the fact that the `foreach` loop advances an array's internal pointer during every iteration, we can replace the statement that reads:

```php
<?php print $field->content; ?>
```

To the following:

```php
<?php

        if($id == 'title'){
            print '<a href="';
            print $fields['path']->content;
            print '" rel="shadowbox[Mixed];width=800;height=600">';
            print $field->content;
            print '</a>';
        }else{
    print $field->content;
        }

    ?>
```

The preceding code basically says that whenever we are about to print out the contents of the title field, we should wrap it within an anchor element and use the contents of the `path` field to get the correct link. Note that we *can* directly use `path`, because we set it to be an absolute URL, which prevents potentially broken relative path links.

With those changes saved, we are finally ready to put together all the pieces by embedding this view within the **articles** node.

Embedding the View

You are already familiar with the process of overriding template files for specific nodes, so go ahead and create a `node--article.tpl.php` file in your theme folder and open it up for editing.

The process of embedding a view is fairly straightforward, but does require the use of PHP. For the sake of this example, we are going to add the view to the bottom of the page so that the list of reviews doesn't get in the way of the content itself.

Scroll to the bottom of the file and make the changes, as shown as follows:

```php
</div>

<?php print render($content['links']); ?>

<?php print render($content['comments']); ?>
```

```
<div class="article-review-list">
 <?php
    print views_embed_view('Article_reviews', 'page_1');
 ?>
</div>

</div> <!-- /.node -->
```

Note that we have wrapped the new view within a `<div>` and given it a class in order to provide some control over how it is styled. Next, we use PHP to fetch the relevant view, `Article_reviews`, and then display the correct page, `page_1` (Note that this should reflect the **Machine name** of the display you want to access).

Save the changes and then browse to an article page that has a review or two. You should see something similar to the following screenshot:

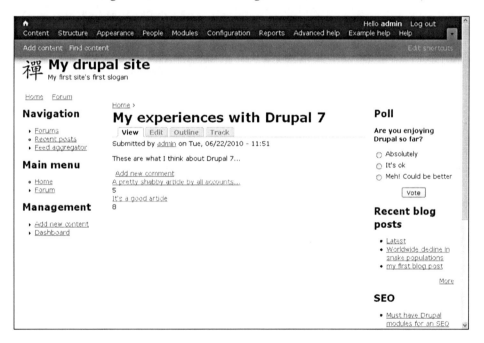

Notice that now there are two article reviews shown below the body of this article—accompanied by their rating value. Ok, it's pretty plain, because we haven't done much styling. We would suffix the rating with something like "*out of 10 stars*" to give it a bit more meaning—whatever you like. Clicking on a link will bring up the review itself in a shadowbox overlay so that the user can browse through the list of review titles and select the ones they would like to read in full, without ever having to leave the article itself.

That's it. Hopefully you've enjoyed creating something fairly new. Remember that having built this to apply to articles is exactly the same as applying this to products. You could also take things further by creating more views that aggregate rating information to display an average rating at the top of the review list—possibly in an attachment display.

It's important to note that changes to Drupal, Views, CCK, Shadowbox, and any other software and scripts used in this more technical example might mean that you need to make changes to the procedure or possibly even the code itself.

Summary

Drupal makes it easy to achieve most of the day-to-day requirements of a website. The past nine chapters have each covered specific topics more or less in isolation. This chapter took a big leap forward by demonstrating how we can create more sophisticated features by combining a range of technologies, modules, and software to create something entirely new.

Initially, we laid the groundwork by showing how panels can be used to combine different combinations of views, widgets, and other content into one themable page. This is an important part of making complex pages. Look at some of the Internet's big, successful websites, and you'll notice that they don't often leave individual site features in isolation. For example, a login page can also be combined with other content, FAQs, special offers, and so on. For mixing and matching, you can't beat Panels.

Having seen that previously, distinct parts of Drupal can be combined using Panels, we then undertook a more advanced task that highlighted a range of skills—theming for nodes and pages, views with arguments and relationships, integrating third party scripts for shadowbox overlays—that could be combined to produce an entirely unique, flexible, and powerful review feature.

The procedure we highlighted to present article reviews can be modified in any number of ways. For example, if you decide to sell products or services, consider downloading the UberCart module and then use what we learned here to provide a review system for customers to use.

At this point, we have reached the end of the development phase of the book. The final chapter focuses on how to manage and maintain a site.

Keep going; there's light at the end of the tunnel!

11
Deployment and Management

By now, the majority of the development for the new site is complete. You should also feel confident that, from a development perspective, you can respond to whatever demands the site throws at you and operate Drupal with proficiency – although the site still has to go live.

One of the problems with presenting a chapter like this is that we can't possibly hope to cover each and every nuance of the huge array of different platforms on which Drupal can be deployed and run. Internet Service Providers (ISPs) offer wildly varying packages that are either totally bereft of any type of helpful functionality or packed full with all the latest gadgets.

As a result, we will look at the functionality that is in common use. In the event you do not have access to the same software, the text will clearly demonstrate the tasks you need to perform. Hopefully, you can still successfully operate with the software *you do have access to*. For example, by using XAMPP, we already have certain technologies that we can make use of on the development machine such as phpMyAdmin.

 It may be helpful to read through this chapter before selecting a hosting package (assuming you haven't already) in order to get a feel for the type of functionality that may prove to be useful.

Once the site is deployed, there are also a few other web-related activities inherent to Drupal that we should take the time to look over quickly. As a result, this chapter will talk about:

- Deployment
- Backups
- Website activities—including paths, XML sitemaps, and user maintenance
- Updates

Armed with the information presented in this final chapter, you will be a well-equipped Drupal website administrator operating a live website. Ultimately, the experience gained from running a live website in itself should prove to be far more valuable than this book. Hopefully, you will find the entire experience richly rewarding and share your hard-won knowledge with the rest of the community in the future.

We're on the home stretch...

Deployment

While it is not a huge problem to make modifications to a site after deployment, there is no point in making things difficult by having to recode some pages or make design changes later, when you can get them done now.

Here is a checklist to use in order to ensure that, from a user's point of view, the site works nicely:

Use at least two different browsers.	One browser may implement some features that others do not—you might find that something you rely on heavily works on your browser of choice but not on others. Use at least Firefox and IE.	[ ]
Resize your browsers for a variety of pages.	This helps to determine whether you have HTML elements that have not been set correctly. For example, some sections may use the full page width, while others expand only to a certain limit.	[ ]
Access pages from slow as well as fast connections.	You might find that certain pages load very slowly over a dial-up connection. This might mean you need to rethink image and page sizes.	[ ]

Check all links – text and image.	Often, links break during deployment because of differing file paths or file permissions. You should:
	
	  • Check all links and buttons on each page
	  • Check all links in blocks
	  • Check that large as well as small images display appropriately
	  • Check that any ads link correctly
		[ ]

Check each page's look.	This is important, because not all browsers can render certain style sheet settings.	[ ]

Use each page.	This is vital for ensuring that users can:
	
	  • Register accounts
	  • Manage their accounts
	  • Add content depending on permissions
	  • Correctly access content depending on their roles
	  • Make use of all the site's facilities
	
	Ensure that:
	
	  • The search engine works correctly
	  • Contact e-mails can be sent properly
	  • Privacy and conditions of use are shown along with any important copyright information
		[ ]

Try to break the site (as a restricted user, of course).	Just as important as ensuring that everything works properly (if not more important), is ensuring that nothing can be broken at will.	[ ]

If you can perform everything listed in this checklist with several browsers, with no problems, then you can be reasonably certain that the site will hold up when it goes live. If everything looks good, you can begin with the preparation process. In no particular order, ensure that there is:

- A full copy of the site
- A copy of the database
- A file system and database on the live server

Let's take a look at how this is done.

The live server

Your web server needs to have a MySQL database and sufficient space to hold all the Drupal files. It should also have some sort of administrative panel that gives you convenient access to the various facilities that are available on the website (such as logs and error reports, FTP, database administration, e-mail facilities, security, and more).

The best, in my opinion, is cPanel, which provides a comprehensive administration center that uses advanced web 2.0 features to make your job a lot easier than some of the more basic admin panels out there:

One example of this is cPanel's drag-and-drop file management interface, which is far quicker and more convenient than other server administration software that requires a page refresh each time a file is copied or moved—often, you can only move one file around at a time, which is tedious, to say the least.

In order to transfer files across to the live server you can use either FTP or the server's native file handling software that will come with an upload option. If you don't have access to an FTP account, then don't panic—it will still be easy to upload your files to the host site. However, no FTP account may be an indication of a poor service, so be careful to ensure that everything else required is available.

Take a look at the administrative interface and see if there is a section for creating and controlling MySQL databases (hopefully, phpMyAdmin is available). For example, the demo site's host has the following **Manage Mysql** link in the **Databases** section that provides an interface used to create databases. It also provides phpMyAdmin in order to administer those databases:

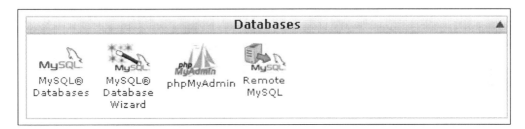

After ensuring the live server has the facilities you need, it's time to begin the process of preparing your development site for transfer.

Preparing for deployment

Before transferring anything, make a master copy of the site. Zip up and store the exact version of the Drupal directory that you send across.

> At the moment, the target URL for the Drupal index page will be something like http://www.domain_name.com/drupal/. If you want it to be http://www.domain_name.com/, then zip the files without the parent directory so that files are extracted directly to the public_html folder on the live site.

While we are on the subject, you may also clean up the Drupal file system properly, so that you don't end up saving and transferring erroneous files.

Access your site from a browser and perform the following five important tasks:

1. *Disable all caching and clear all caches*—hopefully, these haven't been enabled during development anyway.

2. *Disable clean URLs*—in case the new server isn't set up correctly. You can enable it later.

3. *Set any logging options (such as database logging) to small values and run cron*—to clear out old log files that are no longer needed and cut down on the transfer size of the database.

4. *Remove redundant posts*—try not to transfer over a whole lot of stuff that will be deleted anyway.

5. *Clear out unused images and other files*

While it might seem a bit excessive to do all this at the moment, there are a couple of good reasons for it. Firstly, having any sort of unused files lying around on your host file system is a poor security practice. Secondly, why clutter up a brand-new installation with caches and files you don't need? Working on a lot of files over the course of the development phase, adding and removing functionality, and so on, adds a lot of unnecessary size to the upload, if you don't trim away what isn't needed.

Now, open up the configuration file, `sites/default/settings.php`, and remove the username and password from the `$databases` array. For example:

```
$databases = array (
  'default' =>
  array (
    'default' =>
    array (
      'driver' => 'mysql',
      'database' => 'drupal',
      'username' => 'drupaluser',
      'password' => 'drupalpassword',
      'host' => 'localhost',
      'port' => '',
    ),
  ),
);
```

Should be changed to:

```
$databases = array (
  'default' =>
  array (
    'default' =>
    array (
      'driver' => 'mysql',
      'database' => '',
      'username' => '',
      'password' => '',
      'host' => 'localhost',
      'port' => '',
    ),
  ),
);
```

The current database name and password will change to the ones set when you create a new database on the host, but there is no point in transferring any type of sensitive information like this—especially because people often prefer to use the same username and password for a variety of things.

Once this is done you can then make a master, zipped copy of your Drupal site—call it RTP (Release to Public), or something similar, to distinguish it from other versions. If you don't have a zip facility, consider downloading something like 7-Zip (`http://7-zip.org`)—which is a free utility that will get the job done easily.

Deploying the site

Assuming there are images and a fair bit of data held within the site, you can be sure that the size of the upload is quite substantial. For this reason, you need a reasonably high speed connection—dial-up connections can be slightly erratic over a long period of time.

By far, the easiest method would be to use a native upload feature from the host's file manager over a quick connection. If this is available, simply use it to upload the archive file across to the host server. The demo site has this facility, as shown in the next screenshot:

Notice that the file is being uploaded to the `public_html` folder, because this is the document root from which all web pages on this server are served.

Alternatively, assuming your site has an FTP account enabled, either attempt to use FTP's drag-and-drop facility, which is exactly the same as moving files around on your PC in Windows or make use of an FTP utility.

When in doubt, simply get in touch with your host service and ask them for information about how to transfer files. The administrative interface and file manager for the vast majority of the sites are easy to use, and you will have no problems uploading the files. Because of this, we won't waste time discussing FTP utilities in detail. Simply ensure that, ultimately, the ZIP or gzip file ends up in the document root of your host's server.

Remember not to leave the ZIP folder lying around in the document root once it has been extracted and the site is installed. Delete it as soon as it is no longer needed.

Extract the archive file to the public_html folder—a good web server package will include zip facilities that will handle .zip and .tar.gz files. With these files extracted, there is now a replica of the files from the development machine on the live server.

Next, set up the database using the database handling facilities on your server. Make sure that you assign the new database a user.

Drupal needs almost all the privileges available to its database user. Ensure that you grant **ALL** privileges, otherwise there may be problems down the line.

It's important that you take careful note of the database, username, and the password you specify, as these are required to correctly configure Drupal a bit later on.

In particular, be aware that live servers often prefix database names with a unique identifier. So, if you called a database drupal, the actual name might end up as something like wwwdr_drupal. The database interface will clearly display the database and usernames for you to see after the creation.

With a new database available for use on the live server, it's time to populate it with the data from the development site. For that, we need a database backup and you will need to skip ahead to the section on *Backups* (since regular backups are part and parcel of good website maintenance) later in this chapter, if you are unfamiliar with how to make a database backup.

With access to a copy of the database, go to phpMyAdmin on the live server (if you don't have access to phpMyAdmin, contact your service provider and find out how you can import the database), and follow along:

1. In the left-hand panel on the phpMyAdmin home page, click on the name of the database you have just created.

2. In the new page that opens up, click on the **Import** tab along the top of the page.

3. Click on the **Browse** button for the **Location of the text file** option.

4. Locate the database backup file you want to import and click on the **Go** button, as shown in the following screenshot:

Assuming the file executes successfully, you can now take a look through phpMyAdmin to ensure that the live server's database has got the same tables and data as the development server's database.

In the event that something goes wrong, ensure that the backup file was created with **utf8** encoding and that the version of MySQL being used is sufficient for Drupal 7 (discussed in the **Requirements** section of INSTALL.txt within the Drupal download).

Configuring the site

With the database in place, go back to the settings.php file in the sites/default/ folder *on the live site* and alter it according to the live system's setup—ensure that you add precisely the names and passwords required by your *live database* to $databases.

> File permissions on the live filesystem may prevent you from accessing settings.php initially. Take note of the permission settings before altering them to allow you to edit its information. As soon as you are done, return the permission settings to their original state—to prevent others from writing to the file.

Once the configuration settings are set appropriately, try browsing some pages. With a bit of luck, you will see everything more or less as it was on the development machine.

Access problem?

Try to log into the administrator's account. I suspect that more than a few of you will come across a somewhat nasty surprise in that the browser will, no doubt, tell you that it cannot find the page you are looking for. If this is the case, it is more than likely because the .htaccess file was not successfully ported to the live site.

> You must ensure that Drupal's .htaccess file is present on the live site. .htaccess in the Drupal parent folder contains instructions and information vital to the healthy operation of the site.

When viewing the contents of .htaccess file on the live site (most likely in the document root depending on how the things are set up), you should see something like the following:

```
#
# Apache/PHP/Drupal settings:
#

# Protect files and directories from prying eyes.
<FilesMatch "\.(engine|inc|info|install|make|module|p
rofile|test|po|sh|.*sql|theme|tpl(\.php)?|xtmpl)$|^(\
..*|Entries.*|Repository|Root|Tag|Template)$">
  Order allow,deny
</FilesMatch>
```

```
# Don't show directory listings for URLs which map to a directory.
Options -Indexes

# Follow symbolic links in this directory.
Options +FollowSymLinks

# Make Drupal handle any 404 errors.
ErrorDocument 404 /index.php

# Force simple error message for requests for non-existent favicon.
ico.
<Files favicon.ico>
   # There is no end quote below, for compatibility with Apache 1.3.
   ErrorDocument 404 "The requested file favicon.ico was not found.
</Files>

# Set the default handler.
DirectoryIndex index.php index.html index.htm
```

If the file is absent or is blank, then copy and paste the contents of the development server's .htaccess file to the live site's .htaccess file. This should resolve the problem and you should now be able to browse the live site's pages.

Filesystem settings

Recall from *Chapter 3, Configuration and Reports* that in order to correctly access and store files, it was necessary for us to set certain file paths. It may be that these file paths are no longer valid on the live server (depending on what you originally specified), and, more likely, certain folders are no longer writable on the live server—for security reasons, new folders created on a Linux server are generally not writable, even though Drupal requires them to be in order to function.

If you find that you start receiving warnings about being unable to access or overwrite files (often images used by Drupal's native image handling), then it is likely that file system permissions are the problem. To resolve this matter, view the warnings, which will indicate the culprit folders and modify their permissions using cPanel's (or whichever file manager is relevant for you) file manager.

Which reminds me:

 If you are receiving warnings printed on the screen, remember to disable them at **Logging and errors** in the **DEVELOPMENT** section of the **Configuration** overlay. Otherwise, systems errors and warnings can be used by hackers for malicious purposes.

Now, all that's left is to test out the site in its entirety. In particular, ensure that the site's administration features all work correctly. It's a good idea to redo the *site checklist*, shown earlier in the chapter, to confirm that users will not encounter any problems when browsing.

Often, users will find that they encounter problems and providing a webmaster's e-mail address is a good way to let them complain if they do. Open lines of communication between you and your users will help foster strong ties and improve the quality of your site—consider using the `Feedback` module for this purpose.

Backups

There are plenty of reasons to make backups of both the filesystem and database. As mentioned several times throughout the course of the book, always back up anything that is at risk of being damaged, whenever you modify code, add a new module, or even implement upgrades. It sounds like a real pain to do this because the majority of the time, nothing goes wrong with the application. Sooner or later though, for some unfathomable reason, if you don't make backups, you *will* get stung in precisely the most painful spot!

Especially, corrupting or breaking a database, which in turn leads to a loss of precious data, can be a real pain in the backend of your application. So, while it is fairly easy to back up the files on the filesystem by making copies of the directories in question, or indeed, by copying the entire `drupal` folder (whatever you have named it), it is of paramount importance that you learn how to back up the database too.

It is a good idea to back up the entire site at fairly regular intervals, as well as backing up the database more frequently. These backups should be clearly marked, so that you know when they were made, making it easy to determine the correct one to use in the event of some sort of disaster. You might also consider holding these backups away from the main filesystem, perhaps on a CD or remote backup server, so that you don't have to rely on your host's disaster-recovery policy—you have your own.

As mentioned, most good hosts provide software such as cPanel to help administer your site. A standard cPanel administration page looks similar to the following screenshot:

Notice that a few options (bottom section) provide backup facilities. Clicking on the **Backups** link brings up the following page that can be used to back up not only the database, but all the files along with any other important bits of information about your filesystem:

The backups are generated and stored on the host server to download or use whenever you wish. Remember that it is prudent to transfer a full site backup over a secure connection, in case the transfer is eavesdropped. In addition to this standard facility, hosts often provide a regular backup service to a remote server. However, this service will often be subject to charges.

More often than not, it is the data in the database that needs to be regularly backed up instead of the whole site, and luckily there is a very simple contribution designed for precisely this purpose—the Backup and Migrate module.

Head over to the Drupal site and download, install, and enable the latest version of Backup and Migrate. This will provide you with the facilities to make *regular scheduled backups* and maintain a log of as many recent backups as you deem appropriate using the **BACKUP** page:

This module also comes with the ability to manually backup/export the database or even import/restore a database. It's easy enough to learn your way around by playing with it. Be warned: make sure that you create a separate backup of any valuable data *before* playing with this module in case you inadvertently import bad data and lose what you already have.

Website activities

There are plenty of different tasks that still lie ahead. For example, are you sure that malicious people out there can't hotlink to your site and chew bandwidth? *What is hotlinking? What is bandwidth?* These questions constitute only a very small part of the types of concerns that must take focus once development is completed.

While the subject of this book is to *build a site*, this task is only one side of the coin. As we saw earlier in the section on *Backups*, hosts often provide a standard administration interface such as cPanel or Plesk, and it is recommended that you spend some time finding out what is available for use and how to use it. Knowing what is available is important because it means you are better able to plan *how you work*.

Another important thing to note here is that most hosting services will offer a full array of statistics for your website—information like where people have come from, how many accessed the site, which pages are being accessed, and so on. Drupal comes with modules that do pretty much the same thing, so check to see whether the site's native statistics are sufficient or whether you need to consider installing a new module—like Google Analytics.

There are other matters that relate more closely to Drupal itself that become very important for a live website.

Path and Pathauto

By default, Drupal labels pages by number (specifically, their node ID)—for example, `http://www.mydrupalsite.com/node/25`. This is not particularly descriptive to either humans or search engines, so the `Path` module ships with the Drupal core as a way to provide meaningful aliases for content. Providing relevant aliases (in other words, a descriptive phrase that describes the content) can be a real benefit when it is time for Google to rank your pages.

Head over to the **Modules** section and enable **Path**. This will create a new **URL aliases** page under **SEARCH AND METADATA** on the **Configuration** overlay that contains a list of current aliases and an **Add alias** link. Initially, there will be no aliases present, so the list is not too interesting. The **Add aliases** form looks like this:

Let's say that `node 29` (from the previous screenshot) contains information about a **pride of lions**. Then the alias provided, `pride-lions`, is clearly a good one both in terms of being descriptive of the content and in terms of being a relevant keyword because the term **pride of lions** appears in the content of this post several times (for argument's sake).

Notice too that aliases can be applied to pretty much any type of page — including forums and taxonomy term pages. If, for example, you want to show a page that contains all the posts tagged with **conservation** and **wildlife** (let's say these are taxonomy terms 2 and 7) but provide it with a user-friendly name (perhaps because it will be a prominent page accessed from the navigation), you would specify `taxonomy/term/2+7` as the existing path and provide a suitable alias, perhaps `wildlife-conservation`.

 It is far easier for users to find a page called `wildlife-conservation` than to try remembering the taxonomy values of each of the terms.

Take heed of the fact that selecting a **Language** (assuming you have a need for multiple languages and have enabled the `Locale` core module first) means that the alias provided will apply only to that language's content. In other words, aliases should be provided for each individual language or left as is to apply to all of them at once.

It is also important to note that while it is possible to give the same node multiple aliases, for example, assigning `node/25` the alias `lions` and `kingofthejungle`, this should be avoided because search engines take a dim view of this practice and may drop page rankings accordingly. The reason being that malicious webmasters could write a single page and copy it a million times to slightly different URLs — to give the impression that they are important producers of content for that topic, when in fact they are not.

The interface here should be quite intuitive for you now — aliases are listed at the bottom of the page with the option to **edit** or **delete** each one. A **FILTER ALIASES** box is also provided to reduce the number of visible aliases to only those that you are interested in. For example, entering **lions** in the **FILTER ALIASES** box returns the one result, while entering **tigers** returns an empty set.

It should be noted that aliases don't have to be single words — multiple words and relative paths are often more intuitive. It's very useful to be able to use aliases like `cats/lions` rather than just `lions`. Also, `king-of-the-jungle` is better than `kingofthejungle` for both readers and SEO.

Ideally, all content should be provided with a path alias right from the start. Path does provide the option to add an alias during node creation, but why should we manually fill this out each time when we can have Drupal do it for us? Consider automating the process with the Pathauto module.

To see it in action, download the Token module (required by Pathauto) along with Pathauto module. Install and enable the Token module and then do the same for Pathauto. With Pathauto enabled, revisit the **Add aliases** form:

Note that there is now a list of tabs along the top of the overlay that allows us to configure how Drupal generates aliases for our content. The **PATTERNS** tab allows you to decide on the default path formats for a range of different data types:

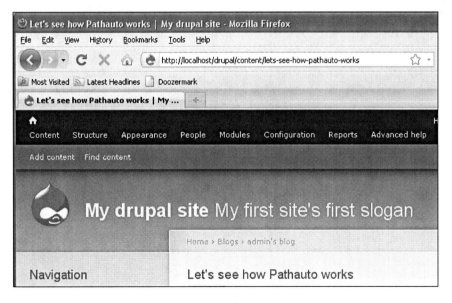

The default patterns provided are all very sensible, but if you want to change them, take a look at the **REPLACEMENT PATTERNS** for each path in order to see what tokens are available for you to use.

Posting a blog with nothing altered shows that an alias has been automatically generated from the blog title (**Let's see how pathauto works**):

`Pathauto` doesn't force you to automatically generate an alias—users still have the power to specify their own ones, if necessary, by scrolling down the content creation page and disabling the **Automatic alias** option before entering a new alias in the **URL path settings** section:

Head over to the **SETTINGS** tab in the **URL aliases** overlay. Without boring you too much with the vast array of settings to consider, it's worth looking at the two main sections:

- **GENERAL SETTINGS**—Use this section to specify generic properties of path aliases. Settings such as maximum and minimum alias lengths, word separator character, update actions, and strings to remove are all provided here.

- **PUNCTUATION**—Instruct `Pathauto` to handle any non-alphanumeric characters in a number of ways. By default, characters such as braces, brackets, and quotes are all removed, but they can be replaced by a separator or left as it is.

Search engine optimization and website promotion

One of the most common goals for a website is to appear high up on the big search engine rankings. As you should know, having a good ranking increases the chances of potential users finding your site among the mass of other sites. *So what can be done to rank as highly as possible without actually having to pay anyone?*

There is no straight answer to this, unfortunately. However, there is a core set of tasks you can take up that *should* help—they might vary in importance, but it is probably worth performing all of them:

Optimization	Explanation
Write web-enhanced copy	Admittedly, you cannot control the content of other people's comments and pages, but this would still apply to any and all standard pages or articles you write—including your personal blog.
	Make the content of these pages clear and concise (so that people can read them quickly), and ensure that you use the relevant keywords that you would like to see showing up in the searches where appropriate.
Use meaningful path names	It certainly helps to have everything named meaningfully, not least because search engines do look at filenames. Instead of naming a page 19, give it something appropriate like expert-opinion.
	Path and Pathauto, discussed earlier, help in this regard.
Use meaningful anchor text	IMPORTANT: Search engines in particular Google, place a large amount of emphasis on the anchor text used in links. Make sure all your links have meaningful text associated with them. For example, you could rewrite the following sentence:
	`Donate to the Wildlife community <a href ="<yourlink>">here</a>.`
	to:
	`Donate to the <a href ="<yourlink>">Wildlife community</a> here.`
	The reason for this is that the word **here** is not particularly meaningful to a search engine, even though humans can easily make the connection. For the sake of your rankings, simply move the link to the key phrase **Wildlife community** to place more emphasis on it for the search engine.

Optimization	Explanation
Manage links	A high level of importance is placed on the perceived popularity of a website. Search engines can judge the popularity of a website by looking at how many incoming and mutual links are there to the site – as well as how popular the linked sites are.
	For this reason, you should ensure that you link only to the sites that you feel are suitable partners – don't be fooled by offers to buy millions of incoming links because these generally use poor quality sites that are not highly rated. This can actually damage your perceived popularity by Google.
	Effectively, you should search for as many relevant link pages as possible, or actually speak to the relevant sites to determine whether you can provide mutual links. The more links you have from popular sites, the better your ranking will be. You can also try to get one-way links to your site – these are also rated highly by search engines.
Write meaningful alt tags for images	Search engines don't see pictures like humans do, but they still try to glean information about them. Give them meaningful names and ensure that you enable the **Title** and **Alt** fields, as discussed in *Chapter 7, Multimedia*.
Submit to search engines and online directories	Make sure your site is listed wherever it is relevant. Some hosting packages provide an automated SE-submission facility, which will automatically forward your site to search engines for indexing.
Read up and contribute to lists, forums, and online tutorials	There is a lot of helpful information out there. Do some research and come up with an SEO policy that is right for you.
Good meta keywords and descriptions	Google often uses the meta description of a web page as the text in its results. So while the actual content of the meta description may not directly affect your SEO, it plays a huge roll in helping human readers decide which search result to click on based on what they read.

The XML Sitemap module that automatically generates a site map according to the sitemaps.org specification is pretty important:

 Submitting a site map is highly recommended (by Google among others) for controlling and improving the efficiency of how your site is indexed by major search engines – a must for Drupal SEO.

There are a number of additional features that are provided along with the site map module, as evidenced by the number of options that come with the module download in the **Modules** overlay:

Take a moment to look around these options once they have been enabled. It is possible to have your site maps regularly and automatically submitted to the major search engines, which is a great help if your website is very dynamic and has a lot of new content and structure.

Possibly the single most important thing you can do to promote a website (and this is not specifically related to SEO) is to get other people talking about it. You need to create a buzz by getting well known bloggers or subject experts to talk about it (and link to you in the process). Even if it means talking about them, cajoling, and stroking their egos—most popular bloggers are keenly aware of the value that their links or reviews hold for other sites.

Bloggers are not the be all and end all either—there are plenty of review sites that specifically look to write reviews about up-and-coming, exciting websites. Finding and engaging with them is a worthwhile endeavor.

Social media sites are also a good place to go—mentioning your blog on sites like Twitter, Facebook, Digg, or LinkedIn exposes your pages to a whole new target audience. Online networks can also be invaluable and you should consider joining sites like LinkedIn in order to meet other people with similar business interests who may be willing to join in strategic partnerships with you.

Writing articles and submitting them to directories or news sites can also have an impact on your traffic. Creating a newsletter or RSS feed also serves to create a more tangible link with the users who do visit your site, and RSS feeds, in particular, can have quite far reaching effects if they are picked up by a variety of aggregators.

Updates

From time to time, it becomes necessary to upgrade your installation of Drupal in order to keep your site up-to-speed and trouble free. The `Update manager` module ships as part of the core and is an extremely useful tool for keeping up-to-date because it notifies you any time it detects a possible or required Drupal update. Actually, this goes for each contribution too—modules and themes are also under constant development (well, many of them) and the **Available updates** page under **Reports** will notify you of any and all outstanding and important changes:

Every now and then, for example, a security issue may be identified, and it is important to upgrade in order to avoid falling prey to malicious hacking—in this case, the report will tell you in no uncertain terms, **Security update required**.

All software, proprietary or open source, has weaknesses. Weaknesses are something you are not able to escape. What counts is how they are dealt with once they are found. In the case of Drupal, there is an entire community of people watching for bugs, reporting them, fixing them, and then offering the solutions to all users.

As of Drupal 7, the procedure for implementing updates both to Drupal and the contributed modules has been simplified enormously. The process of implementing updates is discussed here, but is predicated on the assumption that you have already made a special backup or have a recent backup already saved.

Note that there is an **UPDATE** tab shown on the **Available updates** overlay—it's also present on the **Modules** overlay. Clicking on this brings up a list of the projects that have available updates:

You can browse through this list and decide which updates to implement. It's generally a good idea to use the latest stable release, and it's very important to ensure that you implement any and all security updates. For the purposes of this discussion, we'll select the **Pathauto** update and click on the **Download these updates** button.

Your website will then trundle off to Drupal and fetch the specified updates, before informing you of their status:

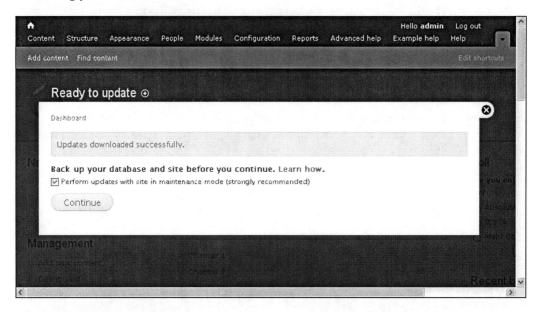

With the updates now uploaded to the local site, we can implement the update by clicking on the **Continue** button.

Note that the option to perform this update in maintenance mode is automatically checked. Leaving this selected will temporarily render your website unavailable to users while the updates are in progress. It's a good idea to leave this as is to prevent people from accessing the site while updates are in progress (they may experience some odd behavior or the site may be temporarily broken), but if, for some reason, you can't afford the downtime, then unselect this option.

Once the update has been performed, you will be presented with a success page and a list of further options:

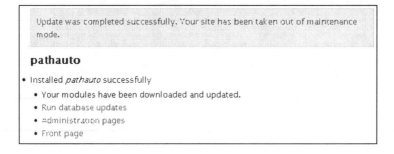

Of critical importance is that you **Run database updates** (also known as the update. php script). After ensuring that the database update process completes with no errors, you will be able to verify that Drupal or the module(s) have been correctly updated by viewing the available updates overlay or the module list.

If, for some reason, these updates are not working, you can perform updates manually by downloading the new project and extracting it to the modules folder on your site. Once this is done, you will need to run the update.php script yourself by browsing to it at http://www.mydrupalsite.com/update.php—there's also a link to it on the **Modules** overlay. This page also has plenty of useful tips and guidelines to help:

Drupal database update

Use this utility to update your database whenever a new release of Drupal or a module is installed.

For more detailed information, see the upgrading handbook. If you are unsure what these terms mean you should probably contact your hosting provider.

✓ Verify requirements

▶ Overview

Review updates

Run updates

Review log

1. **Back up your database.** This process will change your database values and in case of emergency you may need to revert to a backup.
2. **Back up your code.** Hint: when backing up module code, do not leave that backup in the 'modules' or 'sites/*/modules' directories as this may confuse Drupal's auto-discovery mechanism.
3. Put your site into maintenance mode.
4. Install your new files in the appropriate location, as described in the handbook.

When you have performed the steps above, you may proceed.

Continue

By paying regular attention to status updates provided by the update manager, you can be sure to keep your site operating securely and smoothly.

Summary

This chapter has rounded off the picture painted by the rest of the book by taking a look at some of the most important website-related chores that you will have to undertake. Knowing how to automate backups at the click of a button will be an invaluable tool in the coming weeks and months as you develop and maintain a fledgling site or two.

Implementing a user and search engine-friendly site is one of the most important things you can do to get your new site noticed. `Path` and `Pathauto` can help to make URLs easier to read and parse for humans and bots alike. Submitting a site map will also go a long way in ensuring that the major search engines index your content correctly and efficiently.

Finally, keeping your site up-to-date with the latest core distribution and modules is extremely important for maintaining a bug-free, secure web platform.

With the end of this chapter, we come to the end of the book. Congratulations on getting here, and I wish you all the best in your future endeavors on the web. Remember that there are plenty of online quiz questions and exercises available at site prebuilder (`http://www.siteprebuilder.com`), if you are interested in testing your knowledge and exploring Drupal a little further than we had space to do here.

Leveraging jQuery

jQuery, `http://jquery.com/`, is a library of JavaScript functions that make developing AJAX and other JavaScript features quick and easy. With the trend for rich, dynamic, and responsive web pages (Web 2.0) now well established, it is no surprise that Drupal keeps up with the times. Accordingly, jQuery has been built into the Drupal core, and you can find the main library files in the `misc` folder of your installation.

This appendix has been included to give you a basic overview of how jQuery can be leveraged to create new and interesting effects to enhance your content. Since jQuery comes as part of Drupal, and various Drupal modules rely heavily on it, why shouldn't we, the site administrators, cash in on its ready- and waiting- functionality?

Before we can go ahead and start adding dynamic and powerful features, we need to know a little bit about how jQuery works, so let's take a crash course. I should warn you that this section really is a crash course — to become proficient in utilizing jQuery, you will need to practice. Consider purchasing *Learning jQuery: Better Interaction Design and Web Development with Simple JavaScript Techniques by Chaffer and Swedberg* (ISBN 978-1-847192-50-9), *Packt Publishing*.

jQuery Basics

How jQuery works can be split into two main parts and summed up as:

 Find elements; do something with them.

If some of the code in the coming section appears quite complex, remember the previous statement and it should help to simplify things.

Because different parts of a web page can be loaded up at different times, we need to wrap any jQuery statements inside the `ready()` function to cause the jQuery JavaScript to be executed only once the page is fully loaded—this prevents the jQuery application from breaking, in the event it is run before everything (specifically, its target page element) is present:

```
jQuery(document).ready(function(){
   // Your code here
   });
```

Let's take a look at a simple jQuery statement to highlight the general syntax we use:

```
Clicking on this will <a href="#">trigger an alert</a>
<script type="text/javascript">
jQuery(document).ready(function(){
   jQuery("a").click(function() {
     alert("Hello world!");
   });
});
</script>
```

The first line is straightforward HTML, with a single hyperlink created using the `<a>` tag. Next, we have the JavaScript wrapped in the `<script>` tags followed by the `ready()` function. The statement:

```
jQuery ("a").click(function() {
   alert("Hello world!");
});
```

tells jQuery that it must find all the `<a>` tags on the page, and when someone clicks on the link, it should execute the function (containing the `Hello World` alert).

Looking at it more generically, the statement `jQuery ()` is actually an alias for a jQuery object. It can be created using a number of CSS style selectors. A selector can be the name of a tag, as used in this instance, it can be the class name of a tag (that is, `<a class="classname">`), and even the ID of a tag. So, if for example, you had an `<input>` tag, it would be easy to apply effects to this tag by creating a new object like this:

```
jQuery ("input")
```

Bear in mind though that applying effects to a tag like this means that you might get some unexpected results because jQuery will apply whatever effects you specify to *the entire set of tags that match the selector throughout the page.* If you want to limit the scope of the effects to a single piece of HTML, you would use the ID selector (note the leading #):

```
jQuery ("#uniqueid")
```

and this would act on the unique tag that has the matching ID. For example:

```
Clicking on this will <a href="#" id="uniqueid">trigger an alert</a>
```

This jQuery object has a number of predefined methods that can be used to provide all sorts of functionality and effects. The one we used in the previous example was `click()` to bind a specified function to the mouse click event but there are many more. To look over a list of what's available, go to `http://docs.jquery.com/Events`.

jQuery also has a whole lot of effects. For example, if you wanted a link to disappear after being clicked once, you could make use of the `hide()` method provided by jQuery to remove it:

```
jQuery ("a").click(function() {
    jQuery (this).hide("slow");
});
```

Again, there are a large number of effects that can be achieved, and you should refer to `http://api.jquery.com/category/effects/` for a complete list.

Now, one of the most powerful features of jQuery is that its methods actually return the jQuery object itself. This means that you can apply one method after the other in a process known as *chaining*. To get a nice combination of effects, simply add one after the other in a line:

```
...

.new{
background: #eded11;
font-weight: bold;
font-size: 20px;
align: left;
}

...

jQuery ('#uid').click(function() {
    jQuery (this).addClass("new").fadeTo("slow", 0.2);
});
```

Here, we have chained together two methods, namely, `addClass` (`addClass` applies a class definition, specified as `new`, to an element) and `fadeTo` to slowly reduce the opacity of the tag to 0.2 times normal (that is, 20 percent).

Let's take a look at how all this turns out on an actual web page.

jQuery in action

As much as we are demonstrating jQuery in action, this section also shows off `.info` in action. Open up your current theme's folder and add a new file entitled **jquery_test.css** with the class definition that will be used in the example:

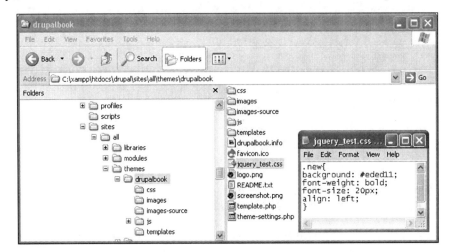

Next, create a new JavaScript file, entitled **jquery_test.js**, to house the jQuery call and add it to the same folder:

Next, edit the theme's **.info** file to ensure that the theme can locate the new CSS and JavaScript files. For example:

```
regions[page_top] = Page top
regions[page_bottom] = Page bottom
regions[sidebar_first] = First sidebar
regions_hidden[] = sidebar_first

stylesheets[all][] = jquery_test.css
scripts[] = jquery_test.js


; Information added by drupal.org packaging script on 2010-05-23
version = "7.0-alpha5"
project = "drupal"
datestamp = "1274628610"
```

Save the changes and then create a page with some HTML, against which the jQuery can act:

Take special note that the **id** attribute shown here matches the identifier specified in the jQuery statement—**uid**. In order for the new **.info** settings to take effect, the theme registry should be reloaded—ensure that this is done before trying anything out.

The page initially looks quite ordinary because no effects are applied until the link is clicked. In this case, we have:

Once the link is clicked, however, things change somewhat:

Notice that the style information has been applied, and that the text is now quite faded—just as we expect from having the chained methods applied to the tag.

That wraps up this brief overview of the exciting world of jQuery. There is much, much more for you to learn, and one of the best places to start is with the entire jQuery overview, found at `http://docs.jquery.com/Main_Page`. This will give an excellent overview of what is available and what can be achieved—there are plenty of jQuery tutorials and demonstrations that can be found on this site too.

Index

file system
about 98
blog files 100-103
private files 99
public files 98, 99
filesystem, Drupal site
backups 370, 372
settings 369, 370
Filtered HTML option 213
filters
about 261
example 261, 262
Firefox
URL 308
footers 279
foreach loop 356
formatting
about 211
example 212
Filtered HTML option 213
PHP evaluator option 216, 217
forum moderator users 119
Forum module
about 54
containers 55
example 51, 55
forum settings, managing 54-57
forums 153
forums section, Drupal community
about 19
general category 19
newsletters category 19
recent posts 20, 21
services category 19
support category 19
tips 20
URL 20
free taxonomy 197

G

gAMA information 301
garland stylesheet 303
General Public License. *See* GPL
GIF
about 300
drawbacks 300

Gimp
about 300
URL 300
GNU
URL 23
Google Analytics 373
GPL 23, 24
Graphics Interchange Format. *See* GIF

H

headers 279
hide() method 389
hierarchy
about 207
deep hierarchy structure, building 208, 209
example 207, 208
htdocs directory 29, 33, 41
HTTP request 25
HyperText Transfer Protocol request. *See* HTTP request

I

ICO format 314
image fields
about 220
adding 221-223
images
about 220
adding, to content type 220-223
fields 220-223
GIF format 300
Gimp 300
JPG format 301
limitations 300
PNG format 301
styles 224
working, with 299-301
image styles
about 224
blogs, posting 228, 229
example 226, 227
large 223, 224
medium 223, 224
thumbnail 223, 224

Thank you for buying
Drupal 7

About Packt Publishing

Packt, pronounced 'packed', published its first book "*Mastering phpMyAdmin for Effective MySQL Management*" in April 2004 and subsequently continued to specialize in publishing highly focused books on specific technologies and solutions.

Our books and publications share the experiences of your fellow IT professionals in adapting and customizing today's systems, applications, and frameworks. Our solution based books give you the knowledge and power to customize the software and technologies you're using to get the job done. Packt books are more specific and less general than the IT books you have seen in the past. Our unique business model allows us to bring you more focused information, giving you more of what you need to know, and less of what you don't.

Packt is a modern, yet unique publishing company, which focuses on producing quality, cutting-edge books for communities of developers, administrators, and newbies alike. For more information, please visit our website: www.packtpub.com.

About Packt Open Source

In 2010, Packt launched two new brands, Packt Open Source and Packt Enterprise, in order to continue its focus on specialization. This book is part of the Packt Open Source brand, home to books published on software built around Open Source licences, and offering information to anybody from advanced developers to budding web designers. The Open Source brand also runs Packt's Open Source Royalty Scheme, by which Packt gives a royalty to each Open Source project about whose software a book is sold.

Writing for Packt

We welcome all inquiries from people who are interested in authoring. Book proposals should be sent to author@packtpub.com. If your book idea is still at an early stage and you would like to discuss it first before writing a formal book proposal, contact us; one of our commissioning editors will get in touch with you.

We're not just looking for published authors; if you have strong technical skills but no writing experience, our experienced editors can help you develop a writing career, or simply get some additional reward for your expertise.

Building Powerful and Robust Websites with Drupal 6

ISBN: 978-1-847192-97-4   Paperback: 380 pages

Build your own professional blog, forum, portal or community website with Drupal 6

1. Set up, configure, and deploy Drupal 6

2. Harness Drupal's world-class Content Management System

3. Design and implement your website's look and feel

4. Easily add exciting and powerful features

Drupal for Education and E-Learning

ISBN: 978-1-847195-02-9   Paperback: 400 pages

Teaching and learning in the classroom using the Drupal CMS

1. Use Drupal in the classroom to enhance teaching and engage students with a range of learning activities

2. Create blogs, online discussions, groups, and a community website using Drupal

3. Clear step-by-step instructions throughout the book

4. No need for code! A teacher-friendly, comprehensive guide

LaVergne, TN USA
08 November 2010
204046LV00006B/82/P